Slave Women
in the New World

Studies in Historical Social Change

SCOTT G. McNALL AND JILL S. QUADAGNO, EDITORS

Slave Women
in the New World

GENDER STRATIFICATION
IN THE CARIBBEAN

Marietta Morrissey

University Press of Kansas

Published by the University Press of Kansas (Lawrence, Kansas 66045), which was
organized by the Kansas Board of Regents and is operated and funded by Emporia State
University, Fort Hays State University, Kansas State University, Pittsburg State
University, the University of Kansas, and Wichita State University

Library of Congress Cataloging-in-Publication Data

Morrissey, Marietta.
    Slave women in the New World: gender stratification in the
Caribbean / Marietta Morrissey.
    p.   cm. — (Studies in historical social change)
    Bibliography: p.
    Includes index.
    ISBN 0-7006-0394-8 (alk. paper)
    1. Women slaves—Caribbean Area—Social conditions. 2. Social
classes—Caribbean Area—History. 3. Sex role—Caribbean Area—
History. I. Title. II. Series.
HT1071.M655   1989
305.4—dc19   89-5454
                                                             CIP

British Library Cataloguing in Publication Data is available.

Printed in the United States of America
10 9 8 7 6 5 4 3 2 1

The paper used in this publication meets the minimum requirements of the American
National Standard for Permanence of Paper for Printed Library Materials Z39.48-1984.

FOR JEFF

CONTENTS

PREFACE

Feminists generally agree that a major impediment to the formation of theory in the social sciences is the lack of attention to women's position. This is especially true in studies of the Third World, where women's frequent absence from formal labor markets has excluded them from scholarly examination. Recent study of informal labor markets and domestic work has begun to correct this neglect. It has also forced sociologists to rethink the fundamental unit of analysis in social science and to ask whether societal and world-level theories usefully illuminate the position of women, at least as these theories are now constituted.

This book is an analysis of slave women's position in the British, Dutch, French, Spanish, and Danish colonies of the West Indies, extending from 1600 through the 1800s. It is a critical work: I question whether historical generalization and sociological concepts about slavery and its Caribbean form can be accurate, because women slaves have generally been ignored in scholarly research and discourse. I present evidence as well that slave women's experience was sufficiently divergent from that of slave men to warrant reassessment of major analytical work on Caribbean slavery. It follows that lower-level generalizations and units of analysis—gender, class, and the household—are more revealing than higher-level categories if formal labor and commodity markets are not the exclusive media of social and economic exchange.

In search of fresh information about slave women's lives and experience, I have consulted early histories and travelers' accounts, most fully for the British, Spanish, and French West Indies. I have focused particular attention on slave women's work at home, in the fields, and as domestics; pregnancies, births, and women's general health; family organization and incentives for building kinship networks; and white attitudes toward women slaves as mothers and as workers. These same topics oriented my survey of the extensive contemporary research into and analysis of Caribbean slavery.

The research was guided as well by my understanding of the agenda of macro historical sociology and its application to feminist studies. The most meaningful task of those engaged in historical comparison is the construction of sufficiently discrete and specific analytical categories to account for the unique experiences of social groups, in this case men and women. Still, accepted bodies of sociological literature informed my questions about slave women: the emerging cross-cultural study of women's social and economic position, Caribbean slave studies, and dependency theories. The theoretical speculations drawn from these perspectives were challenged in significant ways by the primary data. But the research confirmed a fundamental assumption: that Caribbean bondwomen share with other groups historically and cross-culturally relative powerlessness in their communities and victimization through several forms of inequality and exploitation.

Sociologists generally find that with extensive but incomplete "data sets" like this one more hypotheses are rejected than supported. I have followed this conservative course, qualifying observations that appear to be unique to a society, region, or historical era (Narroll 1968). Only if a sociological concept or hypothesis is supported for most available cases have I considered it a likely constituent element of gender stratification in New World slavery.

EPISTEMOLOGY AND CONTENT

It is an orienting assumption of this work that social scientists' efforts to build alternative theories of social change in the Third World are often frustrated by the application of imprecise and inappropriate concepts and research questions [see also Skocpol (1984, 1987), Schwarz (1987), and Tilly (1984)]. Epistemological gaps in earlier analyses of the Third World also raise substantive issues that have influenced my thinking about gender and Caribbean slavery. For example, dependency theories began with what is certain: that capitalism affected noncapitalist class formation and economic growth. But noncapitalist regions and workers in the nonwage sector, in particular women, were largely ignored. Yet many questions about the underdevelopment of Caribbean economies in the mid and late nineteenth century go back to the slave era and involve women's roles in production and reproduction.

A larger point is implicit here that shapes the goals of this analysis and places it among emerging studies on the intersection of capitalism and noncapitalist groups and economies in the Third World. Slaves more than other Caribbean social groups and slave women more than men met international capitalism through mediators linked to the capitalist world. Bondmen and women had few social or economic exchanges with capitalist world traders or manufacturers except through estate owners and managers. Yet the slaves' daily lives were influenced by international capitalist forces, with ever more dramatic consequences. Slave women were more firmly entrenched than bondmen in seigneurial and peasantlike social relations. But precisely because of capitalism's invasive impact, female slaves were increasingly differentiated from and dominated by males, even as slaves of both genders moved together into routinized plantation work and more highly rationalized relations with slaveholders.

Any such study of slaves and women reflects the paradoxes, the twists and turns, of social relations endemic to Third World capitalism and its articulation with noncapitalist social and economic systems. Slave women were in a constant, dynamic struggle with men—both slave and free—over the foundations of their social experience: Did gender or their status as slaves define social relations? The complex response to this question forms the central hypothesis of this work: Women's slave status in the Caribbean gradually robbed them of a domain, the household economy, making them more nearly units of agricultural labor, like men. But females' lack of access to skilled agricultural work diminished their social status and authority, and gender became an increasingly salient expression of stratification within communities of Caribbean slaves and among free men and women.

An Outline

In Chapter One I provide an overview of the last three decades' major theoretical debates about New World slavery. Comparative slave treatment, the viability of the slave mode of production, and the slaves' phenomenological status are discussed in relation to gender stratification. I then offer a general theoretical perspective for the study of Caribbean slave women, grounded in emerging conceptions of household economies in mixed and articulated systems of production.

In Chapter Two I compare cash crop production and its impact on slave women in the U.S. South and the Caribbean. A more traditional agrarian, gender-based division of labor was found in tobacco, cotton and rice cultivation in the United States than in sugar culture in the West Indies. Although women performed field labor throughout the New World, the crops, climate, and related smaller scale of production in the South generally granted bondwomen a greater diversity of agricultural tasks and more differentiation of work from that of male slaves than in sugar production. In the Caribbean, production of cash crops, particularly sugar, was conducted on a large scale. Women's agricultural work varied little from men's. The complex and increasingly mechanized process of sugar refining increased productivity demands on both males and females and created more high-status skilled positions for bondmen.

In the following chapter I treat the changing proportion of slave women in Caribbean populations from the seventeenth through the nineteenth centuries. A pattern emerges, resulting from the shifting supply of African women, slaveholders' beliefs about female labor productivity, and in the Spanish West Indies religious and moral ideologies militating against women's presence on plantations. At first, equal numbers of males and females were common, followed by a preponderance of males and then a majority of females. Gender ratio appears to have had relatively little impact on fertility, family formation, or sexual mores. The particular configuration of modes and systems of production in Caribbean slavery blunted the relationship between gender and other forms of social organization that we have come to expect from the study of related social formations.

Women's work is examined in Chapters Four and Five. Female slaves had a broad role in household maintenance, gardening and the cultivation and marketing of provisions, and field labor and domestic work. I make several general points: that women's control of subsistence production and trade gave them authority and social status; that household tasks, including child care, were the province of women; and that domestic labor in the homes of slave masters and other whites was more attractive to slaves than field labor and yielded both privileges and occasional manumission. Abolition of the slave trade brought increased absorption of males and females into agricultural labor. Erosion of income-generating avenues followed, degrading women's economic position. Female slaves lost access to the cultivation and marketing of provisions and to domestic and other work that enhanced their status, income, or resources. And as field laborers, women were rarely employed in status-accruing skilled work. Their situation contrasts with that of women slaves in the United States, whose economic power and hence social status was less, along with their participation in production of commodity exports.

I discuss family organization in Chapter Six. Studies of United States slaves have revised the view that slaves did not form nuclear families. A similar revision has occurred in the examination of Caribbean slave communities, with a substantial number of nuclear families discovered in a variety of national and historical settings. I review several theories of family formation in the region, concluding that nuclear families increased marginally in many settings where gender ratios decreased and sugar production and labor productivity had ebbed. But other conditions are necessary to this development: serious amelioration programs and/or opportunities for males to garner status, authority, or income. Finally, I review and question the currently popular understanding of the slave family as a vehicle of Caribbean slave resistance and revolt. The slave family is more appropriately viewed as a retreat from the brutalities of slavery, perhaps more for male family members than for females.

I treat fertility in the seventh chapter. Why did Caribbean slave women have so few children? Creolization of the population and improving age and gender ratios are less meaningful in explaining fertility changes in the Caribbean than expected. I suggest a materialist approach to childbearing, whereby women's loss of control over income-generating activities such as the growing and trade of provisions and "hiring out" affected birth rates. Slave women exercised fertility control through contraceptive use, abortion, and infanticide. I also discuss slave mortality. Women lived longer than men and generally enjoyed better health. Slave infants were prone to particular diseases, for example, tetanus, contributing to extremely high infant mortality rates.

The focus of Chapter Eight is fecundity and the physiological reasons why male and female slaves failed to conceive children and why women were often unable to bear them. Disease, malnutrition, and overwork were all likely causes of subfecundity among Caribbean slaves. The low capacity of slaves for reproduction appears to have worked in tandem with voluntary fertility control, thus explaining the low birth rate among the region's slaves. Circumstances improved with amelioration of living and health conditions and diminishing labor demands. But, although women were required to work more often in field labor and to increase their productivity, improved conditions of childbearing had little impact on the birth rate.

In Chapter Nine I examine slave women's sexual relationships with European males, their punishment and abuse by slave masters, and their participation in rebellions and insurgency against the slave system. A paradox forms around white men's fascination with black sexuality and the imposition of dramatic and cruel punishments on female slaves. Women slaves often rebelled against these and other forms of exploitation through armed revolt, but more commonly they used indirect means. These included support of male militancy, poisonings, flight, and control of reproduction.

In Chapter Ten I offer a series of conclusions about the position of Caribbean slave women and relate them to emerging themes in women's studies. First, although it is clear that bondwomen's place varied in New World slavery, it was also consistently subordinated to that of both whites and male slaves. This observation reinforces our growing understanding that settled agriculture fundamentally changed women's social position, generally in the direction of increased oppression and exploitation. Industrialization has had a similarly significant impact on gender relations by creating new bases for hierarchy in the differentiation of skill levels, which only in the late twentieth century have been modified to admit women in large numbers, and by increasing women's social autonomy from male authorities in families and other primary social groups. Slavery embodies both the degradation of agriculture, with its increasing demands on women's physical labor, and early industrialism, with skill hierarchies that excluded women from higher status occupational positions and increased female social independence.

Higher-level sociological and feminist theoretical perspectives must capture the material dynamics outlined and the seemingly independent ideological trends and movements that shaped the lives of slaves. The construction of appropriate theories hinges in part on the resolution of epistemological tensions between the fixity of social structure and the impact of action. The study of relatively powerless groups, such as slaves, is crucial to this enterprise, for their effect on the seemingly impenetrable confines of the plantation economy was both profound and constantly frustrated by the brutality of the institution and the ruthlessness of its stewards.

I gratefully acknowledge the contributions of many institutions and colleagues to the preparation of this manuscript. I conducted much of the research at the Harvard and Yale University libraries. The Inter-Library Loan librarians at Texas Tech University secured many other materials for me. I appreciate as well the assistance of the Yale University Latin American Studies Program for granting me Visiting Fellow status for the summer of 1984 and the American Philosophical Society for a travel grant. A Faculty Development Leave from Texas Tech University allowed me several months of uninterrupted time to write.

I thank Orlando Patterson and members of his 1981 National Endowment for the Humanities Summer Seminar on the Comparative Study of Slavery at Harvard University for many ideas and much lively discussion that has influenced the focus and direction of this work. Others who have offered support and advice include Stanley Engerman, M. G. Smith, Richard Sheridan, Janet Chafetz, Jeffrey Gamso, Gary Elbow, Michael Craton, Martin Murray, Scott McNall, Jill Quadagno, and Pamela Brink. Gary Elbow also generously drew the regional map that appears at the beginning of the book. The editorial staff at the University Press of Kansas has been attentive and helpful. And I note with special gratitude the confidence and good will of my family, my many women colleagues in sociology, and the faculties and staffs of the Sociology Department and Women's Studies Program at Texas Tech University.

Slave Women
in the New World

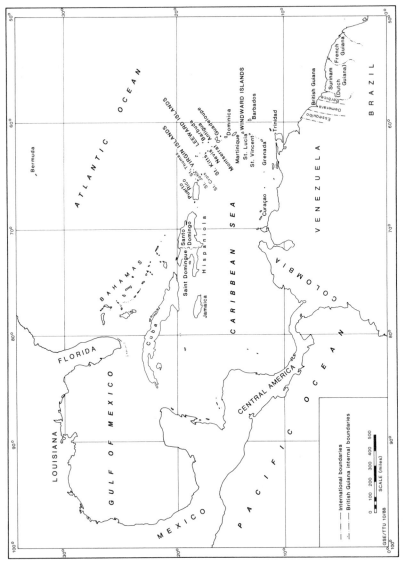

Caribbean and Northern South America, c. 1800

CHAPTER ONE

A Theoretical Overview

The recent academic study of women has brought about a profound critique of theory and methods in social science. Substantive areas have been revolutionized by consideration of women's work and influence on culture and social life. And women's studies has led to recognition that traditional, gender-bound analytical perspectives both hinder and inspire critical thought. Feminist influences on academic writing and research are distinct but not wholly separable from Marxian and other analytical strategies emphasizing the feelings and actions of underlying populations.

A parallel explosion of research and commentary on New World slavery has focused little on women. Extensive work on the demography of slave societies in the U.S. South and the Caribbean touches some dimensions of females' experience, but in an indirect and shallow way. A major rethinking of New World slavery to account for women's experience has only just begun. This book is meant as a contribution to that reconceptualization, an attempt to probe and recast major theoretical questions about slavery in light of research findings on Caribbean slave women's position. It is also an effort to understand the work, family organization, and social status of Caribbean bondwomen.

Several notable recent works on women in the West Indies have laid the groundwork for new analytical strategies and constructs, with fresh data on slave women and pertinent theoretical insights. Mathurin (1974) follows Jamaican slave women through several significant eras, introducing new material on women's roles in production, reproduction, and other areas of social life. Nanny and other Maroon and insurgent women slaves have come alive through the research of Kopytoff (1976) and Tuelon (1973). Barbara Bush's (1981) contrast of free and slave women's social status in the British West Indies reminds us that skin color, gender, and social position together conditioned slave women's experience. Reddock (1985) raises the contradiction between production and reproduction, moving away from the simple categorization of slave women's low fertility as an act of resistance or insurgence. Gautier (1985) touches all of these issues in her exposition and analysis of bondwomen's lives in the French West Indies and, through discussion of women in Africa, traces indigenous sources of gender stratification among New World slaves.[1]

1

In a broader sense the last twenty years of slave studies have laid the groundwork for a complete and critical study of slave women. Three debates have preoccupied scholars, each dominating the literature for nearly a decade [see Davis (1974) for a discussion of these and related questions]. The theme uniting these controversies is whether social structural entities, for example, the state, the law, and the symbolic and economic orders, define slaves' experiences or whether slaves' institutions and relationships, often informal and considered illegitimate by economic and political authorities, capture the essence of slavery. These and related debates are significantly altered, if not resolved, by examination of women's place. And in moving beyond these disputes in light of women's position, we lay the foundation of a broader analytic for studying slavery.

Let us turn, then, to three major areas of controversy in Caribbean slave studies: (1) the comparative treatment of slaves, (2) the continuing profitability of New World slavery, and (3) the phenomenological status of slaves.

COMPARATIVE TREATMENT OF MALE AND FEMALE SLAVES

Historical accounts of New World slavery present a broad variation in the treatment of slaves, but horrific physical abuses of human beings were found throughout the Caribbean. There is general scholarly agreement that Spanish slave codes were more liberal than the British and French codes and that in the seventeenth century Spanish and Portuguese slave colonies exhibited relatively patriarchal master-slave relationships, that is, ones mediated by noneconomic ties. In 1946 Tannenbaum formalized the proposition advanced earlier by Freyre and nineteenth-century observers that imperial cultures and religious beliefs influenced slave treatment.

> There were, briefly speaking, three slave systems in the Western Hemisphere. The British, American, Dutch and Danish were at one extreme, and the Spanish and Portuguese at the other. In between these two fell the French. The first of these groups is characterized by the fact that they had no effective slave tradition, no slave law, and that their religious institutions were little concerned about the Negro. At the other extreme there were both a slave law and a belief that the spiritual personality of the slave transcended his slave status. In between them the French suffered from the lack of a slave tradition and slave law, but did have the same principles as the Spaniards and Portuguese. If one were forced to arrange these systems of slavery in order of severity, the Dutch would stand as the hardest, the Portuguese as the mildest, and the French, in between, having elements of both. (Tannenbaum 1946, p. 65)

A plethora of studies reinforcing Tannenbaum's hypothesis followed (see, for example, Klein 1967; Elkins 1976). Critical reaction to Tannenbaum's thesis was extensive (Sio 1965; Goveia 1960; Davis 1966). Genovese (1965) broke new theoretical ground in acknowledging regional and temporal variation in slave treatment and argued that imperial economic goals were more powerful determinants than culture or religion. And, he argued, the comparative development of industrial capitalism within the contours of a changing global economy influenced master-slave relationships and thus the treatment of slaves. Hence the experiences of slaves could shift dramatically with the fortunes and structural position of the metropolitan bourgeoisie and the state, as they did in the British West Indies during the seventeenth century (Dunn 1972). Or local industrial, agricultural, and commercial entrepreneurs could challenge imperial authority, as in Cuba, transforming a relatively "benign" form of slavery into a highly centralized and brutal system, demanding unprecedented levels of slave productivity (Knight 1970; Moreno Fraginals 1977, 1978).

Newer understandings of the foundation of variation in the treatment of slaves in comparative capitalist development are fuller and more complex than Tannenbaum's earlier analysis. Indeed, many scholars are now contemptuous of discussing "treatment": Slavery is profoundly inhuman and to detail its cruelty, superfluous and insensitive. It is agreed, however, that variations in daily experience occurred—in time, from one slave society to another, and across plantations on a single island. The theme of treatment has also broadened to include comparative labor productivity, diet, and living conditions, which are more readily quantifiable and more sensitive to variation within and among units of analysis than physical treatment of slaves.

Several traditional areas of scrutiny reveal differences in the treatment of males and females and warn us against the wholesale rejection of Tannenbaum's thesis until the position of females has been more fully and deliberately studied. Certainly women experienced many of the psychological and physical abuses endured by men. Few punishments of males were not inflicted on females. But the general atmosphere of cruelty and the physical abuse of slaves by masters had slightly different expressions and implications for men and women.

There were, of course, variations in laws pertaining to the punishment of men, women, and children. The Spanish codes accorded more rights to slave women than did the British, French, Dutch, or Danish. But enforcement was neither universal nor consistent; throughout the Caribbean both male and female slaves were treated sadistically. As elsewhere where women have been violently abused, pregnant women were especially vulnerable to brutality (Davis 1966, p. 233). James (1963, p. 13) graphically describes an example of such terror: "'When the hands and arms were tied to four posts on the ground, the slave was said to undergo 'the four post.' The pregnant woman was not spared her 'four-post.' A hole was dug in the earth to accommodate the unborn child.'' This disturbing passage suggests other dynamics too often ignored in discussion of the treatment of slaves. The white male master's relationship with black women slaves was intrinsically more complex than that with male slaves, influenced by gender conflicts, sexual tensions, and his ownership of her unborn children (Jordan 1968; Clinton 1982; Bush 1981; Hine 1979).

Two issues emerge, both suggesting an ambivalence among female slaves toward superordinate whites. First, sexual relationships between white male masters and female slaves were frequent in the Caribbean, particularly where white women were scarce (Morner 1973; Davis 1966; Mathurin 1974; Bush 1981). These liaisons were an important source of mobility for slave women and sometimes resulted in freedom for themselves and for the children born of such unions. Combined with the rigidity of the master-slave tie, sexual unions may have meant more mistreatment, especially sexual abuse, of women than has generally been acknowledged.[2] Davis (1966, p. 228) cites the case of Brazil, where greater demands on slaves for productivity brought harsher treatment and more sadism in sexual relations between masters and slave women. In a similar way the master's attitude toward slaves' unborn children was necessarily contradictory and varied in time and place. Children were evidence of the sexual freedom that Europeans exaggerated, admired, and feared in slave communities, and—whether fathered by white or slave males— must have stirred sexual tensions and guilt. Pregnancy also marked a conflict between the planter's goals of labor productivity and reproduction of the labor force, suggesting another possible source of sadism and violence.

It is often remarked in documents of the day that women were harsher masters than men, especially toward female slaves. If this is true, the complicated relationship between free and slave women, both subordinates of white men, becomes significant (Clinton 1982; White 1985; Mathurin 1974); if false, the scapegoating of women masters by men in discussing abuse is itself rich in sociological implications (Gautier 1985, p. 35).

Finally, there are aspects of the treatment of slaves that only variations in metropolitan ethos seem to explain. For example, women were fewer in the Spanish West Indies than elsewhere and significantly lower priced. Supply factors do not wholly account for this discrepancy (Klein 1978). Neither does demand, for males' and females' levels of labor productivity were close. Early commentators believed that Spanish moral and religious beliefs discouraged the presence of women on estates, as proximity was believed to foster promiscuity (Humboldt 1960, p. 188). This contention is consistent with the argument that Spanish religious leaders respected the integrity of slaves' souls (Tannenbaum 1946). In the absence of other explanations, this ideologically based perspective must be considered to account for the predominance of male slaves in the Spanish Caribbean, although it is likely that slaves' treatment otherwise varied little with the national origin of slaveowners.

Living conditions and food consumption also differed for men and women. Estate managers and planters allocated resources to men and women equally, whereas children were to receive less. However, we do not know if ration plans for food, building supplies, huts, furniture, and other material goods were mediated by overseers or if slaves themselves redistributed goods, with more allotted to men and other privileged social groups. The question is especially pertinent to areas where food was not rationed but grown on provision grounds.

In the West Indies slaves generally had small garden plots, or "polincks." Usually less than an acre, the gardens were apportioned to slaves for cultivation of legumes, grains, vegetables, and herbs. Livestock were occasionally tended as well. Unfortunately, records are sparse on how lands were divided and distributed. It appears that each adult slave received a provision plot, making possible land consolidation by families.[3] Patterson (1976, p. 56) argues that women saw an advantage in living without mates with whom to compete for domestic authority and the social and economic rewards of successful farming and marketing. Slave women could group the provision grounds of their children, suggesting that in Jamaica, at least, children, too, controlled small parcels of land for food cultivation. Craton (1982, p. 50) qualifies Patterson's interpretation:

From the very few records and descriptions of the grounds that have survived, it seems clear that the plots were allocated to heads of household and that these were predominantly male. The working of the grounds (and the smaller garden plots around the houses) was normally a family, almost proto-peasant, activity. Men, women, and children worked together as a household unit. . . . But in the division of labor the men decided what should be grown and did most of the planting and reaping, the children carried and weeded, and the women tended the house plot and domestic animals, cooking the provisions and carrying the surplus to market on Sunday.

Mintz (1974) agrees, contending that nowhere in West Indian slave history is the claim of women's authority or control of the growing or marketing of provisions validated.

Other commentary suggests a middle ground between Patterson's assertion of women's economic power and Craton and Mintz's depiction of gender hierarchy traditionally associated with agricultural production. Women did sometimes control provision grounds, but more often men were in charge. Women's dominance in marketing is broadly asserted and upheld by historical evidence. A repetition of the West African pattern is suggested, with men performing heavy agriculture and women trading produce. Jones (1982, p. 254) argues that the division of labor among New World slaves provided more gender equality than is common in agrarian societies and that "the more freedom [U.S.] slaves had in determining their own activities the more clearly emerged a distinct division of labor between the sexes."[4]

The relatively few nuclear families among Caribbean slaves suggests a greater production role for female slaves in the West Indies than in the U.S. South. This often translated into household authority and subordination of adult sons to the economic needs of their mothers and her other offspring.[5] But with extensive evidence of male status in economic and social arenas, from their monopoly of skilled jobs to occasional intergenerational repetition of males' names, female heads of households may have suffered economic hardship along with relative autonomy, much as they do in industrial societies today.

The authority to disperse provision land and food among slaves was especially significant, for slaves everywhere in the Caribbean were often malnourished and generally underfed. With notable status within the slave community, males probably claimed more food from provision grounds or rations. It appears that young males were given more food than females, the elderly, the ill, and the disabled. Male labor productivity was generally assumed to be greater than females' and that of other apparently feeble groups, and, with males' superior place in the stratification system of slaves, differential access to rations was in all likelihood considered appropriate and legitimate by other bondmen and women. There is evidence, however, that female slaves and other categories of presumably weak workers were at some times as productive as male agricultural workers (Higman 1976a). Moreover, women slaves generally did arduous physical work throughout pregnancy. Were working women less able to meet nutritional requirements than men? And to what degree did male slaves themselves contribute to this inequality?

Males and females also enjoyed differential access to shelter in many settings. Masters sometimes built houses and allocated them to slaves, equally to households with and without male heads. Elsewhere slaves built their own huts. The historical record discloses cases of single women prevailing on others in the community to construct dwellings for them (Bennett 1958, pp. 32-33).

We can infer more certainly that living conditions—poor sanitation in slave villages, lack of adequate ventilation and warmth, and inadequate access to proteins and other nutrients—affected males and females differently. For example, females outlived male slaves, even in settings in which the females' work loads were extraordinarily heavy and increasing (Craton 1971, 1977). The consequences of brutal living conditions for women's fertility, pregnancy, and childbirth and for early infant survival were enormous, as emerging research reveals. It has long been assumed that women's promiscuity depressed their fertility and led to reproductive diseases (Sheridan 1985, p. 226; Bennett 1958, p. 53). This is a regrettable bias, reflecting both a lack of certainty about slave women's sexual patterns and a lack of interest in what are surely more profound influences on reproduction—nutrition, sanitation, and physical comfort (Dunn 1977; Debien 1974).

A final quantifiable index of the differing treatment of male and female slaves is productivity. It appears that women were as productive as men in some periods of Caribbean slavery, for example, immediately preceding emancipation in Jamaica when, in the absence of young men, women, children, and older slaves often sustained prior levels of productivity. In general, the marginally lower prices paid for female slaves suggest lower productivity than was achieved by males. But the prices of male and female slaves varied little across Caribbean slave societies and time periods. It seems, then, that slaves of both genders labored more intensively over time in conjunction with the escalating demands of plantation agriculture and that female slaves were always considered useful workers and fully exploited.[6]

The often heated and intense discussion of slave treatment has, then, bypassed important gender issues. Specifically, the differential treatment of male and female slaves in terms of physical abuse and cruelty, food consumption and shelter, and labor productivity has not been systematically studied. Yet differences emerge that alter the course of debate.

First, although general slave treatment coincides with changing fortunes of sugar monoculture and European patterns of consumption, women's treatment may not. The experiences of women are as much a function of the complex structure of status inequality influenced by colonial ideologies as of global or national conflicts and competitions. Women's position is further removed from global disputes than men's because of their subordinate position within a community of slaves and by gender itself, mediated in the master-slave relationship by racial differences.

SLAVERY AND INDUSTRIAL CAPITALISM

The second major area of theoretical debate within Caribbean slave studies concerns the continuing productivity of slave-based agriculture. A long tradition of research and commentary held that plantation slavery was finally inefficient, destroying soil fertility and the producer's competitive edge in international commodity markets. This process was especially marked, it is argued, in the Caribbean, where the Industrial Revolution mandated intensive production techniques. In 1944 Eric Williams (1966) claimed that Caribbean islands boomed and fell in productivity and profitability. But contemporary observers question this relationship, contending that planters were not shortsighted but often adopted productive techniques to preserve the ecosystem in order to sustain profits and productivity. The latter view has received considerable attention in recent years and now commands the field (Anstey 1975; Drescher 1977, 1987; Engerman 1973; Eltis 1987; Solow and Engerman 1987).

The differential impact of external and internal dynamics on the rise and demise of Caribbean slavery has preoccupied Marxist scholars as well. They have generally supported Williams's theory, regarding seventeenth- and eighteenth-century imperialism as a means of primitive capital accumulation. The possibility that master-slave relations do not mirror the labor-capital ties that define capitalism has, however, generated a great debate. The key question posed is whether labor relations or market relations are the essence of capitalism.

The most extreme statement of the market position is well known through the work of Wallerstein (1974, 1980) and others, who date the start of modern capitalism with fifteenth-century international expansion (for a review of this and related literature, see Chilcote 1984 and Wallerstein 1976). The world systems and "dependency" emphases constitute more than a semantic break from the classic Marxian definition of capitalism by production relations. They imply a dynamic that emphasizes profit making, or surplus accumulation, over other noneconomic aspects of human relations. Hence Genovese's characterization of the slave-based economy in the U.S. South as seigneurial is rejected. Following the market definition of capitalism, noncapitalist dimensions of New World slavery, including seigneurial aspects of master-slave bonds, were disrupted by mercantilism and finally transformed into capitalism (Genovese 1965, 1976).

Hindess and Hirst (1975) have taken the structuralist epistemology of much dependency theory to buttress a more orthodox Marxist definition of slavery. They argue that slavery, like capitalism, is a mode of production that may articulate with (dominate or be dominated by) another mode of production. But slavery's basic dynamics, founded on class relations, retain an integrity, modified perhaps by other dominating modes but finally preserved.

An odd conceptual alliance appears, then, between, on the one hand, Drescher, Engerman, and others who see slavery as a modern system of group relations compatible with industrial capitalism and, on the other hand, orthodox Marxists, who agree, by virtue of an epistemology that links holistic economic systems or, in Marxist parlance, modes of production. These views split, of course, on the question of internal contradictions. Marxists contend that systems hold and foster the seeds of their own failure.[7] Neoclassical economics allows for infinite growth and development in an economic system, dependent finally on the creativity and energy of its leaders.

At the same time, dependency theory has reinforced Williams's view of slavery. A continuum has formed from the Williams/dependency perspective to the Marxist/neoclassical economics approach. Proponents of the Williams/ dependency position define New World slavery as capitalist by virtue of its integration with fourteenth- through nineteenth-century international market relations. They also stress a cycle of productive expansion and decline influenced by worldwide trade. The Marxist/neoclassical view simultaneously emphasizes class relations and the long-term economic viability of the slave regimen. Its proponents recognize the strength and intensity of international economic exchange but consider its influence limited.

The implications for the study of women slaves in this multidimensional debate are significant, if heretofore unexplored. In the Williams/dependency analysis slave traders and owners found that women were undesirable because of their presumed deficiencies as laborers. Other reasons have been proffered for the dominance of men among African slaves by early observers, all focusing on the low supply of women rather than the high demand for men (Humboldt 1960; DuTertre 1958). But these explanations have received relatively little attention. They do not reinforce the influential principle introduced by Williams—that physical strength was at a premium on New World slave plantations and males' superiority in this regard was accepted and sought by slaveholders. Yet, with the end of the slave trade, young men were no longer available, and women and children often outnumbered men in the field, performing ably.

If, with the changing composition of the field labor force, Caribbean slave productivity remained constant, perhaps women were excluded for other reasons. Indeed, the price of female slaves was rarely more than 5 percent less than that paid for males. This important point suggests that slave owners saw less difference in the productivity of males and females than modern observers infer. Recent analysis of mid-nineteenth-century productivity in Jamaica demonstrates that women at least sometimes maintained the levels of productivity achieved by the formerly male-dominated work force. Supply and other factors must then be scrutinized to explain slave owners' apparent preference for male slaves, and the entire thrust of the Williams/dependency perspective must be questioned.

If weaknesses in the Williams/dependency view are highlighted in our analysis of Caribbean slave women's position, the other major perspective on New World slave economies also presents conceptual problems. Proponents of the Marxist/neoclassical economics position fail to acknowledge powerful tendencies toward dissolution in Caribbean slave societies rooted less in market constraints and pressures than in the social relations of slavery, including gender. At the end of the slave trade, when women slaves could not be purchased, their roles in field labor, food production, and reproduction were increasingly difficult to fulfill. These and other contradictions in New World slavery intensified and finally wrought a new mode of production, a no less complex mixture, this time of capitalist plantation labor and peasant-based production and trade of commodities. No amount of capitalist ingenuity and aggressiveness could forestall the crises of slavery, neocapitalist economists' claims notwithstanding. But failure to attend to women's position in this complex drama makes it impossible to identify the forces that brought collapse and renders significant efforts to define and describe the slave mode of production cumbersome and overly abstract.

What contribution can the study of Caribbean slave women make to a *synthesis* of these two dramatically different perspectives on New World slave economies? World systems theorists have lately emphasized the household as a point of convergence (Smith et al., 1984). It has been argued that, although capitalism may dominate and finally change noncapitalist social relations, these relations must retain their internal dynamics to encourage capitalist production (Wolf 1982; Mintz 1978; Dupuy 1983). And it is within the household that precapitalist social relations and their ties to larger, dominating production systems are found. For example, the slave mode of production in the West Indies often provided for its own subsistence by slave-controlled growing of provisions or cultivation of food as another estate crop (Mintz 1974, 1978; Tomich 1976; Dupuy 1983)[8] and in some locations through other income-generating activities, such as "hiring-out" of slaves to individuals and firms beyond the plantation. Such subsistence activities became more difficult to initiate and maintain with growing demands on slave labor. A rapid, linear destruction of the slave mode did not ensue, as the self-sufficiency of the slave population had to be nurtured for capitalism to operate smoothly and to grow. But the production of provisions, especially on slave-controlled lands, and other autonomous economic activities unrelated to the production of cash crops were constantly besieged.

I am suggesting, then, that it was not the inefficiency of slave production that brought slavery's end but the near impossibility of sustaining the slave population and increasing productivity. Whether this was a necessary economic tension or primarily the product of political and other external events is beyond the scope of this work.[9] But women's changing situation can help to explain more precisely why slave societies gave way to internal and international pressures and rivalries. In general terms it appears that women had a long-standing and major role in food production and household maintenance. As their labor was required increasingly in commodity agriculture, slavery was perceived as inefficient and attacked by sectors of European and Caribbean states (Williams 1966). If women's productivity was not seriously at issue, why did the slave mode of production falter? International competition and soil infertility have been argued by Williams and dependency theorists.[10] Rejecting this view, as Marxist/neoclassical advocates have done, we must look elsewhere for explanation.

I contend that an aging population of slaves, composed disproportionately of women, was asked to bear too many burdens in domestic, subsistence, and commodity production. Had rejuvenation of the population been possible, these tasks and more might have been accomplished. Caribbean slave women were never highly fertile for many reasons, including overwork and generally poor living and work conditions. At the end of the slave trade, slave masters ameliorated conditions, just as they demanded more labor from women of childbearing age. Productivity was maintained and mortality declined, but the birth rate failed to improve except where production had long since peaked and productivity demands ebbed. Voluntary and involuntary fertility combine here, we can safely infer, to show the limits of slaves' endurance and energy.

Demographic history has recently focused on such problems in Europe, Latin America, and elsewhere. Because the household is a seemingly inappropriate category of analysis for bonded people, we may easily miss the primary locus for decision making, contradiction, and crisis within Caribbean slave societies. The two dominating perspectives on the economic dynamics of slavery have focused on these major questions: Was New World slavery a capitalist, noncapitalist, or transitional system of production? Did external or internal forces bring decline and decay? Neither focus intrinsically deters us from consideration of women as an oppressed group among slaves; indeed in combination they enhance it. Yet women's position has been wholly ignored in theoretical debate. Tragically, the enormous and painful role played by women and other presumed weak groups in maintaining a still vital economic system has been underestimated; the costs of perpetuating this exploitation are obscured; and as a consequence major conceptual questions about slavery's functions and demise remain unresolved.

The household is a significant category for slavery in the New World as elsewhere, for it is there that many gender inequalities were expressed. Males and females had differential access to household economies, in particular, provision grounds. At the same time, Caribbean slave women experienced a high level of control in the growing and marketing of provisions. This economic sector fueled plantation production and eventually was destroyed by it. Women's economic power ebbed with productivity demands in the commodity sector, finally becoming less significant as male-dominated wage labor became the foundation for family economies in the postemancipation era.

Where collectivized growing of provisions by slaves under the supervision of estate managers was the norm, as in Barbados, both male and female slaves had little access to social status and authority. Still, gender equality was reduced by male control of skilled labor, the principal means of generating status and economic resources. Other areas, such as Cuba, that imported food represent a later stage in the movement of slave-based cash crop production throughout the New World. Labor had become a source of gender inequality, with male strength and its legacy from an earlier period of agricultural production as its foundation.

THE PHENOMENOLOGICAL STATUS OF SLAVES

The social position of slaves has long perplexed and fascinated Western social scientists. Traditionally slaves have been conceptualized as property. Such definitions have generally had three dimensions: The slave is the property of another human being; his or her will is subject to another's authority; his or her labor and services are obtained through coercion (Davis 1966). Slave laws have generally treated slaves as animals, machinery, and other objects. Elkins (1976) introduced another dimension in the categorization of slaves as property: their dehumanization.

Davis and others have questioned this view, holding that slaves were never treated wholly as property. Masters recognized the humanity of slaves in several ways. Tannenbaum (1946) had earlier compared the treatment of slaves across European colonial governments. He argued that, although New World slaveholders treated slaves as property in law and practice, they sometimes saw slaves as *human* property. In the Spanish West Indies, for example, slavery was an external condition, beyond the souls of masters and slaves. "The distinction between slavery and freedom is a production of accident and misfortune, and the free man might have been a slave" (Tannenbaum 1946, p. 46). In the British, French, Dutch, and Danish West Indies slaveholders perceived bondmen and women as fully comparable to other forms of property.

There has long been discontent with the notion of slaves as chattel. Patterson (1982) calls for a sociological definition of slaves, one resting less on relationships codified by law and more on the symbolic expression of social relations. He describes slavery by three characteristics: (1) masters' use of force against slaves, (2) the dishonoring of slaves, and (3) slaves' natal alienation. The last point pertains most directly to social position. "The slave [was] denied all claims on, and obligations to, his parents and living blood relations but, by extension, all such claims and obligations on his more remote ancestors and on his descendants. He was truly a genealogical isolate" (Patterson 1982, p. 5). Put more strongly, the slave was "socially dead." Slaves formed social bonds, of course, but they were not recognized as legitimate by the state or social elite. Family and friendship ties had meaning only within the slave community; in the symbolic order slaves were "bond-less."

Perspectives of the slave as property or as natally alienated hold or imply that males and females were viewed in structurally similar terms.[11] As property, males and females alike were bought and sold, with profitability always overwhelming considerations of sexuality, friendship, and affection. Within the slave community slave men lost authority over women and children, itself sometimes conceptualized as a property relationship. "Natal alienation" similarly obliterates the meaning of informal relationships between master and slave and within the slave community. But, as Davis (1966, p. 59) notes, "bondwomen have always been the victims of sexual exploitation, which was perhaps the clearest recognition of their humanity." Slaveholders often sired and later freed the children of slave women, suggesting reciprocal relations accompanied perhaps by affection and respect.

Much recent literature on slavery has treated the informal social ties of slaves, emphasizing their strength and endurance. In the U.S. South the frequency of nuclear families has been proven (Blassingame 1972; Genovese 1976; Fogel and Engerman 1974). Gutman (1977) has demonstrated that kinship ties endured and remained important to slaves over several generations. In the West Indies a high incidence of the formation of nuclear families has been found in some areas, eras, and units of production (Craton 1978, 1979; Higman 1976b, 1978). Of significance is the shift in focus away from the state level and its manifestation of the slaves' position in law, and the social structure, with its symbolic and cultural expressions of the slaves' status, to the slaves' community. In other words, "history from below" is advocated, with slaves' creation of culture more significant than that of more powerful social and political forces.

The deep epistemological debate over how to study oppressed people is confounding. Both sides claim a close affinity with underlying classes and groups. The study of state and social structure seems to ignore the values, behavior, intentions, and actions of slaves. On the other hand, slaves' culture and struggles were always impeded and framed by symbolic and legal orders. Variations on this debate have, of course, preoccupied scholars in all the social sciences, including women's studies. Its resolution may not be possible, and efforts are certainly beyond our scope here. A suitable goal is to establish some limits of both approaches for the study of Caribbean slave women's position.

Theories based on elite and state conceptions of the position of slaves manifest a fundamental and serious weakness in their failure to qualify the assertion that male and female slaves were equal before the law and in the symbolic order of the society. Slave status per se differentiated the free from the enslaved; no slave, male or female, ever attained greater status than any free human being. But this equality did not translate into equity among slaves precisely because slave masters treated male and female slaves differently. Slave men, by virtue of their greater access to resources (skilled positions, hiring out, provision gardens), had status and authority over slave women and children. And women's greater access to manumissions, domestic work, sexual unions with masters, and the potential for bearing free children gave them an advantage over slave men. Clearly a dialectic of gender and sexual relations must be superimposed on status for status to be an effective construct for understanding the position of slaves.[12]

Are women and men, even among slaves, equally subject to natal alienation? On the face of it, yes; women, men, and children could be bought and sold away from kin. But feminist studies have reminded us that the mother-child bond is unique and places women in a structural position that generally involves more social ties than men enjoy, especially when men are not in institutionalized familial roles. Again, focus on the categorical nature of the position of slaves has deterred us from discerning contrasts in informal social ties among males and females.

Scholars who have stressed slaves' creation of culture have also erred conceptually by failing to consider women. Ironically, the ways in which this position has been expressed have directly opposite consequences. Craton (1979), Jones (1982, p. 258), Bush (1986), and others have contended that families formed among slaves not only as a gesture of autonomy but also as an act of political protest. Masters discouraged family formation in a variety of ways. To have a family was to flaunt an independent spirit. To a degree this interpretation is contrary to findings on the U.S. South and the Caribbean. At some times slave masters encouraged marriage and reproduction. On the other hand, many observers have contended that slave women, especially in the Caribbean, failed to have children as an act of alienation and political protest (Patterson 1969; Brathwaite 1971; Bush 1986; Gautier 1985). It has been argued as well that marriage and lasting conjugal unions were anathema to slaves, particularly as youths (Patterson 1969, p. 164). Yet Caribbean slave masters themselves discouraged marriage and childbearing.

My first line of criticism of the proposition that marriage or fertility—or its absence—was a form of political protest is simply that its advocates can't have it both ways. Second, proponents of this approach seem to be claiming that slaves accepted their owners' ideologies in failing to marry and have children. More important, however, we cannot possibly know how slaves felt about the impact on masters of their decisions to create children or kin. Historical parallels are not very informative on these questions, and they are sadly absent in the literature, especially literature on the United States. Genovese (1976) and Gutman (1977) have used music, folklore, and evidence of kin networks to demonstrate the dearness of kin to slaves, but this hardly establishes the intentions of slaves to create kin, particularly in response to political motivations.

I refer once more to recent materialist work on households in articulating systems of production. We *can* establish material incentives for childbearing, family formation, and family maintenance, although, of course, materialist motives themselves are not demonstrable through historical evidence. Following this approach, we can infer that children were economically valuable in the U.S. South and in some Caribbean settings at some times. These material motives are also important in distinguishing male and female status levels, resource bases, and relations with masters.

DEBATES ON SLAVERY, MARXISM, AND WOMEN'S STUDIES

Three extensive and complicated areas of debate and discussion within Caribbean slave studies form the theoretical basis of this book and suggest research questions. First, women's treatment differed from men's in both physical terms and in reference to the quantitatively determined areas now under heavy scrutiny—food, shelter, clothing, housing, provision grounds, and the like. But were these differences systematic, either in Tannenbaum's terms of religious and cultural variation or in the stages of capitalist development suggested by his critics?

Second, the economic basis of Caribbean slavery has been at issue. Was it a self-propelled mode of production or a form of international merchant capitalism? I set forth a synthesis of these approaches, focusing on the Caribbean slave household as a locus of subsistence production, where females enjoyed some status, authority, and economic power. When household production was limited, males were more powerful, as indicated by their access to skilled jobs and postemancipation proletarianization.

Finally, the social and cultural status of slaves has been debated by those who favor a structural explanation based on symbolic and legal orders and by those advocating the study of the culture of working peoples. Structural explanations, based on slaves as property or as natally alienated, tend to equalize males and females when such an analysis is not warranted by the data. Those who recognize the integrity of slave culture interpret slaves' emotions and political intentions, also without basis. A materialist strategy that acknowledges slaves' economic motives for status in a society with strong structural barriers to mobility and social change is advocated.

My responses to these areas of debate are drawn from a broad Marxian perspective and favor specific analytics and categories. New World slavery is, for me, best understood as a series of social formations, combining non-capitalist modes of production, including slavery, with mercantile capitalism. Locating the interconnections of modes of production in households advances the analysis of slavery, patriarchy, and gender. Some phenomena are best described as rooted in ideologies, the material bases of which are unclear but finally determinant. The Marxian study of Caribbean slave women benefits from reference to other sources and perspectives that have focused on gender directly.

Women's studies has blossomed in recent years and has presented a surprisingly uniform body of literature on the cross-cultural position of women. There is strong agreement among comparativists that the development of advanced agriculture generally diminishes women's status (Boserup 1970; Sanday 1981; Goody 1976; Blumberg 1978). Cultivation of crops for sale generally puts a premium on male strength and undermines the crucial economic roles women perform in hunter-gatherer, horticultural, and simple agrarian societies.

New World slavery marked major advances in agriculture, expressed in the plantation form of production. Males were dominant in skilled tasks and valued for their productivity in field agriculture, despite their only marginal superiority over female workers. Planters' and slaves' overestimation of relative male strength may simply reflect West African and European peasant traditions, where males predominated in part because females' physical capacities were channeled to childbearing. Women slaves in the Caribbean bore few children and were involved in heavy labor in both plantation-based production and subsistence cultivation. Yet this emphasis on production over reproduction translated into status and authority only in the growing of provisions, and then only where carried out on individually controlled grounds and where a male head of household did not preempt females' access to land.

New World slavery in its Caribbean form supports the finding that advanced forms of agriculture had a profound influence on women's economic and social position and with the steady incorporation of industrial elements, plantation organization and technology further altered women's status. Slave women's energy was almost fully applied to agricultural production, and their labor productivity nearly equaled men's. Women's social position too approached men's. Yet gender stratification remained relevant, expressing another tragic irony of Caribbean slavery: that with women working as hard as men, in the same jobs and generally as competently, gender was an important basis of social hierarchy.

The parallels of Caribbean plantation slavery to modern industrial society are conspicuous. As modern wage workers have entered industrial and service employment, the birth rate has dropped and women have been drawn into previously male provinces of work. At the same time, women's economic power and social status have generally diminished, although gains in social autonomy and women's recent movement into higher-level occupational slots have been compensating trends (Chafetz 1984; Blumberg 1978). Caribbean slave women's enlarged role in field labor subjected them to routinized and continuous work, particularly as industrial components modified plantation organization. Independence from male slave authority figures followed. But without the corresponding economic gains that contemporary women have slowly achieved, slave women's autonomy meant little more than isolation and estrangement from kin and other social ties.

Slaves became, then, commodities in much the way Marx understood wage laborers. Increasingly bondless Caribbean slaves were atomized and alienated. New World slavery was indeed a moment in the long-running proletarianization of Caribbean agricultural workers (Mintz 1978). It conferred on bonded workers a status much like the proletarian and foreshadowed capitalism's eclipse of other relations of production after emancipation. Slave women's part in the elaboration of changing modes of production was especially cruel. Victims of an agrarian system with industrial patterns of production, women worked as men but lacked even bondmen's status and authority.

CHAPTER TWO

Women in New World Slavery

The study of women in Caribbean slavery raises questions about the experiences of slave women throughout the Americas. European exploration of the New World led to production of commodity crops and the use of slaves in North America, the Caribbean, Brazil, and on a more limited basis, in other areas of South and Central America. In what ways did bondwomen's lives vary in these settings? What systematic factors underlie slave women's differing experiences?

Historians have considered North American slavery and bondage as categorically different from slavery in the Caribbean and Brazil. For Tannenbaum (1946) differences were rooted in the comparative treatment of slaves in these settings. Genovese (1965) has insisted on the structural origins of slavery in the Americas. Comparative case studies (for example, Klein 1967) point to a variety of specific differences, some situational, others the product of larger socioeconomic and political dynamics of bondage in the New World.

Several important works have appeared in recent years on slave women in the U.S. South (White 1985; Jones 1982, 1986; Hine 1979; Gundersen 1986; Fox-Genovese 1986). Their depiction of southern slave women's position in the slave community and plantation-based production of commodity exports is not substantially different from our understanding of the lives of Caribbean bondwomen. In both cases women worked in the fields and as domestic servants, had relatively little entry into skilled positions, and were responsible for the care of their families and households. Some important differences emerge in slave women's fertility, in the degree of slave women's independent access to income-generating activities, and in slave family organization. In general, it appears that Caribbean slave women worked more frequently and intensely in field labor than their counterparts in the southern United States and wielded more status and authority as household heads and as petty entrepreneurs and traders than slave women in the South.[1]

In this chapter I focus on the bases of this variation, beginning with broad differences in the historical development of the production of commodities for export in the United States and the Caribbean.[2] Production of cotton, tobacco, and rice in the South evolved under different political, economic, and ecological constraints from those accompanying production of sugar in the Caribbean. These contrasting conditions generated diverging demands on the slave work force, manifested in differing gender-based divisions of labor. They also created demographic circumstances more conducive to the organization of nuclear families, the endurance of kinship ties, and childbearing among slaves in the United States than among their Caribbean counterparts.

The comparison of southern mainland and Caribbean commodity production advances the development of a theoretical perspective on the situation of Caribbean slave women. Mercantilism and the related articulation of capitalist and noncapitalist modes of production set the contours of New World plantation slavery. The resulting form of plantation-based cash crop production and labor organization equalized the position of male and female workers at the lowest occupational levels and generated hierarchy within higher-status positions. Plantation systems able to take advantage of economies of scale were most likely to exhibit a skill-based hierarchy in gender stratification. Smaller-scale systems of slave-based plantation production generally assigned different work to male and female slaves, suggesting a more lateral, task-oriented division of labor. Some work allocation appears to have reflected earlier European and West African patterns of distribution of work and rewards to males and females.

SLAVERY IN THE UNITED STATES AND THE CARIBBEAN

Slave studies in recent years have focused increasingly on economic and political constraints and opportunities in the lives of New World slaveholders and slaves. Following Williams's (1966) seminal work, many scholars have seen modern slavery as the product of European social structural forces beyond the influence of individual or even group will in the plantation setting. This viewpoint has found fertile ground in comparative work, where scholarship has recently emphasized the profound contrast in the organization and use of slave labor in the South and the Caribbean and its relationship to the economic development of the United States and Great Britain.

Genovese has been an especially strong proponent of this view. In his *Political Economy of Slavery* (1965), Genovese painted a broad contrast among British, Spanish, and French political economies and their colonies in the New World that employed slave labor for the production of commodity crops. Using a Marxist model of capitalist development, Genovese claimed that more highly rationalized relations of production, influenced by mercantile and industrial capitalism, characterized slave labor in the English and French colonies. A quasi-seigneurial system, resembling the feudal manor, was found in the U.S. South and in Spanish colonies. In these places slaves had more highly personalistic ties with slave masters than in British or French colonies. More important, argued Genovese, was that slavery was an engine for capitalist development by the bourgeoisie of Great Britain and France. For the

Spanish and southern slave master, however, it was only a primitive social relation, bogging the South and Spain down in precapitalist backwardness.

Genovese, with Fox-Genovese (Fox-Genovese and Genovese 1983), has since advanced his conceptualization of the slave South, now arguing that "the Old South, more than any other slaveholding country, became a slave society in the strict sense: its politics, economy, and culture were primarily determined by slave, not feudal or bourgeois, relations of production" (Fox-Genovese and Genovese 1983, p. 16). This southern precapitalist slave mode of production was a "product" of mercantile capitalism. Fox-Genovese and Genovese agree with Dobb's (1947) characterization of mercantile capitalism as "conservative," producing perhaps economic growth through slavery but finally preventing industrial development.[3]

British and French colonial slavery had quite different relationships to more advanced forms of production. The Caribbean "slave-plantation system" was an "adjunct" of British capitalism, the "pawn and prize" in the struggle between capitalism and "residual feudalism" in France (Fox-Genovese and Genovese 1983, p. 5). No real economic development occurred in these regions, but the attitude of planters toward their enterprise and labor was more utilitarian and rational than in the U.S. South and their capital contributed to industrial growth and diversification in their imperial centers.[4]

Fox-Genovese and Genovese (1983, p. 60) comment further that patriarchy influenced political and community life profoundly in the South in contrast to the West Indies. Southern planters were generally resident, with whites the majority in most areas. There were, for example, 23,000 blacks and 72,000 whites in Virginia in 1715, a period of prosperous tobacco planting. Maryland, another major eighteenth-century tobacco producer, had a population of 9,500 blacks and 40,700 whites in 1715. Only in rice-growing South Carolina, did blacks outnumber whites in 1715, with 10,500 blacks and 6,250 whites (Harris 1964, p. 84). Of the nearly 10 million people in the United States in 1820 over 80 percent were white. Even in the South blacks were never more than 38 percent of the total population (Harris 1964, p. 85).[5]

The Caribbean offers a dramatic contrast to the South in black/white population ratios. Slaves were generally the majority of the population, particularly as sugar and other forms of cash crop production intensified and spread. In eighteenth-century Jamaica, Saint Domingue, and much of the rest of the Caribbean, more than 80 percent of the population was black. In 1650 blacks made up 25 percent of the British Caribbean population, constituting 91 percent by 1770 (Fogel and Engerman 1974, p. 22). Even in Cuba, Puerto Rico, and other Caribbean islands with relatively large settler populations, intense production of cash crops followed European settlement; production was regionally concentrated and meant the separation of the planters' households and family members from slaves and export agriculture (Scarano 1984; Moreno Fraginals 1978).

The effects of planter absenteeism on the community were many and evident in the ways that culture developed in the West Indies and in the United States (Patterson 1969, 1973; Genovese 1971). White women and children resided with their planter husbands in the U.S. South, fostering the development of formal religious, educational, and cultural institutions among whites. Miscegenation was also less common, although the exploitation of black female sexuality by the white elite was frequent, seeming to be intrinsic to New World slavery (White 1985; Jones 1986).

Southern whites held on to the institution of slavery until 1861, displaying greater tenacity and political will than Europeans in the West Indies. Indeed, the international merchant class and many prescient West Indian planters had moved their money to other pursuits and joined the forces of opposition to slavery by the turn of the nineteenth century (Williams 1966; Ragatz 1963). Those who held on saw their ranks thin and outside support dwindle. Southern whites, on the other hand, understood that their lifestyle and their livelihood depended on slavery. They sought separation from the metropolitan center as a means to continue what was finally, for both southern and West Indian planters, an economy and labor system out of line with world trends and forces (Wallerstein 1976; see also Wright 1987).[6]

CROPS, CLIMATE, AND CHANGING TASTES

Differences in metropolitan political economies conditioned settlement patterns and other points of contrast between the Caribbean and U.S. South but cannot account fully for the ways in which local and regional economies emerged in the Americas. Ecological factors were extremely significant— temperature and soil conspired to make less lucrative crops suitable to the temperate mainland and the greater riches of sugar nearly inevitable for its West Indian producers. The emerging and differentiated European market for luxury foods affected the prospect of the successful production of various commodities (Mintz 1979–1980). Geography also contributed to the contrasting development of the West Indies and the U.S. South, encouraging settlement on the expansive mainland and warfare and piracy in the Caribbean Sea. These immutable physical factors intermingled, and as production of commodity crops developed on the slave-based plantations of the Americas, "inexorably and very rapidly—the island and mainland plantations evolved into two separate communities" (Dunn 1972, p. xiii).

Tobacco, Cotton, and the U.S. South

The tropical climate of the West Indies and the temperate zone of the Atlantic coast of North America were both well suited to tobacco cultivation, which has traditionally been carried out on small plots and requires diligent and continuous care. A single planter or task force must carry the operation through from planting to harvest to preserve and nurture the quality of every plant (Ortiz 1947). Tobacco is thus less labor intensive than many other New World commodity crops, and the work of tobacco production is spread out through the entire year rather than concentrated in a few intense months, as in much other cash cropping.

Tobacco was grown by white farmers in Cuba and the other early Spanish territories, along with food and other cash crops. The English settlers of Barbados used slash and burn techniques to produce both cotton and tobacco for export (Dunn 1972, p. 5).[7] Eventually slaves were introduced to tend tobacco, as its cultivation spread in the seventeenth century through the Caribbean region and to the Chesapeake Bay area on the east coast of the United States. Wallerstein (1980, p. 164) called tobacco "the poor relative" of sugar, "an early starter and an early loser." In the Caribbean sugar production quickly surpassed tobacco. Yet tobacco production prospered in the Chesapeake area, in the states of Virginia and Maryland, where a "superior crop at lower prices" than could be cultivated in the Caribbean was developed (Wallerstein 1980, p. 165).

Tobacco leaches nutrients from the soil even more forcefully than does sugar, requiring a move to new territory every quarter century. The large expanse of land on the mainland was thus conducive to the soil replacement requirements of the crop. Planters could preserve the quality of the product and their land by rotating tobacco with staple crops, at the same time ensuring some degree of food self-sufficiency (Stampp 1956, p. 129). The annual work cycle began with preparation of the beds for planting during the winter months. In May the shoots were transplanted. "Worming, topping and suckering" of the plants occurred in summer. Finally, during the summer plants were "split, cut and left in the fields to wilt." The processing phase then began, with drying and curing of the plant in the tobacco house. The following year, after starting a new crop, the tobacco was stripped from the stalks, tied into bundles, and "prized into hogsheads" (Stampp 1956, p. 49).

The European labor force was more extensive in the Chesapeake Bay area than in the Caribbean. The enclosure movement had encouraged British migration, and from 1600 to 1700, 500,000 English emigrated to North America. In contrast, 150,000 emigrants from Spain arrived in the Spanish Caribbean settlements from 1509 to 1790 (Harris 1964, p. 82). Kulikoff (1986, p. 4) notes that the seventeenth-century Chesapeake was "full of opportunities." The many servants who migrated to the area worked in tobacco cultivation and related endeavors, often completing their service to become proprietors themselves.

Falling tobacco prices and a decline in white immigration led to an increase in the use of slave labor in the late seventeenth century. In 1650 slaves made up only 3 percent of the Chesapeake population, but 15 percent in 1690, as chattel slavery became crucial to tobacco production in Virginia (Kulikoff 1986, p. 319).[8] In 1690 Maryland and Virginia accounted for two-thirds of the black population in the United States; in 1790 Maryland and Virginia had 56 percent of U.S. slaves, even as the slave population was moving southward to work in cotton farming (Fogel and Engerman 1974, p. 44).

Plantations were relatively small in the Chesapeake Bay area, with estates in Virginia generally covering about 500 acres in the mid-seventeenth century, increasing to perhaps 1,000 acres in 1750 (Eaves 1945, p. 21). The average holding in Virginia and Maryland numbered fewer than 13 slaves (Fogel and Engerman 1974, p. 22).[9] On the basis of his survey of several counties in the Chesapeake Bay area, Kulikoff (1986, p. 330) speculates that in the 1730s half of the slaves lived in units of 10 or less, with only a quarter on estates with more than 20 slaves. Each slave cultivated from two to three acres, meaning that much land was generally devoted to other crops and uses (Eaves 1945, p. 22).

The tobacco industry declined with a succession of crises and recessions in the eighteenth century (Kulikoff 1986; Fox-Genovese and Genovese 1983, pp. 53–55). The center of tobacco growing moved westward to Virginia's Piedmont region. Many planters, along with their slaves, migrated farther south. Other slaves were sold to cotton planters in Georgia, Mississippi, and Alabama by farmers in the Chesapeake Bay area and South Carolina. From 1790 to 1860, 835,000 slaves moved south from exporting states (Fogel and Engerman 1974, pp. 47–48).

Cotton production was found in the United States from the first years of the seventeenth century. Green seed, or upland, cotton, grew bountifully in the southern climate, but its widespread cultivation was hindered by early difficulties in processing. The hand removal of cotton fibers from the thousands of seeds in a pod, or boll, was a slow and arduous job. When the separation of fiber and seeds was mechanized in 1793, with the invention of the cotton gin, southern plantation production of cotton boomed. In 1709, 3,000 bales were produced in the United States, rising to 178,000 bales in 1810, to 732,000 bales in 1830, and to more than 4 million bales in 1860, when cotton constituted more than two-thirds of U.S. exports (Fogel and Engerman 1974, p. 44). Cotton production eventually spread through Georgia, Alabama, Mississippi, Missouri, Louisiana, Tennessee, Arkansas, and Texas. The U.S. slave population grew from 700,000 in 1793 to 4,000,000 in 1860.

The intensity of work in the cotton fields was higher than in tobacco farming, and tasks were more compatible with large-scale planting. Cotton seeds were planted in the winter, close together in shallow beds or furrows. When the seedlings were 3–4 inches high, they were thinned or "chopped" with a hoe. The cotton plant blossoms when it is about a foot high; the petals fall off several days later and flat green bolls are left. The bolls then take up to two months to mature into egg-shaped pods that, when they split, reveal several compartments of cotton. In the deep South, the bolls were picked from the plant in July. The cotton fiber and seeds were then separated laboriously by hand or, finally, in gins.

Work was generally assigned in a mix of gang and task labor, depending on the size of the estate and the work force. Gangs of workers often plowed and hoed the cotton fields under the direction of a driver. Or they were assigned a plot of perhaps 150 square feet to tend, following the task system. Slaves generally picked a daily quota of cotton during the harvest (Stampp 1956, p. 55). The number of slaves per agricultural unit grew as cotton production prospered, with most cotton estates utilizing the labor of at least 30 slaves. The optimal number of slaves per unit immediately before the Civil War was 50 "on the black-belt soils of Alabama and Texas, and more than 200 in the alluvial lands of the Mississippi flood plain" [Wolf (1982, p. 280); see also, Fogel and Engerman (1974, p. 200)]. Nevertheless, about half of U.S. cotton was grown by small farmers with from one to twelve slaves.

Cotton processing was done on large estates or at ginning operations serving a group of smaller-scale farms. The fibers were pulled away from the seeds as the boll passed through a roller with wire teeth or a saw edge. After the ginning was completed, the cotton fibers were packed for transport to textile mills in the North, in England, and to a lesser extent, in southern cities.

Other Southern Cash Crops

Other commodity export crops were also grown in the slave South. Rice production dominated plantations in South Carolina in the seventeenth and eighteenth centuries, taking advantage of the large West Indian market for rice to feed the slaves (Fox-Genovese and Genovese 1983, p. 52). In South Carolina blacks outnumbered whites, constituting 60 percent of the population in the early 1700s, and perhaps 50–55 percent when cotton became an important crop there in the nineteenth century (Genovese 1979; Wood 1974). Rice was also grown in coastal Georgia and the Carolinas.

Rice is a delicate crop planted in shallow ground, but its cultivation is relatively simple. Planting began in March and April. In the summer slaves weeded, flooded, raked, and dried the fields. In the fall the rice was cut and milled. The process of threshing and pounding with mortar and pestle was borrowed from West African techniques of rice cultivation and introduced by the slaves. Finally the rice was screened and packed (Stampp 1956; Wood 1974). When not engaged in planting or harvesting, slaves cleared and refurbished the trenches and banks that made up the infrastructure of the rice plantation.

Slaves hoed during the summer in unison but performed other work by task, allowing time to themselves when their work was done. The number of slaves per unit was low in the early 1700s, perhaps from eight to twelve, comparable to the share in selected Maryland counties cited by Kulikoff (1986). However, the slave population was unevenly distributed and increasingly concentrated. Wood (1974, p. 159) presents the example of South Carolina's St. George County in 1727, when two-thirds of the slaves lived on 18 plantations in groups ranging from 25 to 94 slaves, with more than 20 percent of the slaves on the largest 3 plantations. Rice planting was considered brutal because of the disease climate of the coastal swamplands and the general intensity of work. Indeed, South Carolina has been compared to Barbados, the origin of its early explorers and founders, because of the black majority and their tendency to lose population in the mid-eighteenth century rather than to gain slaves as elsewhere in the South.

Sugar production also acquired some significance in the U.S. South, beginning in Louisiana in the late 1700s with the emigration of slaves and former planters from then newly independent Saint Domingue. The state provided 95 percent of the U.S. sugar crop. Sugar was cultivated as well in Texas, Georgia, and Florida, all following the difficult planting regimen imposed on slaves in Louisiana and the Caribbean. The complex routine of processing sugar, described in the next section, required a few highly skilled workers. The cultivation of cane required labor of most plantation slaves, who worked in gangs to plant, weed, and harvest the cane and deliver it to the processing mill.

Although sugar and rice were important regional crops, tobacco and cotton utilized more land and slaves and were generally more profitable than other cash crops grown in the South. The difference in slave population engaged in each major cash crop in 1850 is marked, although by the mid-nineteenth century the peak period of tobacco and rice production had passed: cotton, 73 percent; tobacco, 14 percent; sugar, 6 percent; rice, 5 percent; hemp, 2 percent. United States southern production of commodity exports, primarily tobacco and cotton, made the South a center of New World slavery by the time of the Civil War. Fogel and Engerman (1974, p. 29) estimate that by 1835 the United States had nearly 2 million slaves, 36 percent of the slaves in the Western world.[10]

Sugar and the Caribbean

Sugar cane was grown in South Asia in 4 B.C. Crude processing came later, in perhaps the sixth century A.D., yielding sugar "crudely similar to the modern product" (Mintz 1979–1980, p. 58). By the twelfth century sugar production was well established in the southern and eastern Mediterranean, gradually moving westward to Portugal and Spain. In the 1200s sugar was a delicacy enjoyed by British royalty. By the eighteenth century it was a common spice, enjoyed throughout Western Europe by working people as well as the nobility (Mintz 1979–1980; Dirks 1987, pp. 10–11). In the interim sugar production had moved from the Mediterranean to the Canary Islands and Madeira to Brazil in the sixteenth century and to the West Indies in the seventeenth century. With it came slaves and an enormous expansion in the cultivation and productivity of sugar.

Among West Indian islands Barbados made a dramatic transition to sugar by 1640. The Dutch introduced sugar following their expulsion from Brazil and brought with them production techniques and markets. A more profitable crop than tobacco, sugar attracted Barbados's planters, who feared over-production of tobacco in the region and in North America and a consequent drop in prices.[11] The small island of Barbados was well suited to sugar production. Unlike many of the other West Indies islands, Barbados was flat and thus easily defended from the military and private force and violence dominating the Caribbean Sea at the time. Escape of slaves was also less likely there than in more mountainous nearby islands. Barbados's less "enervating" climate made it a suitable outpost for English settlers, who found Caribbean temperatures generally difficult to withstand (Sheridan 1965; see also Wallerstein 1980, p. 163).

Still, European settlement was sparse, and profitable sugar production required large-scale planting. Hence labor shortages were a problem in Barbados, and slave labor expanded quickly once introduced (Green 1988; Dirks 1987, p. 16).[12] In the 1670s slave-based sugar production started in earnest in the smaller Leewards and in French Martinique and Guadeloupe. The typical slave labor force was then 50 to 100 slaves on 100 to 200 acres. Although annexed by the British in 1655, the larger Jamaica did not become a major sugar producer until the eighteenth century, when the other large islands, first Saint Domingue and later Cuba, were able to take advantage of established planting techniques and the relative peace of the area to become sugar producers on an unprecedented scale. Average estates in late sugar producers covered more than a thousand acres, and plantation labor forces often exceeded 300 slaves. The intensification and spread of sugar cultivation brought the fortunes that intrepid Europeans had sought in moving to the West Indies, bounty more notable than that enjoyed by southern planters (Klein 1986).

New World sugar production was extremely complex by virtue of the complication and precision required in processing. Sugar cultivation itself involved a relatively simple technique. Slaves laid cane in holes in the ground in the fall for harvesting 16 months later. The harvest was a frantic and busy time, for sugar spoils immediately after cutting. Field slaves cut the cane and loaded it onto carts for the processing mill during an intense few days (Dirks

1987). While field gangs recovered from the hurry and deprivation of the harvest, a small skilled team of adult male slaves processed the cane into brown sugar, rum, and in some settings, white sugar. The demanding and precise refining regimen began as the cane was ground in mills powered by cattle, wind, or water, and juice was extracted. A boiler then heated the juice in successively smaller and hotter coppers, cooling the juice at just the right time for crystals to form. This delicate work was followed by drying the sugar and draining off molasses for rum (Dunn 1972; Schnakenbourg 1980).

The slave labor force spent the remainder of the year engaged in replanting and waiting for the results of a second planting, from either ratooning (growing a second or even third sprout from the original cane) or new cane plantings. Either way the soil had little rest and the field gangs had considerable time away from planting. As on southern cotton plantations, dead time was spent on road work, repairing buildings, and cleaning equipment. Craton (1974, p. 129) argues, however, that Caribbean planters resorted to highly repressive methods to keep their relatively large, under-employed work forces under control when they were not directly engaged in sugar cultivation.

Sugar refining, like cotton ginning, had to be done on or near the plantation for the planter to realize large profits from cultivation. The ginning process was sufficiently simple that the nineteenth century brought no major technical innovations to increase the volume of cotton grown or processed. Increased productivity came later, primarily with mechanization of planting and harvesting. For sugar, technical progress was slow until the nineteenth century and was centered in processing machinery and techniques. Two innovations were especially important. First, steam-powered mills, developed in Jamaica, increased production and labor productivity. This was followed by the development in Cuba of the mechanized mill, which improved the quality and the amount of juice extracted from the cane (Moreno Fraginals 1978). Mechanization led to the separation of agricultural and industrial functions in Cuban sugar production, with centralized mills (*centrales*) drawing sugar for refining from surrounding farms. As a result, increased world demand for sugar could be satisfied, but only by raising productivity demands on the slave work force, constricted by the 1807 close of the slave trade.

Mercantilism and Plantation Agriculture

The New World production of commodity crops for export meant the development and refinement of the plantation as a major means of agricultural production. Beckford, Mintz, Best, Dirks, and others have drawn on the earlier work of Edgar Thompson (1975) to suggest that plantation production represented a qualitative shift in planting techniques, allowing for large-scale production of a single crop, generally for export. It has also been argued that labor was frequently coerced and usually imported, because free laborers in an open resource situation would prefer to work for higher wages or to have their own firms rather than work for low plantation wages (see Dirks 1987 for a review of this argument).

Examination of New World plantations raises some serious questions about (1) the degree of coercion intrinsic to plantation economies and (2) the advantage of economies of scale for New World plantation producers of some commodities. Southern tobacco cultivation, for example, undermines generalizations about scale. Small-scale production prevailed in the Chesapeake Bay and Piedmont areas along with subsistence planting and crop rotation. Unit costs decreased as the number of plants increased but only up to a point that was quickly achieved and followed by overplanting. Only the need for slave labor and production of tobacco for export made tobacco consistent with the commonly held conception of a plantation crop.[13] Indeed, Ortiz (1947) developed the dichotomy between Cuban sugar production, a large-scale crop cultivated by African slaves, and tobacco, the crop of, first, the Indian horticulturalist and, later, the skilled European farmer.

Sugar, cotton, and rice could have been produced with free labor. After the emancipation of slaves and the heavy capitalization of plantation production by emergent multinational corporations in the late nineteenth century, sugar was produced by wage laborers (Beckford 1972). Why was slavery necessary to earlier New World plantations? The logic of mercantilism encouraged broad-scale production facilitated by protective political devices. And the political strength of mercantile interests guaranteed the enormous costs of acquiring and seasoning slaves. The lack of success of some indentured servants and their eventual scarcity further supported the use of slave labor. But even within the confines of mercantile political and economic strategies, variations in labor organization and planting technique can be found, conditioned by the metropolitan stage of economic and political development and the exigencies of particular crops and climates.

These factors also influenced technical developments within plantation economies. Relatively high levels of capital investment and industrial sophistication could be achieved in the production of sugar, given both the means of processing and the political economy of Caribbean planting. In contrast, production of tobacco involved little sophisticated technology; nor did it yield the capital necessary for many forms of technical or agricultural change. The mix of political-economic and ecological factors affected women's role in cash crop production and determined their level of participation in field agriculture, their labor productivity, and their entry into higher-skill processing jobs. Scale of production and general division of slave labor conditioned the gender division of labor.

GENDER ON NEW WORLD PLANTATIONS

Women were sold into the Atlantic slave trade in increasing numbers during the seventeenth and eighteenth centuries in response to the New World demand for slave labor and African supply factors. Women had long played an important role in African slavery; most modern sub-Saharan African slaves were women. Long recognized as reproducers and keepers of African lineages, women, it is now understood, played a principal role in production. African slave women did "most of the agricultural and virtually all of the domestic work. The value of women slaves was based on a sexual division of labor which assigned much of the productive labor to women" (Robertson and Klein 1983, p. 11).[14] The gender division of labor differed in the New World primarily by bringing males into agriculture, particularly into skilled positions. The domestic component lessened as well in large-scale cash cropping, and the nature of the agricultural work changed, becoming more repetitive (Terbourg-Penn 1986).

A continuum can be constructed of New World plantation economies on the basis of their size and apparent capacity to take advantage of economies of scale and of their level of technical innovation and sophistication in refining agricultural raw materials. The latter issue influenced the creation of stratification among laborers on the plantation and the demand for increased output of the raw agricultural crop. On one end of the continuum was tobacco production, conducted on a relatively small scale. Technical innovation and machinery were minimal. Improvements in quality and yield resulted primarily from the use of fertilizers and crop rotation. Changes were also made in the construction of drying and curing houses. But this too was a rudimentary kind of transformation, involving little or no machinery (Eaves 1945). Women planted and tended tobacco; indeed, few escaped field labor on many farms and estates (Kulikoff 1986, p. 399; Gundersen 1986). The skills involved in tobacco production were only reluctantly passed on by Chesapeake farmers to a presumably incapable slave labor force, and male slaves were deemed the most suitable recipients of tobacco culture. Yet, because many farms in the Chesapeake Bay area were small and nearly all produced food crops, slaves' work was generally more diversified than in the production of most New World cash crops. Women did many different kinds of domestic, horticultural, and agricultural work, and as the native-born proportion of slaves increased, kinship networks developed and fertility increased (Kulikoff 1986, p. 73).

Cultivation of rice and cotton represents the midpoint on the continuum of organization of large-scale cash cropping in the New World. Produced on a larger scale than tobacco, rice and cotton production nevertheless allowed for at least some task allocation rather than planting exclusively by gangs, as in

New World sugar cultivation. In rice culture gender determined the division of some agricultural labor, with women performing the winnowing of grain and the separation of the rice from its kernal with a mortar and pestle, much as they did in West Africa. It is likely that other tasks were allocated by gender: heavy work to males and horticulture, animal husbandry, and domestic work to females, much as in other agrarian settings. Rice was not refined but shipped in its crude state, eliminating a major basis for gender stratification. Even with the "primitive" conditions of coastal rice production in the South, "it was not unusual for families to remain intact over the generations, and to maintain contact with kin on nearby holdings" (Jones 1986, p. 15). Natural population increases developed at the turn of the eighteenth century but were reversed with the mid-eighteenth-century spread and intensification of rice cultivation. A later return to black population growth suggests that the work demands and conditions of rice culture were compatible with moderate fertility levels to the extent that planters modified their productivity demands and were responsive to the needs of workers in a stressful physical environment (Wood 1974, pp. 143–166; Jones 1986).

Southern cotton farming varied in its gender-based division of labor by size of holding. Small farms required diverse tasks of women, as field labor was mixed with household and other agricultural chores. On large estates women's options were more narrow, and they were rarely allowed to develop artisanal abilities.[15] Slave women's domestic tasks on behalf of the master's family were seldom considered skilled. Slave women also had important roles in the small-scale production of cloth and textiles carried out on most estates and farms. Spinning and weaving were constant accompaniments to other tasks. "This form of labor occupied female slaves of all ages at night, during the winter and on rainy summer days, whether or not they were pregnant or nursing a baby, and whether they were formally designated as cooks, house servants, or field hands" (Jones 1986, p. 24). Such work remained secondary to cotton cultivation, however, and could be carried out only when women were not engaged in field labor. The larger and more productive the plantation, the more exclusive and significant women's role in cotton production and the less meaningful their work in other forms of production for use or exchange.

Sugar cultivation forms the last point on the continuum of New World slave-based cash cropping, with men and women cruelly and continuously exploited (Mathurin 1974; Gautier 1985; Bush 1981, 1986; Olwig 1985). Economies of scale were possible in West Indian sugar cultivation and were driven finally by technical improvements that allowed massive amounts of cane to be processed quickly. With the close of the slave trade, slave labor including that of women, was precious. On the large estates women worked long and hard, with little opportunity for less burdensome tasks.[16] The intensity of cultivation and harvesting depleted their physical energy and well-being, influencing fertility, as the general exigencies of constant work and locational instability diminished their prospects for family continuity.

Conclusions

The situations of bondwomen in the Americas are strikingly similar. Where plantation agriculture approached industrial forms of organization, males' and females' labor was not sharply differentiated. The expanded scale and technological apparatus of the plantations increased highly skilled tasks and allocated them to males. Where agriculture was on a smaller scale and processing nonmechanized, more traditional agrarian gender-based divisions of labor emerged. Males' and females' agricultural work in these settings was both more diversified and differentiated by gender. European and West African farming techniques and modes of agrarian organization influenced the ways in which labor was distributed, both in the production of cash crops and in related aspects of labor.

The comparison of the production of commodities for export and its impact on gender stratification is useful in establishing the interaction of ecological and social structural variables in any social formation. The political economy of colonial powers was meaningful to New World social organization only if planters and their agents were able to create profitable enterprises in a given physical environment. The ecosystem was often surprisingly malleable to the invention, creativity, and greed of the mercantile planter.

The larger issue raised by this discussion of New World plantation slavery is how little gender mattered in the production of raw commodities. Women lost ground in plantation agriculture, particularly if they had previously worked in simpler agrarian, horticultural, or hunter-gatherer forms of production. These systems separated male and female but recognized the contributions of both genders as essential. In plantation agriculture much of male and female work was the same. Gender-specific realms lost significance as gender hierarchies were established in the distribution of skilled work in the technically sophisticated processing and refining of commodities. In this sense New World plantations marked a watershed, in which on a large, regional scale the need for field labor overwhelmed production for use, women's province in both Europe and West Africa.

CHAPTER THREE

Gender Ratios and Caribbean Slavery

During the eighteenth century sugar surpassed other forms of commodity production in the West Indies in profit making and area cultivated. Tobacco, coffee, cotton, and various spices were grown on small islands and in isolated regions of major sugar producers, but sugar ruled (Williams 1966). Sugar production on large estates and plantations spread throughout the Caribbean, driven in part by inefficient cultivation techniques and the search for new, fresh soils. By the mid-nineteenth century the areas from Brazil northward to Surinam and British Guiana through the West Indies and northwest into British Honduras had become centers of production of commodities for export, primarily sugar.

Imperial stewardship diminished in significance as large-scale sugar production became more competitive and uniform (Beckford 1972). Sixteenth- through nineteenth-century Caribbean history is replete with wars and skirmishes among colonial powers for access to these remarkably productive lands. But over time shifting imperial policies had relatively little impact on slaveholding or on the economic fortunes and social organization of plantations.

Slavery supplanted all other labor systems, most notably indenture. Africans constituted the principal worker pool. Europeans were relatively few in number and less adaptable to strenuous forced labor in New World climates than Africans or indigenous peoples. The native Caribs and Arawaks resisted European conquest and were in most areas eradicated. Finally, plantation size grew and labor forces increased. Slaves became more valuable and productive. And more dimensions of slave life, from housing to cooking and child care, were collectivized. Slaves were progressively subjected to routinized and rigorous work schemes and made socially bondless with the rending of kinship ties. Women progressively lost control of economic activities that had given them status and power.

Mintz (1978, p. 85) offers a period schema for West Indian slave societies that encapsulates these transitions. First, from ca. 1500 to 1580 the Spanish introduced the cultivation of sugar cane to much of the Greater Antilles, utilizing enslaved aborigines and Africans. From ca. 1640 to 1670 British and French states and entrepreneurs entered the Lesser Antilles, enslaving indigenous peoples and using the labor of African slaves and indentured

Europeans. The Dutch and then the Danes followed similar patterns of colonization and exploitation of land and enslaved labor in the Virgin Islands.

In the third stage, the apogee of Caribbean sugar planting (ca. 1670–1770), British and French planters dominated the region's production and used African slave labor exclusively in the cultivation of sugar. Unprecedented labor productivity and output were achieved by slave labor in English Jamaica after 1655 and in French Saint Domingue after 1697. Finally, from ca. 1770 to 1870 Hispanic sugar producers reached new levels of output, principally in Cuba, with mixes of "enslaved, 'contracted' and coerced labor'' (Mintz 1978, p. 85). Puerto Rico experienced a similar if less successful sugar boom, as did British Guiana and Trinidad, and, largely with indentured East Indian labor, Dutch Surinam.

Curtin's (1969) chronology lays the groundwork for discussion of demographic change within each sugar-producing society. Slave imports grew, with unequal gender ratios contributing to a natural population decrease. The labor exploitation associated with achievement of full production in much of the region also fostered population loss. Finally, declining production and profits altered the character of slave imports, now for replacement only. The Creole population then grew, gender ratios fell, and the gap between births and deaths narrowed.

Planters generally expressed a preference for male slaves, who were more readily available than females. This pattern was least pronounced in the period from 1500 to 1580, but roughly equal gender ratios are found for the seventeenth century as well. By the third stage, the late seventeenth and eighteenth centuries, the numerical predominance of males was well established and continued for areas then commencing slave-based sugar production. Finally, throughout the region increased local births and the purchase of females changed gender ratios and signaled a decline in production.

How Many Women?

There is virtually no task in Caribbean commodity production not at some time carried out by female slaves. Indeed, in the declining years of sugar production women generally outnumbered men and sometimes, with older slaves and children, achieved at least as high levels of per capita labor productivity as earlier generations of young, robust males (Higman 1976a; Klein 1978). Women had a prominent place in African slavery, with slaves used in domestic service and incorporated into lineages (Klein 1986, p. 13; Robertson and Klein 1983). Yet women slaves were often scarce in the Caribbean. Their participation in agriculture and related domestic tasks followed a pattern shaped by the shifting world economy and the peculiar ideologies of colonial powers.

There is little in the historical record to prove that African men and women reached the Caribbean in equal numbers in the fifteenth and sixteenth centuries. But several data are suggestive. Most Caribbean commodity planting began on a small scale with slaves employed in a variety of agricultural tasks, often involving the resident slaveholder. This general pattern prevailed well into the late 1700s for Cuba, British Guiana, Surinam, Puerto Rico, and Trinidad. Puerto Rico, for example, had a nearly equal number of male and female slaves in 1821, along with an extremely large cohort of children under age 10 (Turnbull 1840, p. 558; Flinter 1834, p. 213; Baralt 1981, p. 79). Moreno Franginals (1978, p. 38) argues as well that Cuba's slave gender ratio was nearly equal in the early 1800s. And Trinidad in 1779 had only slightly fewer females than males, with 5,396 boys and men counted island-wide and 4,613 girls and women (Millette 1970, Table 1).

Seventeenth- and eighteenth-century Caribbean societies also had a large number of women, although we are dependent on the observations of visitors and records from single plantations for information. Richard Ligon (1657, p. 47), an early European visitor to Barbados, noted that many male slaves had two or three wives. Thomas Atwood (1791) made the same observation about late eighteenth-century Dominica. This pattern of conjugal organization is consistent historically with gender ratios approaching equality or with a preponderance of women, although polygamy was sometimes found in Caribbean slave societies where men clearly outnumbered women (see, for example, Carmichael 1834, vol. 1, p. 298).[1] Europeans also had a tendency to call polygamous what were in fact multiple casual unions (Bennett 1958, p. 35). Of 992 slaves in Montserrat in 1678, 292 were children (Fergus 1975, p. 16). In the late eighteenth century French West Indian slaves married, raised children, and enjoyed feasts for children's baptisms and marriages provided by masters (Peytraud 1973, p. 207; Gautier 1985). Again, these phenomena are compatible with ratios of equality. Firmer evidence of low gender ratios for early Caribbean slavery comes from Bermuda, where 1721 census figures show that the number of slave men and boys nearly equaled slave women and girls (Packwood 1975, p. 74).

Apparent numerical equality of male and female slaves changed everywhere with the intensification and expansion of monoculture, thus departing from U.S. slave history in a fundamental way. Slaveholders in North America continued to purchase female slaves and to encourage conjugal families. More important, the United States ceased purchasing slaves earlier. During the 1700s and into the 1800s, a majority of the slave population in the British and French West Indies was born in Africa; as late as 1800, 25 percent had recently arrived from Africa. The native-born population constituted a majority of U.S. slaves as early as 1680 (Fogel and Engerman 1974, p. 23). This "creolization" of the U.S. slave population led to its feminization.[2]

West Indian slave owners continued to seek young male slaves. As a result, the ratio of male to female slaves changed, often dramatically. For the British and Spanish West Indies, contemporary observers estimated that about one-third of slaves were female in the mid-eighteenth century (Edwards 1966, vol. 2, p. 138; Humboldt 1960, p. 188). An example from arriving slave ships to Cuba supports a nearly 4:1 male to female ratio: from 1763 to 1765 La Real Compañía delivered 3,983 men and boys and 1,054 women and girls (Marrero 1983, p. 6).[3] Craton (1977, p. 72) contends that among slaves on trading ships to the British West Indies, 60 percent were male, suggesting a slightly more equitable gender distribution. Records for British trade from 1791 to 1798 indicate that females made up 38 percent of the 83,000 slaves taken from the entire western African coastal region (Klein 1983, p. 30).

A similar range of percentages is found for trade to other Caribbean slave societies. The roster of a slave ship reaching St. Thomas in the eighteenth century listed twice as many men as women (Westergaard 1917, p. 140). From 1779 to 1789, 49 Danish ships left the Guinea coast with 15,000 slaves, 36 percent of whom were female. The gender ratio among children was 145 boys for every 100 girls. Similar findings are available for the Dutch trade: About 38 percent of slaves traded at the turn of the eighteenth century were women. Among the children, there were 193 boys for every 100 girls (Klein 1978, p. 30). Among slave imports to Surinam until 1735, more than 70 percent were male (Price 1976, p. 12). More than twice as many male as female slaves were imported to the French West Indies (Nicholls 1985, p. 122), with perhaps two-thirds of a ship's slaves being male in the 1740s (Gautier 1985, p. 80).

More extreme gender imbalances in the slave trade and general population are reported for particular settings. Perhaps no more than 5 percent of slaves in Saint Domingue were female in the eighteenth century (Debien 1974, p. 366).[4] Geggus (1978, p. 7) argues, however, that masters exaggerated the scarcity of females to deflect attention from more fundamental causes for the low birth rate, causes such as undernourishment and overwork. On the other hand, by the late eighteenth century many males had left the plantations to join Maroon and other insurgent groups (Nicholls 1985, p. 122). Moreno Fraginals (1978, pp. 42, 87) estimates that, as the Cuban sugar boom began, from 1790 to the 1820s, 76 percent of imported slaves were male; at the same time males constituted nearly 85 percent of slaves on sugar and coffee plantations (see also Deerr 1949–1950, p. 277). Some Cuban plantations had no female slaves (G. Hall 1971, p. 27; Bremer 1853, vol. 2, p. 334; Gurney 1840, p. 160).

Maleness was not enough, of course. Youth was perhaps more valuable to slaveholders. The incredible achievement of Caribbean slave societies, especially the greatly productive late eighteenth-century Jamaica, Cuba, and Saint

Domingue, was to amass an almost wholly productive population.[5] Moreno
Fraginals's description of nineteenth-century Cuba is telling:

In short, the plantations of the time were prison-like places, virtually
without women (only 10.23 percent), children (8.15 percent), or old
people (3.13 percent). They were sugar-producing jails in which there
were no family relations and in which there would be recurrent outbreaks
of aberrant sexual behavior. The maintenance of a plantation economy
based on a demographic structure of this nature demanded the free and
unlimited entry of slaves. (Moreno Fraginals 1977, p. 192)

This productivity yielded immense profits and for slave masters finally
confounded demographic conditions. Recent commentary, influenced by
Williams's presentation of the internal contradictions of slave-based commodity planting under the aegis of mercantile capitalism, emphasizes the
belief among slaveholders that young male slaves were more productive than
other categories of workers and thus highly desired. And, it is suggested, this
rapid utilization of highly productive workers was compatible with the "get
rich quick" mentality of international mercantile capitalism (Williams 1966;
Craton 1974; Moreno Fraginals 1978).

Although this approach provides an outline for explanation, it is not
sufficient for our understanding of young males' predominance among late
eighteenth- and early nineteenth-century Caribbean slaves. Exceptions to
general demographic patterns suggest that seemingly feeble categories of
workers were as productive, or nearly so, as young males (Higman 1976a;
Moreno Fraginals 1978; Dunn 1977). Certainly they were often as numerous,
as Caribbean planters surely observed. For example, two Jamaican estates
belonging to Richard Beckford varied widely in gender ratio in 1756:
Hartford Pen had 41 slaves— 24 men, 6 women, 8 boys, and 3 girls—
although Beckford's larger Roaring River estate had 92 women and 36 girls,
almost equaling the number of men (84) and boys (43) (Sheridan 1964, pp.
48–50). On Saint Domingue, at la Sucrerie Bouge in the parish of la Croix-
des-Bouquets, a 1796 inventory reveals 37 men, 52 women, 21 boys, and 21
girls. In 1768 at the larger Beaulieu plantation in Citronniers à Léogane, of
141 slaves 87 were male and 54 female (Debien 1974, pp. 95, 137).

Even Cuba offers exceptions to the rule that males predominated strongly
among Caribbean slaves in the eighteenth century. On Arango y Parreño's
model estate, La Ninja, 180 men and 160 women shared nearly all tasks in the
cultivation and processing of sugar. Of 71 cane cutters, 69 were female
(Moreno Franginals 1978, p. 17). More typically we find many Cuban estates
where, although men significantly outnumbered women, female slaves were
numerous. Turnbull (1840, pp. 285–288) recorded visits to two such Cuban

estates: Santa Ana, with 90 slaves, including 30 women, and La Pita, where 48 women were found among 161 slaves.

Lacking comparable data, we cannot claim the value of these women as workers or that of younger and older slaves. But the frequent historical exceptions to the conventional understanding of the superiority of male workers in strength and number are suggestive. Moreover, low gender ratios in the United States and the apparent success of North American plantation agriculture mean that purely materialist arguments are insufficient, as is the proposition that slave masters understood labor needs—rightly or wrongly— in materialist terms. Finally, there is scattered testimony to women's superiority as workers that undermines the supposition that men were more able or more generally preferred (Klein 1983, p. 34). Bryan Edwards, writing in 1819 (1966, vol. 2, p. 88), claimed that West Indian planters found Eboe females better workers than their male counterparts. Ortiz (1975, p. 198) suggests that Cuban planters considered women to be of "more constancy and strength in work than men."

Relative slave prices raise further questions about why males so often outnumbered female slaves on West Indian plantations. The price of slaves in the British West Indies differed relatively little for males and females, rarely more than £10. There was apparently only minor variation in this pattern over time. Ligon (1657, p. 46) noted that males in Barbados were valued at £30, women at £25–27. By 1789 male and female field slaves were priced at £80–100, imported slaves, £50 (Watson 1975, p. 139). Galenson (1982, pp. 502–503) found that from 1673 to 1723 female slaves were valued at about 85 percent of male slaves at auction markets in Barbados. The price gap between male and female slaves closed as the overall quality of bondmen declined. Edwards (1966, vol. 2, p. 154) claimed that in the British West Indies the price was £50 for an "able man in prime," £49 for an "able woman"; £47 for a young man, £46 for a young woman; and £40–45 for a boy or girl.[6]

For the French West Indies data on male and female slave prices are scant. Debien (1962, p. 18) cites records from a Saint Domingue plantation where men were valued, on average, at 2,166 livres and women at 1,875 livres; girls, priced at 947 livres, were more valuable than boys, who sold for an average price of 771 livres. Males and females were also sold for about the same price in the slave market in Danish St. Thomas in the eighteenth century (Westergaard 1917, p. 140).[7] The major exception to the claim that male and female slaves were nearly equally valued comes from the Spanish West Indies. There women slaves were consistently sold at about one-third the price of male slaves in the late 1770s and the 1800s (Moreno Fraginals, 1978, p. 191; G. Hall 1971).

The argument for young male superiority in agricultural production to explain planter preference for males is acceptable—although not sufficient—

for those settings in which prices of male and females were nearly equal. In the Spanish West Indies, however, particularly in Cuba, females could be purchased for much less than males, and slaves were rabidly sought. The relative absence of females under these circumstances makes it doubtful that planters' perception of male capability alone explains the predominance of bondmen. Why were women not more readily procured in the Spanish West Indies?

Two explanations are common and complement one another. First, the short-term profit-making goals of Caribbean sugar production are supported by the materialist approach, calling attention to male productivity, and best represented in the path-breaking work of Moreno Fraginals (1978). He has argued that Cuba's late eighteenth-century drive to compete against other Caribbean sugar producers brought unprecedented exploitation of slaves and a strong conviction among slaveholders that incremental differences in productivity among age and gender cohorts made the difference in overall production. The price of women slaves was low simply because there was little demand for them.[8]

Several early commentators explained the relative absence of women slaves in other ways. Bryan Edwards (1966, vol. 2, p. 134) reported the findings of the British Committee Council in 1789 that few women were available for purchase. Four factors influenced slave traders to procure men, according to Edwards: (1) African polygamy, discouraging the sale of women; (2) the growing number of male criminals, punished by sale into international slavery; (3) retention of women slaves as wives; and (4) the presumption that only young women had the needed strength for field work.[9]

Saco (1893, p. 38) proposed that Spanish West Indian planters and traders were influenced by the facility of acquiring male slaves and the belief that the slave trade would soon end. Slave owners and traders also found males to be stronger and females too often disabled by childbirth, pregnancy, and child care. Finally, Saco claimed, Spanish religious and moral opinion held that the presence of slave women on estates would lead to unsanctioned unions and free sexuality. The last factor is accepted by others seeking to explain women's relative scarcity among Cuban slaves (see, for example, Corwin 1967, p. 15).[10] Humboldt (1960, p. 88) summarizes the position this way: "Until the last years of the eighteenth century, female slaves were extraordinarily few on the sugar plantations, and most amazing is a concern based on 'religious scruples', opposing the introduction of females who cost in Havana less than males, and forcing the slaves to celibacy to avoid moral disorder." Such moralistic attitudes seem absurd in a highly immoral slave society. But it has been argued by Klein, Tannenbaum, and others that the Catholic influence differentiated Spanish treatment of slaves from the French and British. For example, clerics and religious leaders, trying to rationalize slavery, more often provided religious training for slaves than did British churches. Spanish priests frequently performed marriages of slaves in Puerto Rico and Cuba;[11] marriage among slaves was illegal or the sanctioning of such marriages forbidden by the church in most of the rest of the region.[12]

The foundation of this approach is that the Spanish slave laws, rooted in the Justinian codes and dating from the fifteenth century, respected slaves' individual rights, including the salvation of their souls (Klein 1967, p. 57). These concerns were blocked by planters as the Cuban sugar boom progressed and material interests finally overwhelmed ideological ones. Nevertheless, discussion of women's place and the number of women in slave societies provides some support for Tannenbaum's and Klein's positions.[13]

The relative supply of male and female slaves may finally be most damaging to the materialist argument for why men prevailed among West Indian slaves in the eighteenth and nineteenth centuries. Were women available to European traders for sale in the West Indies?

There is some fragmentary evidence supporting Edwards's argument that African polygyny required a surplus of women, whether slave or free. Klein (1983) used Curtin's figures on internal prices of women slaves to suggest that they were more highly valued by Africans or that the limited supply of women available for foreign trade drove up their price. "Thus, it has been suggested that the role of women in the economy and society gave them higher value, especially as slaves, than men. In contrast, it has been suggested that male slaves were not easily absorbed into the local labor systems, and thus represented a potential threat in terms of access to women and arms" (Klein 1983, p. 36). Regional variation and local stratification may have further complicated the picture. Geggus (1978, p. 23) found evidence of few women from areas far from the African coast, the number increasing with proximity to coastal trading centers. "Traders transporting slaves from the interior may have concentrated on the higher priced males, while on the coast, in order to make up the cargoes demanded, the local peoples were raided less selectively." Geggus speculates further that in areas of intense slave trading, such as the African coast, leaders may have kept down the supply of salable males to drive up their prices.

Reasonable doubts have been raised, then, that male strength was the key to male predominance among Caribbean slaves. And perhaps nothing raises such serious doubt about the strength argument as a shift in the gender ratio precisely when productivity needs were most profound.

CHANGING GENDER RATIOS, CHANGING LABOR SUPPLY

Caribbean slave gender ratios shifted markedly twice. Commodity producers of the sixteenth and seventeenth centuries probably purchased male and female slaves in roughly equal numbers. This likely gender balance was disrupted and male slaves favored in the eighteenth century as commodity production spread and intensified. Another dramatic population change occurred in the early 1800s. The British abolished the slave trade in 1807, and other European nations followed suit through the first half of the nineteenth century. Caribbean slave populations matured, bringing about gender ratios approaching equality for many settings and the eventual prevalence of female slaves.

Increased competition for available slaves before the abolition of the slave trade meant that fewer slaves were purchased by Caribbean slaveholders. Creole slaves generally had higher rates of fertility and lower mortality than Africans, contributing to a greater number of women (Higman 1984). Up to 50 percent of Africans perished in passage to the New World or during their first years there (Dirks 1978, p. 148). Africans made up a declining proportion of Caribbean slaves in most established sugar-producing societies through the eighteenth century: 6 percent of the total Jamaican slave population was imported in 1700, 5 percent in 1740, 4 percent in 1780, and none in 1808 (Craton 1971, p. 17). In Cuba African males made up nearly 80 percent of slaves from 1746 to 1790 but only 31.69 percent from 1845 to 1868, with African females constituting 8.51 percent of slaves from 1746 to 1790 and 21.29 percent of slaves in the 1845–1868 period (Moreno Fraginals 1977, pp. 191-193). Females also lived longer, often by 5 percent (see, for example, Craton 1977, p. 75; Dunn 1987, p. 813). Even when males generally predominated in the French West Indies, female slaves followed the African pattern and outnumbered males among slaves older than 60 years (Debien 1974, p. 342).

It is commonly assumed that women's longevity resulted from a capacity to endure, an explanation commonly used for women's comparative longevity in the twentieth century. Dunn's (1977, p. 45) description and commentary on a Jamaican estate mirrors this accepted view: "At Mesopotamia, as was generally the case on West Indian estates, the females proved tougher than the males and better able to survive the trauma of slavery." Diseases more common to women appear to have been less often lethal than those suffered by men (Sheridan 1985, p. 186). Siguret (1968, p. 223) speculates that higher female life expectancy may reflect relative pressure for productivity on male slaves with an increased proportion of female slaves, so that "feminization and creolization accompany male mortality."

Women's relative strength and working capacity were substantial, but, as Siguret implies, ambiguity surrounds the relative contributions of female physical advantage and greater male labor productivity to the age gap. Scattered data support conflicting viewpoints. For example, in the 1870s mortality rates for Puerto Rican female slaves under 45 years of age were greater than for males; after the age of 45 years, male mortality surpassed that of females. "These data suggest that . . . male slaves fared better than females during their most productive years. However, the females who survived the first 45 years of life were more likely to survive through the next 15 years than the males slaves of their cohort'' (Wessman 1980, p. 284). Geggus's (1978, p. 29) findings for slaves in Saint Domingue a century earlier suggest the opposite. There gender was the most important determinant of slaves' health. Sick females were disproportionately 50 years of age or older, whereas ailing males were younger. It may also have been the case that many more girl than boy slaves were born and/or survived the first days of life. Roberts (1977, p. 155) found that gender ratios at birth were lower among Caribbean slaves, at 102 or 103 males for every 100 females, than for contemporary European populations, with gender ratios at birth of 105 or 106 males for every 100 females.

With fewer males available in the slave trade, female slaves were increasingly sold to West Indian estate owners. In Cuba, for example, only two women were imported for every ten men in the eighteenth century. By the 1823 to 1844 period, half of African slaves brought to Cuba through international and interisland trade were female (Moreno Fraginals 1977, p. 87; Kiple 1976, p. 44). French West Indian planters also purchased many African women at the turn of the century (Debien 1974, p. 353). In the 1850s younger slaves were purchased (Craton 1974, p. 124), with children imported to Cuba in massive numbers (Moreno Fraginals 1978, p. 11; Bremer 1853, vol. 2, p. 352; Gurney 1840, p. 162).

The tendencies toward creolization of the slave population and the increased purchase of women dovetailed with a worry among Caribbean planters that slaves had failed to reproduce themselves throughout the region, a serious issue as abolition of the slave trade became imminent. Low fertility among slaves had been a continuing issue for some political interests, expressed in slave codes and other laws from early in the history of West Indian sugar planting. The British slave codes of 1696 required importation of an equal number of male and female slaves to encourage reproduction (Roberts 1957, p. 232). In Cuba concern about gender ratios was expressed as early as 1795 (Humboldt 1960, p. 188). The Cédula of 1798 ordered Cuban planters with only male slaves to buy females. The Royal Decree of 1804 offered a twelve-year extension of the slave trade to the Spanish and a six-year extension to foreigners, with the proviso that slave women be introduced (Corwin 1967, p. 15). Incentives were occasionally offered for the purchase or retention of women. For the Netherlands a royal decree called ''for a cessation of the annual head tax on women, but doubled it for men'' (Lewisohn 1970, p. 195). In 1792 import duties and the annual head tax on female field slaves in Danish St. John, St. Thomas, and St. Croix were also abolished to increase the population of slave women (Olwig 1985, p. 28).

The shifting slave gender ratios are most fully and accurately reported for the British West Indies, after the mandatory slave registration of the early

Table 3.1. Basic Demographic Indexes for Early Nineteenth-Century Bahamas, Montserrat, Antigua, Nevis, St. Christopher, Barbados, and Jamaica

Island	Dates	Total Slave Population	Males per 100 Females	Births per 1,000	Deaths per 1,000	Natural Increase per 1,000
BAHAMAS	1819–22	10,908	104.6	–	–	–
	1822–25	10,036	103.3	26.9	14.2	12.7
	1825–28	9,266	100.2	31.0	14.9	16.1
LEEWARDS						
Montserrat	1817–21	6,558	86.4	31.0	30.4	0.6
	1821–24	6,392	86.0	31.4	32.0	– 0.6
	1824–27	6,270	84.6	34.1	28.1	6.0
St. Christopher	1817–22	19,993	92.3	25.2	28.4	– 3.2
	1822–25	19,667	91.9	28.2	29.0	– 0.8
	1825–28	19,413	91.2	29.3	27.5	1.8
	1828–31	19,198	91.5	28.3	26.3	2.0
Antigua	1817–21	31,627	87.4	18.5	22.8	– 4.3
	1821–24	30,650	87.9	27.1	27.6	– 0.5
	1824–27	30,077	88.8	25.5	25.2	0.3
Nevis	1817–22	9,432	96.6	22.5	25.9	– 3.4
	1822–25	9,274	97.9	23.9	24.9	– 1.0
	1825–28	9,273	97.7	22.9	22.6	0.3
	1828–31	9,201	97.8	23.3	24.6	– 1.3
BARBADOS	1817–20	77,919	86.1	31.7	28.3	3.4
	1820–23	78,581	86.5	34.9	28.5	6.4
	1823–26	79,684	84.9	40.2	28.1	12.1
	1826–29	81,227	85.1	38.0	28.0	10.0
	1829–32	81,701	85.8	40.7	30.6	10.1
JAMAICA	1817–20	344,266	99.7	23.6	24.3	– 0.7
	1820–23	339,318	98.7	22.8	25.9	– 3.1
	1823–26	333,686	97.4	23.0	25.1	– 2.1
	1826–29	326,770	96.5	22.2	25.6	– 3.4
	1829–32	317,649	95.5	23.2	28.0	– 4.8

Source: Higman 1976b, pp. 67–70.

1800s. Table 3.1 reveals that a slight preponderance of female slaves had already come about in most cases. This trend began earlier in some plantations and slave societies than in others. The gender ratio in Barbados began to even out as early as the 1750s, although at the Codrington estates, for which we have extensive records, the genders did not become equal in number until the last third of the 1700s (Watson 1975, p. 130; Bennett 1958, p. 35). Males continued to outnumber females in St. Kitts as late as 1788, but in Nevis the gender ratio was 5 females for every 4 males, and on Montserrat there were probably more women than men (Goveia 1965, p. 124). On the small Devlin estate in Montserrat in 1726, 16 male slaves, valued at from £15 to £40, and 17 females, worth from £10 to £40, were listed. Their total values differed little, with males' worth accumulating to £475, and females to £477 (Fergus 1975, p. 18). In the British Virgin Islands in 1724 women constituted about half of slaves; by 1756 they were nearly 55 percent (Dookhan 1975, p. 28).

An Assembly of Jamaica committee revealed in a 1788 report that the gender ratio among imported slaves was 5 males for every 3 females. Jamaica's gender ratio began to decline in the early nineteenth century, favoring women by 1820 (Higman 1976a, p. 207). Phillips's (1949, p. 8) examination of records from the 1790s for Jamaica's Spring Garden estate reveals a nearly equal gender ratio, with 284 men and 244 women. Dunn (1977, p. 46) reports that at Jamaica's Mesopotamia, males greatly outnumbered females, with a ratio of 148 males for every 100 females; the ratio changed to 88 male slaves for every 100 females by 1818. Surinam's Catharina Sophia estate of 500 slaves achieved a low gender ratio only in the mid-nineteenth century. Gautier (1985, p. 105) reports these gender ratios for the French West Indies in the 1750s: 100, or an equal number of males and females in Martinique; 148 males for every 100 females in Saint Domingue; and 112 males for every 100 females in Guadeloupe. Debien's (1962, p. 18) analysis of prices from one plantation in Saint Domingue shows that girls were more highly valued than boys, although adult men still outpriced adult women. On plantations under British control on the eve of Saint Domingue's revolution, males continued to outnumber females, by a ratio of almost 2 to 1, but, as noted, many more males than females had fled estates (Geggus 1978, pp. 6–7).[14] Men also prevailed in number only slightly at l'Anse-à-l'Ane (Debien 1960, p. 37).

In the Spanish West Indies gender ratios shifted later, reflecting the late commitment of planters there to large-scale sugar planting. Starting in the 1830s at least half of new Cuban slaves were female (Moreno Fraginals 1977, pp. 191–193). In Puerto Rico, in San Germán jurisdiction, the gender ratio remained at 109.7 males for every 100 females as late as 1872, but there were more males where slaves were fewer, a probable indication of a preference for males as skilled workers on small farms and firms (Wessman 1980, p. 279). At Puerto Rico's Ponce market the prices of both slave men and women field hands increased after 1845. Creole male slaves outnumbered females in Ponce, with the gender ratio most skewed among slaves aged 15 to 20 (Scarano 1984, pp. 133, 142). The same pattern is found for British Trinidad and areas of what would later be British Guiana. These last major British Caribbean sugar producers continued to import many slaves until abolition of the slave trade. By the period 1841–1844 males still outnumbered females in Trinidad, Demerara, and Essequibo (Roberts 1977, pp. 154–155).

The importation of young slaves and females had, however, only a limited impact on population growth and stabilization. With the termination of the slave trade, planters at most hoped for a period of high births that would ensure some future population replacement. But closed and generally subfecund Caribbean slave populations could reproduce themselves only as a result of effective pro-natalist state and plantation policies. Caribbean planters generally failed to institute such measures. The importation of a large number of slave women hence brought about their frequent numerical superiority in an "aging and wasting" population (Craton 1978, p. 329; Klein 1986).

TOO FEW, TOO MANY: PARADOXES OF GENDER RATIO IN CARIBBEAN SLAVERY

Many theories have been posited about how gender ratios influence social life. Guttentag and Secord (1983) contend, for example, that a majority of males or females can work to the gender's advantage only when structural circumstances are favorable. Otherwise the gender loses power and social status. Hence, they argue, the long-standing surplus of American black women renders them less powerful than black men. In a similar manner, medieval women gained social ground when high sex ratios were common but lost position when in the late Middle Ages they numerically surpassed men. Guttentag and Secord postulate further that where males hold structural power, their scarcity yields sexual permissiveness, accompanied by traditional gender role ideologies. A scarcity of females in these circumstances results in the rigid gender hierarchy and morality associated with agrarian societies.

Caribbean slavery conforms to neither scenario. Males predominated socially and economically, if less so than in other agrarian settings. When there were more males, in the eighteenth century, nuclear families were proportionately no more or less common than at other times; nor were they less so when women became the majority. Nor did fertility or gender division of labor vary, as one might expect with changing gender ratios.

Guttentag and Secord (1983) present an intuitively sensible idea, true in many cases. Its lack of fit with Caribbean slavery illustrates, however, the strength of authority relations in these social formations. Although not immutable or entirely unique, social relations in Caribbean slavery made difficult certain forms of social and cultural organization, for example, nuclear families, and in this sense transformed gender ratios into grounds for demographic possibility rather than probability.

Potential relationships and trends formed around a cycle of numerical equality of genders, male superiority in number, and female abundance. This pattern reflects supply and demand factors as well as differing male and female mortality rates. There is, however, surprising uniformity in changing sex ratios across colonial domains and within stages of sugar production, technical development, and productivity. The major exception is the Spanish West Indies, where the continued scarcity of female slaves and their low price suggest that Spanish religious and moral ideologies were more influential than materialist studies have recently held. The study of women slaves reveals that earlier hypotheses about comparative treatment, offered by Tannenbaum, Klein, and others, remain useful in at least this respect. It also suggests that ignoring gender makes impossible a full assessment of theory about slavery and a reconstruction of more informative perspectives.

CHAPTER FOUR

Household Economies

In an agrarian setting "labor" is a reified notion; slaves did little that was not work. Males and females conducted material life for most of their waking hours. I describe the scope of slaves' work by treating separately, but as labor, slaves' production directly for the master—in the fields, as domestics, and as artisans—and what they produced for themselves but implicitly for the master—their houses, clothes, and food.

This division contrasts the exigencies of slaves' household economies and the plantation. Home-based production contributed to the success of estates but, especially for the gardening and marketing of provisions, rendered some power, status, and income to slaves. Most other forms of labor had no direct economic or social benefit for bondmen and women. As I argued earlier, slaves were not purely property, bondless, or proletarianized. A key to their status within the slave community and in relation to whites was their independent economic power, never substantial but often effective.

The "household economy" has received attention in at least three academic circles. Comparative sociologists and historians have studied the changing organization and functions of the family in European industrialization (Laslett 1972; Levine 1977, 1983; Tilly 1978, 1984). New economic institutions, particularly cottage industry, generated a nuclear family structure and increased fertility. Freedom from "patriarchal" constraints permitted more family control of income, consumption, and decision making.

World system theorists have expressed a related interest in the specific ways in which international market forces interact with smaller units, in particular, the household (Smith et al. 1984). Since the creation of an international capitalist economy, members of many families and households in the "periphery," or Third World, have produced for at least two of three economic sectors: (1) traditional economies, (2) local capital, and (3) international interests. Conflicts and alliances among elite economic forces are, to a degree, a function of how individual families are managing. At times the conglomeration of interests and mix with local skills creates enormous opportunities for households (see, for example, Salaff 1981); at other times it causes degeneration of family income and social cohesiveness (Bolles 1983).

Finally, scholars have recently expressed great interest in women in contemporary Third World development (Charlton 1984; Rogers 1979).

46

Policymakers have discovered that women often provide the food supply and handle much of the household income. The subsistence and domestic sectors can both advance and discourage technological innovation and political change. The social power of the household has thus been recognized for its potential contribution to larger political agendas.

Three theoretical perspectives, then, orient the following discussion of slaves' household economies: (1) the household as a unit of income and economic management and planning, (2) its complementary and antagonistic roles in relation to the plantation system, and (3) the political consequences of slaves' economic autonomy. Scarcity of data limits our conclusions, but regional trends and patterns emerge clearly and set important parameters for future research.

The historical evolution of Caribbean sugar planting is as significant to this analysis as it was to population change. Changes in plantation size, sugar output, and processing potential resulted in the transition from individual and household provision of goods and services to food rationing, distribution of goods by slaveholders, and collectivization of household tasks. The trends were most notable where sugar production peaked as late as the nineteenth century and less visible before. Important intervening variables are terrain and climate: Some ecosystems were more conducive to individualized growing of food than others.

Women slaves worked in the fields and in slaveholders' and others' households, tended kitchen gardens and provision grounds and marketed subsistence crops, and cared for their own houses and children. As with other dimensions of slaves' experience, women's work varied from one period of commodity production to another. In general, women's field labor was more highly valued as sugar production spread and labor productivity peaked in each Caribbean sugar society. In turn, other areas of production and work appear to have diminished in significance. As boom times ended, women did not necessarily return to household concerns, for females had come to dominate in slave populations and were still needed for field labor.

HOUSES AND THE HOUSEHOLD

In the early days of Caribbean sugar planting, when semipatriarchal relations were maintained between masters and slaves, male and female slaves' social relations were much like those in peasant and other agricultural societies. Slaves lived in cottages of various shapes and sizes. Most were from 15 to 20 feet long and from 10 to 15 feet wide, with wood posts 7 feet high. The outer walls were made of lumber or branches laced with wattle and daub, or occasionally stone (Labat 1930, vol. 2, p. 56; Edwards 1966, vol. 2, pp. 164–165; DuTertre 1958, vol. 2, pp. 482–483; Mintz 1974, p. 266).[1] Roofs were made of leaves from palm, cane, or coconut trees. There were usually two rooms, although sometimes more, with the kitchen in a hallway or outside (Barclay 1828, p. 303; Beckford 1790, p. 228; Handler 1972, p. 68). The earthen floors were often damp, leading to disease (Schnakenbourg 1980, p. 56). In early nineteenth-century Puerto Rico, houses were of wood and raised above the ground (Flinter 1834, p. 247).

Cottage roofs were either flat or arched, although in the French West Indies some were conical, as in West Africa (Debien 1974, p. 221). Simple furnishings included board beds, mats, and occasionally hammocks; a small table and two or three stools; and earthen, iron, and calabash containers and cooking utensils (Edwards 1966, vol. 2, pp. 164–165; Flinter 1834, p. 247; Handler 1972, p. 68; N. Hall 1977, p. 181; Carmichael 1834, vol. 1, p. 129; Labat 1930, vol. 2, p. 56). Skilled slaves often had more elaborate, larger houses that they constructed themselves, at their own expense (Carmichael 1834, vol. 1, p. 124).

Huts were 10 to 12 yards apart in a yard shared by family members and friends. They were arranged in a circle or line, not far from the master's house (DuTertre 1958, vol. 2, p. 483; Labat 1930, vol. 2, p. 57). In the seventeenth century French West Indian slaves were given individual houses, with men's huts larger to allow for future families (Debien 1974, p. 220).[2] More variation prevailed in Guadeloupe. Some families lived together in a house; or parents lived in one house, children in a second, and males of 16 years and older constructing their own huts and cottages for neolocal households. Males generally constructed houses and ''work grounds'' in the British West Indies as well (Moreton 1793, p. 150). Single slaves often had their own cottages in the French West Indies and in Trinidad (Debien 1974, p. 220; Carmichael 1834, vol. 1, p. 124). Slaves generally built their own houses with materials or ''debris'' found on the estate (Bennett 1958, p. 32). French planters wanted the huts of single women to be close to those of other slaves (Debien 1974, p. 220). These circumstances left women dependent on kin and friends for aid in erecting shelters (Bennett 1958, p. 100). But it is likely that, with the extraordinarily high labor expectations for Caribbean women slaves, they occasionally built their own houses.

Women cooked, maintained their cottages, and made and mended clothing. They gathered food from fields and kitchen gardens. Manioc and cassava flours were usually distributed by slaveholders, but grinding stones among slaves' archaeological remains suggest that slave women sometimes milled grain (Handler 1972, p. 68). ''Earthen pots, gourds and calabash dishes'' were presumably made by the slaves, probably by women (Handler 1972, p. 68). Stews, soups, and roasted and boiled legumes and vegetables were eaten. British West Indian slave women boiled ''pots'' at noon and in the evening (Moreton 1793, p. 150). Women and children drew water from nearby ponds.[3]

Clothing manufacture and care involved diverse tasks, although many slaves, particularly children, wore no clothing.[4] Some slaves received material to make clothing, others the clothing itself (Tomich 1976, p. 206; Phillips 1949, p. 10; Levy 1980, p. 9; Pinckard 1970, vol. 1, p. 289). Women made and mended clothing and presumably gathered leaves and straw to shape sleeping mats. The large number of sick slaves on any plantation (perhaps 40 percent of the work force during the harvest) suggests that many more required home care, probably provided by women, as it was in the plantations' infirmaries.

To stress women's responsibilities in household and family work is not to imply that men carried no domestic burdens, especially single men. But the historical record yields few examples of male engagement in household chores. Assuming an entirely equitable division of labor within the slave family—a condition lacking empirical support—the many women heads of household tells us that on the whole, women were more often keepers of the family.

Women's days were nearly endless, especially during the harvest, when sugar cultivation and processing often meant 18 hours of plantation work. Observers wondered at Cuban slave women's good humor, as they completed household tasks while male kin rested (Ortiz 1975, pp. 198–199). Seventeenth-century writer Père Labat (1930, vol. 2, p. 53) noted that females first served the male his meal, then ate with the children. Yet these homemaking activities brought status. Mintz (1974, pp. 239–248) underscores women's authority in her "domain," the domestic realm. Mathurin (1975, p. 2) concurs, for "each woman was the recognized ruler of her hut and her household."

A change in slaves' housing in a succession of booming sugar islands symbolized changes in the domestic lives of slaves and women's work. Slaves in new sugar areas resided in barracklike structures. The slaves themselves built these dwellings but by the direction of and with materials provided by slaveholders.

In Cuba more than half of the estate owners built *barracones* for their slaves (Moreno Fraginals 1977). Each family or single slave was consigned to one of the barrack's many rooms, which opened onto a courtyard. Separate entrances were maintained for men, married women, and single women (Bremer 1853, vol. 2, pp. 312, 355; Moreno Fraginals 1977; Scott 1985, p. 16). A woman cooked cauldrons of rice for the entire large household. In Puerto Rico group houses, or *cuartelles,* were built in parallel lines with a street or lane in between (Diaz Soler 1974, p. 163). Lewisohn's (1970, p. 118) description of houses in eighteenth-century St. Croix reveals a similar pattern: "long motel-like row houses built with one wall between each unit. A family had two adjoining rooms with a connecting door."

Tomich (1976, pp. 222–225) describes the same transition to dormitory-style housing in some areas of the French West Indies in the 1700s. Villages of slave households were less often found in the French islands by mid-century. Fewer slaves lived alone. Even in the British West Indies, where barracks housing was less common, domestic functions were more often centralized. Pinckard (1970, vol. 1, p. 288) describes an estate in Barbados in the early 1800s where the cabins of 15 families formed an octagon around a shared kitchen.

Women were relieved of some domestic responsibilities with this collectivization of residence, but household tasks for the group were assigned to individual females. Flinter (1834, p. 248) observed that a Puerto Rican slave woman cooked for men and women in the field. Clothing still had to be made, along with cooking utensils, bedding, etc., by one or several women slaves. A fundamental division of labor remained, as the work of many women was redistributed to a few. In another sense, however, old patterns changed, for home life was collectivized and rationalized so that the majority of women could join men in agricultural work.

Nowhere is this transformation of male and female labor allocation more apparent than in child care. Children had long accompanied their parents to the field and other work areas, to play, rest, or be carried on their toiling mothers' backs. But their presence was ever less welcome to overseers (Dickson 1789, p. 12), who demanded full attention to cane cultivation from the growing number of female field workers. As sugar production and productivity grew, the care of young children passed to the slaveholder and his administrators. When Cuban slave mothers returned to work after giving birth, their children entered nurseries (*criadas de criolleras*) and were cared for by an old slave woman (Knight 1970, p. 76).[5] Accompanying this trend was a tendency for children to enter the work force earlier and to move to more strenuously worked gangs sooner (Higman 1976a; Moreno Fraginals 1977, 1978).

PROVISION GROUNDS

The slaves' provision grounds have become a source of increasing scholarly interest, particularly as their potential contribution to gender roles and division of labor are discerned (Mintz 1983). An integral part of this discussion is the economic power that provision grounds provided to slaves and the self-sufficiency they brought to a system of production with seemingly little dynamic for growth. Slaves engaged in three systems of food cultivation: (1) kitchen gardens; (2) collectively cultivated, estate-supervised provision grounds; and (3) individualized provision plots. The three held vastly different potential for economic power, status, and income earning, and they contributed in different ways to the continuation of Caribbean slavery.

Kitchen Gardens

Nearly all slaves who lived in cottages or huts planted herbs, plantains, fruits, and other root crops and occasionally kept hogs and poultry (Brathwaite 1971, p. 133).[6] Kitchen gardens were women's responsibility, as horticulture generally is across cultures. Produce was for use, rarely for sale. But some petty trading took place, particularly where collectively tended provision plots or the importation of food precluded agricultural entrepreneurship and where kitchen gardens were the only slave-controlled food source. Such was the case in Barbados, the Leewards, and, over time, Cuba and Saint Domingue. In these settings kitchen gardens were invariably needed to supplement inadequate rations; yet in themselves they rarely provided sufficient nutrition (Mintz 1974, p. 192).

Although universally tiny, the gardens showed some variation in dimension across Caribbean slave societies and stages of sugar production. Because in the seventeenth-century French West Indies the houses were 10 to 12 yards apart, the kitchen gardens could occupy only several square feet (DuTertre 1958, vol. 2, p. 483). Dwellings were brought closer together in the eighteenth century, 5 to 7 yards between cottages (Labat 1930, vol. 2, p. 57), reducing the amount of space available for gardening and keeping animals. Larger provision grounds then grew in size. In St. Croix about 20 to 30 square feet of land was available *per couple* for yard gardens (Lewisohn 1970, p. 240). There and elsewhere in the region the collectivization of slaves' housing reduced the availability of gardens, but their importance grew because food rations were small and only sporadically distributed.

Individualized Provision Grounds

Greater quantities of produce were cultivated on larger provision grounds or "polincks." The slaves themselves cleared, planted, and tended these lands (Brathwaite 1971, p. 133). Provision grounds were apparently small, even by modern Third World standards. Debien (1974, p. 207) and Tomich (1976, p. 213) conclude that most French West Indian provision plots were smaller than two acres. Edwards (1966, vol. 3, p. 255) wrote that British West Indian polincks covered about a quarter of an acre. In the French West Indies peas, manioc, cabbage, sweet potatoes, rice, millet, and maize were raised (Debien 1974, pp. 183–189); in Jamaica the slaves raised pepper, peas, beans, sweet potatoes, cassava, pineapples, pumpkins, cucumbers, okra, and, after 1792, breadfruit (Brathwaite 1971, p. 133). Produce was more diversified than on common lands or in kitchen gardens. "Each slave cultivated as, and what, he wanted to cultivate" (Mintz 1974, p. 194). Some livestock was kept, generally pigs and poultry (Pinckard 1970, vol. 2, p. 105; Leslie 1740, p. 322; Bremer

1853, vol. 2, p. 333). In the early years of Puerto Rican sugar planting, through the early 1800s, many slaves had horses (Flinter 1834, p. 284).

The amount of time devoted to provision grounds, their value, contribution to plantation agriculture, and role in gender stratification are debated. Nearly all Caribbean slave societies scheduled some time for provision tending by slaves. The French Code Noir granted free Saturdays or half a day on Saturday and supplementary rations (Tomich 1976, p. 205).[7] British West Indian laws permitted cultivation of grounds every other Saturday (Lewis 1834, p. 83), although visitors also report that slaves tended their grounds on Sundays (Moreton 1793, p. 149). Except during the harvest, Jamaican estates generally granted slaves every other Monday for cultivation, as well as Sundays, Christmas, Easter, and the Whitsun holidays (Brathwaite 1971, p. 293; Leslie 1740, p. 322). But often slaves were permitted more time and sometimes spent all of their free hours, including mealtimes, tending their land and marketing crops. In British Dominica, for example, slaves tended polincks one day a week or on Saturday afternoon, from noon to 2:00 P.M. daily, and on Sundays (Atwood 1791, pp. 179, 258–259). Slaves on St. John in the Danish West Indies tended gardens on Saturday afternoons when not harvesting sugar and at noon and on Sundays (Olwig 1985, pp. 18–22). The attitude of slaveholders toward provision growing depended on two factors: the intensity of sugar cultivation and the dependence of slaves, slaveholders, and their retainers on slave-grown provisions.

French West Indian planters imitated the Portuguese in Brazil, with provision grounds the main source of plantation food, although slave codes held that these were for the slave's economic benefit and were not meant to provide sustenance. As late as the nineteenth century, only about 21 percent of Martinique's and 10 percent of Guadeloupe's plantations provided nutrition solely through rations (Schnakenbourg 1980, p. 55). In the Danish West Indies "the Negroes were expected to raise all their own food, except for such low-grade fish or defective Irish beef as might be allotted to them when the food supply ran out" (Westergaard 1917, p. 158; Olwig 1985, p. 54). Even domestic slaves were to feed themselves from provision grounds on many Jamaican estates (M. G. Lewis 1834, p. 82). Under these circumstances slaves often were encouraged to tend their grounds and permitted extra days. M. G. Lewis (1834, p. 23) allowed his slaves cultivation time every Saturday. Martinique's and Guadeloupe's masters insisted that slaves attend to their grounds and purchased produce as an incentive to cultivation (Tomich 1976, pp. 207, 208). Slaves in Martinique were allowed as much land as they needed for cultivation (Tomich 1976, p. 155). Indeed, some slaves in Martinique and Guadeloupe hired or procured slaves themselves to tend their grounds (Tomich 1976, p. 220). The same was true in nineteenth-century Trinidad, where slaves hired one another, paying in provisions (Carmichael 1834, vol. 2, p. 231), and traded and sold provision lands.

The British West Indian slave code of 1800 guaranteed slaves the right to market their crops (Mintz 1974, p. 202; Pinckard 1970, vol. 1, p. 369). Saturdays and Sundays were generally market days in towns, although in some settings, such as eighteenth-century Antigua, formal markets were instituted during the week (Schaw 1939, p. 88). Sunday markets often attracted hundreds to British Leeward towns (Goveia 1965, p. 238). Moreau de Saint Méry (1958, p. 433) wrote that more than 15,000 slaves gathered weekly at the Clugny market in Cap Français, Saint Domingue. Slaves traded goods informally whenever and wherever possible. In Danish St. John no formal weekly markets were found, and much exchange was through barter (Olwig 1985, p. 51).

Whites purchased slave-grown provisions, and in Jamaica, Martinique, Guadeloupe, St. Lucia, and other islands with extensive slave-controlled small-scale provision tending, Europeans were almost wholly dependent on slaves for fruits and vegetables.[8] Provision harvests were often sizable, although not all produce was sold. Beckford (1790, p. 256) estimated that a well-planted quarter of an acre in Jamaica fed a "moderate family" with some surplus. A nineteenth-century traveler to Jamaica claimed that a provision ground could maintain a family of four or five for a year and permit a surplus (Stewart 1823, p. 69). Farley (n.d., p. 62) cites the example of a slave in Demerara who sold rice grown on his plot, earning 50 guilders in three months.. Hilliard d'Auberteuil (1776, vol. 1, p. 58) writes that a single slave in Saint Domingue working a space of 100 square feet for 2 hours daily could feed more than 20 slaves.

How much did the marketing of crops yield to slaves? Long (1774, vol. 1, p. 537) reported that £50,000 circulated in Jamaica, 20 percent of which was in slaves' hands, mostly in small coins. Official French sources claimed that a slave could make from 700 francs to 800 francs yearly from provision grounds and trade (Tomich 1976, p. 218). Schoelcher (1948, p. 35) observed that a nineteenth-century French West Indian slave could amass from $300 to $500 from subsistence cultivation and the raising of livestock.

Lacking other cash estimates, inferences must be made from information about how money was used. Slaves in the Spanish West Indies, with the highest rate of manumission in the New World, traditionally purchased their freedom. For many slaves marketing was the principal means to accumulate cash. Even as sugar production became more demanding and marketing opportunities fewer, Cuban slaves garnered money in a group and drew lots to buy their freedom (Bremer 1853, vol. 2, p. 340). French West Indian slaves who hired others obviously accumulated cash, although goods and services were also traded among slaves. A hierarchy of slaves existed on all plantations, with skilled slaves and those successful in production and trade at the top. They commonly had the finest houses, clothes, and trinkets. There are accounts throughout West Indian slave history of dances and fiestas where substantial outlays of cash and provisions were provided by elite slaves (Ligon 1657; Bremer 1853; Peytraud 1973; Fouchard 1981). "Whites were shocked at how gaily and finely dressed Black women were on Sundays and other Holy Days" (Packwood 1975, p. 92).

This portrait of slaves as yeoman farmers must be tempered with knowledge that individualized provision grounds were often under assault and were collectivized when slaves' labor was needed in sugar production. In the Danish Virgin Islands, for example, fears of slaves' independence and the need for their labor in the cultivation of sugar brought restrictions on the time available for tending grounds and on marketing.[9] Crown rule resulted in the slave code of 1755 and insistence that masters approve all sales by slaves (N. Hall 1977, pp. 178–180; Olwig 1985, p. 23). In response, bondmen and women stole their masters' goods to sell at market; this and other factors led to frequent nonenforcement of mid-century codes (N. Hall 1977, p. 180). Similarly in Saint Domingue, when the seventeenth-century Code Noir forbade internal marketing, slaves traded stolen goods, creating an extensive market that persisted even when rights to formal exchange were restored (G. Hall 1972, p. 181). Slave owners in Bermuda so feared independent activity by their nonagricultural slave population that they retained laws passed in 1623 denying blacks land for cultivation (Packwood 1975, p. 119).

French-controlled Saint Domingue emerged as a major sugar producer, resulting in collectivized growing of provisions under the supervision of the masters (Debien 1974, pp. 178–182). Martinique and Guadeloupe also experienced constriction of slaves' prerogatives in food cultivation. The original system on those islands had permitted slaves to hire themselves out for a free Saturday rather than tend their grounds. Masters would provide rations to slaves who chose to earn cash by hiring out instead of growing and marketing provisions (Debien 1974, pp. 178–182). Slaveholders resisted distribution of rations; therefore a slave who hired out his or her services had to purchase food from other slaves. In the British Virgin Islands as well, increased cultivation of sugar led to a decrease in cultivation time for slaves' provision grounds (Dookhan 1975, p. 47).

In Montserrat restrictions on marketing accompanied those on hiring out (Fergus 1975, p. 20), along with rules promulgated in 1736 against planting cash crops: indigo, cotton, ginger, and cocoa (Fergus 1975, p. 19). The laws of the 1600s and 1700s in Barbados restricted marketing as well (Handler 1974, p. 125). Indeed the Christian churches had tried throughout West Indian slave history to prevent Sunday markets. Clergy interests prevailed in ending formal trade among slaves on Sunday as early as 1736 in Montserrat and in 1824 in the rest of the British West Indies (Mathieson 1926, pp. 126–140).

Cuba represents a complete cycle of planter attitudes toward provision growing from approval and dependence on the product to a policy of eradication. In the seventeenth and early eighteenth centuries provision grounds (*conucos*) were common to nearly all Cuban plantations and were a major source of income used by the slaves to purchase their freedom (G. Hall 1971, p. 68; Klein 1967, p. 154). Provision grounds virtually disappeared in some areas of heavy sugar production during the late eighteenth century, when slaveholders began to import food (Knight 1970, p. 68; Scott 1985, p. 16).[10]

Provision cultivation was generally supplemented by meat and fish rations, but poorly. Slaves lacked time and land for cultivation and badly needed additional protein sources (Dirks 1987). Masters were frequently urged by colonial and metropolitan officials to improve the quality and quantity of rations. Increased demands by Trinidad's colonial officials to feed slaves adequately failed to bring compliance in the early 1800s. "Slaves on large plantations received relatively generous allowances of salt fish but little else, and those on small holdings were totally dependent on their provision grounds" (Higman 1984, p. 211). In Martinique the local state insisted that planters feed slaves and cancelled Saturday workdays and markets. But slave owners successfully evaded these policies, and both provision production by slaves and inadequate distribution of rations continued (Tomich 1976, p. 205). A visitor to the Danish Virgin Islands in 1793 found that slaves provided nearly all their own food "with uncertain supplemental rations of flour, salted meats or fish provided by the plantation" (N. Hall 1977, p. 178). Slaveholders allowed bondmen and women to starve following a bad drought from 1725 to 1726. These slaves' situation was often, then, like that of slaves who received estate-grown or imported provisions.

Estate-Grown and Imported Provisions

Flat and arid settings such as Barbados and the Leeward Islands lacked mountain lands where provisions could be grown but sugar could not be cultivated. In contrast, Cuba and Saint Domingue used slaves in sugar production to the exclusion of food crops. Legally the amount of land given to the cultivation of provisions, whether collectively or by individual slaves, was set. But the laws were ignored where importation seemed to enhance sugar productivity and profits.

In Barbados and the Leeward Islands rations were grown by slaves on estate lands under the supervision of an overseer. Nine-tenths of Barbados's estates fed slaves primarily through estate-grown provisions, "corn and roots" (Colthurst 1977, p. 140). Richard Ligon (1657, p. 22) observed that 70 of 500 estate acres might be available for provisions of corn, potatoes, plantains, cassava, bonavist, and table fruits. In the eighteenth century some estates grew only provisions for sale to their neighbors (Dickson 1789, p. 19). Elsewhere provisions were grown for slaves whose work regimen took them away from individual subsistence cultivation (Olwig 1985, pp. 18, 22).

Rations were unspecified in the early days of sugar production on Barbados, and some food was imported (Levy 1980, p. 9; Handler 1974, p. 10). Sheridan (1985, p. 155) summarized the philosophy of local planters, and its consequences for slaves:

> To the extent that British Caribbean planters were economically rational, they were encouraged by the structure of the Atlantic economy and the mercantile system to concentrate their resources on sugar production, and to depend on imported African slaves, foodstuffs, milling equipment, building materials, and other items of fixed and variable capital. What was considered economically rational, however, could well be nutritionally irrational.

Not enough food was grown, for example, at Codrington on estate lands in the late 1700s (Bennett 1958, pp. 37–38). Droughts and the cessation of imports from the United States during the American Revolution caused many slaves to starve (Watson 1975, p. 46; Carrington 1987). This experience led to more provision growing in Barbados (Bennett 1958, p. 101). A surplus was available to British troops in St. Lucia (Watson 1975, p. 47). By 1815 up to two-thirds of estate lands were in provisions (Levy 1980, p. 9). Abolitionists Sturge and Harvey (1838, p. 10) observed that "Barbados is the only considerable English colony which raises provisions and stock enough for its own consumption and for export."[11]

The distribution of food suggests that consumption by whites of imported food contributed to the undernourishment and death from starvation of slaves. Bean's (1977, p. 586) calculations show that Barbados's blacks were largely self-sufficient in food production in the late seventeenth century, moving toward greater dependence on imports as the slave population grew and planters allocated proportionately less land to provisions. Whites consumed mostly imported foods, about a quarter of available food products from 1680 to 1816, and nearly all of the protein-rich foods.

Like Barbados, Demerara (part of British Guiana) grew provisions as an estate crop. The Leewards imported a large quantity of food, leading to barely adequate sustenance (Mathieson 1926, p. 72; Fergus 1975, p. 15). In some cases, for example, Montserrat, all available land was in cane, although Montserrat and the Windward Islands eventually dropped sugar cultivation and became exporters of food to Barbados and the Leewards (Mintz 1974, p. 187; Fergus 1975, p. 15). Ever less time was devoted to collective provision growing in Saint Domingue. Travelers in the 1700s found no rations distributed and slaves starving (Debien 1974, p. 215).

How much land was mandated for collective provision growing? The Slave Act of Jamaica called for one acre for every ten slaves, excluding "negro-grounds" (Edwards 1966, vol. 2, p. 162). In 1669 Montserrat laws required one acre of provisions for two working persons, one acre of yams for six working slaves, and one acre of corn for four slaves. A 1693 law raised the distribution of provision land to one acre per eight slaves (Fergus 1975, p. 5). The Trinidad Ordinance of 1800 required the planting in provisions of one quarrée (3.2 acres) for every ten working slaves, plus food rations and access to provision grounds and time for their cultivation (Higman 1984, p. 210).

Slaves' access to land and food varied, then, throughout the Caribbean, with small subsistence plots commonly found. Slaves could grow a food surplus or be restricted by a master's or state rules from adequate time to cultivate or market crops. Slave owners distributed rations of locally grown or imported foods in some areas. In this case the risk of malnutrition and starvation was generally greater than where slaves controlled subsistence cultivation.

PROVISION GROUNDS AND THE GENDER DIVISION OF LABOR

How were provision grounds distributed to the slave population? Who was responsible for the work? Who received the product and profits? The evidence suggests strongly that planters and colonial legislatures allotted land to individuals, regardless of gender. In Jamaica, for example, small plots were distributed to males and females (Mathurin 1975, p. 8). Earlier commentators seem to support this contention, assuming that the term "slaves" is generic and does not pertain to men alone. Stewart (1823, p. 64) claims that estate owners were to provide 10 acres of provision grounds for every 100 slaves. The Ordinance of 1785 for the French West Indies clearly states that a small plot should be granted to each slave (Fouchard 1981, pp. 35–36; see also Schoelcher 1948, p. 35). Travelers' and slaveholders' accounts also suggest that women routinely received land. Mrs. Carmichael (1834, vol. 1, p. 174) wrote that in Trinidad "every individual has his own ground, and every mother a fixed portion for each child" (see also Carmichael 1834, vol. 2, pp. 67, 183–185). French abolitionist Victor Schoelcher estimated male and female earnings from the growing and marketing of provisions in the French West Indies at about 400 francs yearly, suggesting that women were some-times independent entrepreneurs (cited in Tomich 1976, p. 218).

There is also evidence that children received grounds in Jamaica (Patterson 1969) and Martinique (Tomich 1976, p. 206). In Trinidad, if a slave was too young to work his or her ground, another slave was ordered by the master to do so, with produce given to the child's family. By age 7, many children were old enough to tend their grounds and sell fruits and vegetables (Carmichael 1834, vol. 2, p. 160).

Patterson (1976, p. 56) is the strongest proponent of the position that women and children commonly had provision grounds and that mothers consolidated the land of their offspring to maximize their social position. This potential power may have induced women to avoid conjugal unions (Patterson 1969, p. 169). Mathurin (1975) also emphasizes Jamaican slave women's economic status and authority, based in part on access to provision growing. Higman (1984, p. 355) acknowledges economic benefits to women from tending provision grounds, commenting that rewards to a slave woman for the birth of a child were of limited value if time was taken away from the cultivation of subsistence crops.

Mintz (1974) takes the opposite view, questioning whether women held provision grounds. Much evidence supports his position that slaveholders and slaves themselves reinterpreted codes and laws on land allocation in order to grant a large parcel of land to a male head of household or a figure of prominence in the slave community. References to provision grounds most frequently mention men, who share the work and results with wives, children, and friends. DuTertre (1958, vol. 2, p. 485) describes the distribution of land to slaves in the seventeenth-century French West Indies but notes that "their wives" have small gardens (see also Hilliard d'Auberteuil 1776, vol. 1, p. 59). Lewis's (1834, p. 405) account of sojourns at his Jamaican estates also suggests that males were in charge. He notes, for example, that no slave could possess more than one house and ground for "his family." Phillippo (1843, p. 219) writes, more ambiguously, that women cooked, waited on men, worked on "their" grounds, and sold "their" provisions, seeming to suggest that males controlled both the grounds and the provisions. A similar observation is made by a traveler to the Danish Virgin Islands, who notes that "many a slave with a family had to spend part of the midday break fetching potatoes from his grounds for roasting" (N. Hall 1977, p. 180).[12] "Households" received land on St. John, according to an eighteenth-century missionary; Olwig (1985, p. 49) suggests that women's right to *use* land was recognized in the slave community.

Early observers in the French West Indies described a male slave's provision ground of one and one-half hectares, tended by three men and a woman, bringing a total of about 20 francs daily (Tomich 1976, p. 218). That polygamous males in Trinidad lived with their wives, whereas a polyandrous female resided with only one mate, suggests that males may have wished to control their labor supply (Carmichael 1834, vol. 1, p. 298). Slaves freely shared food and other goods. But land possession and control were important, with slaves designating heirs whenever possible.[13]

Cultivation of provision grounds generally involved more than a single individual. In Jamaica "the focus for family life was the provision grounds, which the families worked in common" (Turner, 1982, p. 45; see also Mintz 1974, p. 211). Males generally cleared the grounds for cultivation (Debien 1974, p. 208). This heavy, often dangerous work involved felling of trees, hoeing, and removing logs and large pieces of debris from mountainous land (Beckford 1790, p. 256). Males' strength may have given them an advantage; their capacity to create new grounds was a source of social control. In the French West Indies women did much of the cultivation. This pattern began in the Caribbean in Martinique and Guadeloupe, where, imitating the Brazilian system, women tended grounds on Saturdays, while men hired themselves out (Debien 1974, pp. 178–182). Planters discouraged this resource-maximizing strategy, reluctant to distribute rations, to which hired-out slaves were entitled (Tomich 1976, p. 201). Fouchard (1981, p. 43) claims that in Saint Domingue women maintained the savings of households and families. Danish West Indian slaves repeated the African Gold Coast division of labor, with males tending grounds and females marketing crops (Hall 1980, p. 29).[14]

Planters generally did not increase the amount of land in provisions to accommodate new slaves. In the French West Indies new recruits worked on gardens of a mentor and were then given part (Debien 1974, p. 80). Edwards (1966) describes a similar system for the British West Indies whereby new slaves became "pensioners" to older ones. This division of goods and labor created a hardship for the slaves, said Edwards (1966, vol. 2, pp. 154–155), but his workers insisted on the practice (see also Labat 1930, vol. 2, p. 47). Slaves also hired or purchased others to work on their grounds. Slave masters sometimes designated a godchild or other slave to work the grounds of an elderly slave (Carmichael 1834, vol. 2, p. 209). At Mrs. Carmichael's Laurel Hill, a "good" slave was occasionally assigned to a "bad" one to increase production in the latter's polinck (1834, vol. 2, p. 231). The potential for inequality was great in all of these circumstances. Provision grounds were important sources of food, income, and status; and those slaves who lacked land or effective means to utilize it were vulnerable to malnutrition, labor exploitation, and depletion of other resources in exchange for food.

Domestics sometimes depended on rations or, with only occasional provision grounds, bought from or were given food by other slaves (Debien 1974, p. 210). Children and sick and elderly slaves were generally allotted rations, so only the kindness of fellow slaves warded off hunger (Tomich 1976, p. 212). In Barbados, where individualized provision grounds were rare and rations reluctantly distributed by masters, superannuated slaves were turned out on the streets to beg. Rations to the sick and old went unchanged in Saint Domingue with overall increases in food distribution (Debien 1974, p. 209).

CONCLUSIONS

Women had many responsibilities in the slave families they headed and in those maintained by men. Women cooked, helped to build houses and tended them, cared for children, managed horticulture, and carried out much of the cultivation of provisions and perhaps most of the fruit and vegetable marketing. A cruel trade-off finally developed in many areas, as the intensification of sugar production demanded women's presence in the fields. Women's status as field laborers robbed both men and women of the economic autonomy associated with the production and trade of food and reduced their domestic commitments and contributions to household economies.

It is a contemporary judgment that fuller incorporation into field labor was less palatable to slaves than the status associated with tending and selling provisions, even with women's broad and demanding roles in petty agriculture, horticulture, and domestic work. Caribbean slaves left us little about their feelings. There can be little doubt, however, that they were avid entrepreneurs and marketers, roles that have persisted and retained their value in Caribbean societies to the present.[15] And the alternative, the regimen of field labor, is indisputably harsh.

Not all Caribbean plantation societies began with slaves' committing time to the planting and marketing of provisions. Many islands, for example, Barbados and the Leewards, were not well suited ecologically to individualized planting, as were Jamaica, the Windwards, Martinique, and Guadeloupe. Colonists in Barbados and the Leewards imported large quantities of food and provisions, or planters supervised their cultivation on estate lands. Others, such as planters in Cuba and Saint Domingue, moved away from slave-controlled planting with sugar expansion and the rationalization of production.

Women's position in the cultivation of provisions has been debated, but a clear, if complex, pattern is evident. Women were counted by slaveholders when provision lands were allocated. But when the distribution of plots to slaves was made, men's greater status secured them control. Male family heads were granted land. Groups of slaves yielded land and authority to powerful male figures, yet many single women also had provision grounds and may have controlled their children's plots as well. Women, along with other family members, did a considerable amount of the cultivation of provisions. Men's capacity to clear and establish growing areas allowed them to create means of production and hence contributed to their social dominance. Marketing was women's domain, although family members participated in petty provision trading as well.

The picture that emerges from this analysis of slave-controlled production is that males had more power than females in the subsistence sector, derived in part from physical superiority for the accomplishment of some agricultural tasks. Males' higher status is manifested also in slaves' homes, where females assumed domestic tasks and child care.

Jones (1982), White (1985), Gundersen (1986), and others have stressed a "separate but equal" division of labor for U.S. slave women but acknowledge male dominance in the slaves' households. Domestic tasks and horticulture belonged to women; agricultural work, for the slave family or the master, to men. This separation is less pronounced in the West Indies, where women did much agricultural work, although Caribbean slave men apparently did little work in the home. We can conclude that women enjoyed considerably more status in the Caribbean than in North America and frequently held a great deal of authority.

But for women who could not meet performance demands in all areas, the quality of material life was poor and potential exploitation by more powerful groups and individuals great. Increases in the scale of commodity production eventually robbed women of advantage, solidifying their role in field labor and equalizing their status with men in the realm of commodity production but taking from them traditional sources of authority and status, that is, the household, family, and petty trade and production. Physically weak women, along with other categories of apparently feeble workers, lost still more status and quality of life with increased exploitation of the agricultural labor force.

CHAPTER FIVE

Plantation Work

Women worked in two areas that benefited slaveholders directly, field labor and domestic service. Domestic service involved women from the earliest period of Caribbean slavery. Field labor increasingly drew women, because young men were no longer available as the slave trade closed. Women performed nearly all unskilled agricultural tasks, but they were not admitted to skilled or artisanal positions, which yielded more food, resources, and income than unskilled work.

Men's, women's, and children's labor power was increasingly demanded by planters in a process that in some ways mimicked the later proletarianization of the agricultural labor force but differed categorically from wage labor. Scholars have debated the categorization of slavery as capitalist and of slaves as proletarians. Marx defined capitalism in terms of the relations of production, with proletarians freely selling their labor to capitalist owners of means of production. The commoditization of labor, which is intrinsic to classic definitions of capitalism and proletarianization, clearly does not apply to slaves who could not sell their own labor.

Orthodox Marxists and some others see the relations of slaves to slaveholders as sui generis (Hindess and Hirst 1975); others, such as Genovese (1965, 1976), have long stressed the noncapitalist, seigneurial character of New World slavery. Proponents of both these positions contend that integral to slavery is the purchase and sale of labor not by slaves but by slave masters and traders. The study of Caribbean slavery suggests that the articulation of capitalist trade relations with New World slave modes of production intensified the exchange of bonded labor. Other slave societies in history—ancient Greece and Rome, Africa, China—were less fully, if at all, integrated with capitalist relations of trade and production. And they generated less extensive and long-lasting systems of human trade. Once the international slave trade became politically impossible, it ceased, heightening contradictions between production for use and exchange and reproduction (Dupuy 1983; Padgug 1977) and hastening the end of slavery in the New World (Reddock 1985; Brathwaite 1971).

Others have emphasized historically changing patterns of slave labor in the New World, contending that slavery was a moment in the transition to wage-based plantation cash cropping. Mintz (1978, p. 87) stresses that the slave mode of production generally mixed peasant provision production with contract and even free labor:

> The succession of different mixes of labor extraction in specific instances reveals clearly how the plantation systems of different Caribbean societies developed as parts of worldwide capitalism, each particular case indicating how variant means were employed to provide adequate labor, some successful and some not, all within an international division of labor transformed by capitalism, and to satisfy an international market created by that same capitalist system.

Eventually slavery and other labor forms associated with precapitalist or noncapitalist systems of production fell away, and true proletarian labor developed (Beckford 1972).

Orthodox and neo-Marxian dependency perspectives converge in the position that New World slaves were bought and sold in a process—variously labeled—that was exacerbated by the incorporation of the slave mode of production in international trade. And it culminated in the Caribbean in the commoditization of labor in the wage-based system of plantation production that followed emancipation.

The expropriation of land and other means of production, also identified with proletarianization (Tilly 1978), was richly elaborated in the history of Caribbean slavery. Slaves enjoyed less control over income and resource-generating activities, or they received less time and support from masters and other slaves to use petty entrepreneurship for the accumulation of income, goods, and food surpluses for trade. This process was especially pronounced in areas that reached their most productive phases in the eighteenth and nineteenth centuries, that is, Jamaica, the French West Indies, Cuba, Puerto Rico, Trinidad, Dutch Surinam, and the Danish Virgin Islands.

Caribbean slaves exercised control over resources derived from four areas of production and service. Ranked in order of their contributions to slaves' livelihoods and availability to the largest number of slaves, they were (1) growing and marketing of provisions, (2) skilled and domestic labor, (3) hiring out of skilled and domestic services, and (4) prostitution. These areas contrast sharply with the alternative, field labor, which allowed little income earning and gradually erased the authority, power, and status rooted in the maintenance of household economies and in specialized tasks. As individually managed and specialized activities decreased or produced less income and resources for slaves, field labor increased and involved more categories of workers. But this relationship did not move in the other direction. When production and productivity dropped, workers were still needed in field labor because of the decline in the number of slaves and, in particular, of adult males.

The emancipation of slaves rendered a partial reversal, and the true proletarianization of rural labor spanned the nineteenth century in many areas of the Caribbean. Labor needs shrank after slavery ended, in part because of the importation of Asian contract laborers (Rodney 1981). And ex-slaves sought farm land wherever they could.

Free wage labor was restricted largely to males. Females returned to their earlier roles in domestic work, horticulture, and petty food production and marketing. Women's status was elevated once more, although plantation wages were high in comparison to other forms of earnings and were available almost exclusively to men. However, postemancipation farming was more universal and on a larger scale than during slavery and was accompanied by a high degree of formation of nuclear families. The resulting patriarchal division of agrarian labor gave females less authority in the control and management of household economies than they had experienced during slavery.

WOMEN AS DOMESTICS

Almost a quarter of the slaves in Barbados may have been domestics (in "menial service") in the early 1800s (Watson 1975, p. 142). Half of the slaves in Bridgetown, the capital of Barbados, are known to have been so employed at the time (Higman 1984, p. 384). Other British islands that had peaked as sugar producers also employed many slaves in domestic service. About half of the fit adults in Montserrat were domestic servants or tradesmen in the late 1700s (Goveia 1965, p. 146). Bermuda's maritime economy resulted in the employment of most slaves as domestics or house servants (Packwood 1975, p. 14). Similarly, the low level of agricultural development on Spanish-controlled Hispaniola meant that many slaves were day workers, including many domestics.

One wealthy Jamaican proprietor had a domestic staff of 25 to 30, probably constituting 10 percent of his slave work force; these servants worked as grooms, gardeners, livestock tenders, laundresses, and ladies' maids (Stewart 1823, p. 210). This relatively modest share of domestics in the total slave population compares with the French West Indies, where perhaps 10 percent of the work force were generally domestics (Schnakenbourg 1980, p. 51).

Contrasts in the number of domestics on a plantation or in Caribbean slave societies in general rest on variations in intensity of sugar and other forms of production of commodities. For example, domestics were common in Puerto Rico throughout its history as a slave-based sugar-producing area, especially in urban centers. But the *haciendas* of Ponce y Guayama, which produced 60 percent of Puerto Rico's sugar exports in 1841, had few domestics (Baralt 1981, p. 77). The share of house slaves did not vary consistently from small to large estates or among more or less intensely worked areas. Domestics made up the same proportion of slaves at two early nineteenth-century estates compared by Craton (1978, p. 347): the small Rolle cotton estate in the Bahamas and Jamaica's larger Worthy Park. Urban centers always had many domestics (Higman 1984, p. 384).

Other pertinent factors in the assignment of slaves to domestic positions included the quality of the work force and its level of efficiency in completing agricultural tasks. More important, the presence of resident planters wishing to maintain a large home, emulating European elite households, contributed to the distribution of labor on plantations. Resident planters and their families believed themselves especially needy of servants. Mrs. Carmichael (1834, vol. 1, p. 120) reports from Trinidad that a family with three maids and a manservant in England would require ten adults and five or six youths in the West Indies.

In the French islands most house slaves were male, with females concentrated in child care, sewing, and laundry (Debien 1974, pp. 87–91). At Martinique's l'Anse-à-l'Ane in 1746 six men and four women served as house slaves (Debien 1960, p. 24). The position of cook had high status in Trinidad and in the French West Indies and was, again, often held by males. Head servants in Trinidad's "great houses" were men; their primary function was to supervise table service. The head female domestic managed the ladies' maids (Carmichael 1834, vol. 1, pp. 116–117). Most of Cuba's urban slaves were domestics, with women predominating (Knight 1970, pp. 60–62). Britain's sugar islands had the following gender distribution: "Females dominated among the houseslaves. In general, 70 percent of rural domestics were females, although the proportion was as high as 86.4 percent in Anguilla in 1827" (Higman 1984, p. 191).

Domestic servants were usually Creoles. At Jamaica's Mesopotamia estate, for example, of 182 African-born slaves, 11 became craft workers or domestics (Dunn 1987, p. 808). Domestics were also often colored, that is, of mixed European and African heritage. Mulatto girls performed household chores in nineteenth-century Martinique (Tomich 1976, p. 182). At Jamaica's Worthy Park in 1796, 60 percent of domestics were colored (Craton 1977, p. 149). The Maryland coffee estate in Jamaica employed its colored females as domestics, as did the Irwin sugar estate (Higman 1976a, pp. 196–199). Mrs. Carmichael (1834, vol. 1, p. 82) reports that domestics were Afro-European in Trinidad as well. The right of colored slaves to a limited number of domestic and artisanal posts may explain tensions between colored and black slaves at Mesopotamia at the turn of the nineteenth century (Dunn 1987, p. 808).

The domestic was not considered skilled and was generally no more highly valued than the field worker, but privileges often accrued, particularly to women (Mathurin 1974, p. 304; Gautier 1985, p. 211). Some domestics lived in the master's "great house"; others in their own cottages, as on Monk Lewis's (1834, p. 85) Jamaican estates. Clothes, medicine, and food were sometimes provided for domestic slaves, and their clothing was mended and washed. Mrs. Carmichael (1834, vol. 1, pp. 82–85) observed that house slaves in Trinidad were referred to as "miss" or "mister" by whites and other slaves alike. In the Leeward Islands of the British West Indies, domestics received a small cash allowance during the late eighteenth century (Goveia 1965, pp. 140–141); the same was true in nineteenth century Curaçao (Hoetink 1972, p. 68). Gautier (1985, p. 211) reports, however, that in the French West Indies only *coutières* among female domestics could receive cash.

Slaves in many settings strongly preferred service to field labor; Cuban domestic workers feared nothing more than transfer to the fields (Turnbull 1840, p. 51).[1] In some areas, such as the French West Indies, slaves moved in and out of agriculture, never secure in generally more desirable domestic work (Debien 1960, pp. 26, 30). Mathurin (1974, pp. 306–307) claims that agricultural work was used to punish slaves. " 'Common labour' in the field was a threat constantly held over the heads of house slaves who resisted white advances." Domestic status was not necessarily retained within a lineage, a condition that worked against females. Dunn (1987, p. 804) found, for example, that at Jamaica's Mesopotamia, among slaves whose work lives fell in the period from 1751 to 1831, boys who began as domestics later became craftsmen and girls were moved from the house to the fields.

Women slaves often used domestic labor as a means of gaining freedom. In the French West Indies many personal servants were freed informally while abroad with masters; *soi-disant libre* status was not, however, legal manumission, and most slaves discharged in this way returned to the Caribbean to work on the estates and live nearby (Debien 1960, p. 26). It was easier for domestics than for other slaves to acquire freedom in Puerto Rico (Diaz Soler 1974, p. 151). Domestics and tradespeople were also more likely than field slaves to gain their freedom in the British West Indies. In St. Lucia, for example, from 1815 to 1819, 52 percent of manumitted slaves were domestics (Higman 1984, p. 384).

Domestic service sometimes led to manumission by allowing slaves to garner income and other resources. More important, domestic work brought slaves into close contact with slave masters, their families, and other whites, enhancing the opportunity for personal relationships. Many old and ill slaves were freed for "sentimental" reasons. Sexual relationships developed between whites and slaves, often domestics, that sometimes resulted in freedom for women and/or the children of such unions. This was not a certain prospect, however. In Bermuda not a single case is recorded of a white freeing black or mulatto children, his own or a slave's (Packwood 1975, p. 172). Elsewhere it was common (Bush 1981). The Code Noir ordered masters to free their colored children, although like other colonial laws and statutes, this one was often ignored. In Saint Domingue, "there was strong sentiment in favor of emancipating the children of the master throughout the history of the colony, and these children were an important source of the free colored population" (G. Hall 1972, p. 185).

Higman's profile of the nineteenth-century British West Indian manumitted slave supports the suggestion that domestic labor worked for women as a means of freedom, frequently through intimate relationships with masters: The typical freed British West Indian slave was female, Creole, young, colored, and working as a domestic (Higman 1984, p. 383). Going further, Higman (1984, pp. 384–385) argues that "colored females were the only [free] group to show a relatively youthful tendency and this suggests strongly that they were most often the recipients of gratuitous manumission paid for by white fathers."

ARTISANAL AND SKILLED POSITIONS

A rigid division of nonfield labor prevailed on Caribbean slave plantations, with women among domestics and men making up the vast majority of craftsmen, skilled processors, and supervisors. Among domestic positions, only those of seamstress and cook were considered skilled. Other semiskilled positions that were held by women were nurse, head of the nursery, and occasionally animal keeper. These were not positions of status or monetary worth, however, and often were assumed by elderly or disabled slaves. In 1805 on the Tharp estates "by far the most medical attendants were female and were in poor physical condition and valued at less than the average of all plantation slaves" (Sheridan 1985, p. 94).

Males' skilled positions included cooper, carpenter, mason, boilerman, millwright, ranger, and clayer; drivers supervised slaves in the field, head boilermen in the milling area. Tradesmen had less status than artisans and supervisors (M. G. Smith 1953; Curtin 1970, pp. 19-20). At Worthy Park 92.4 percent of skilled positions were held by men at the turn of the nineteenth century (Craton 1977, p. 142). Higman (1984, pp. 192–193) found that in nineteenth-century British West Indian sugar colonies only 7 percent of tradespeople were women but that women occasionally supervised the second and third gangs. Women drivers were "not uncommon" on Berbice (Pinckard 1970, vol. 3, p. 179). At times women managed the boiling and drying of sugar. In general, however, among British West Indian slaves "females were totally excluded from skilled trades other than sewing, and very rarely worked in transportation or fishing, or served as 'watchmen'. Males were excluded only from washing and sewing" (Higman 1984, p. 189). The same relation appears to hold true for other places as well.[2]

The distribution of skilled positions to colored and Creole slaves varied with the location and task. British West Indian colored slaves never outnumbered blacks in any occupation examined by Higman (1984, p. 194), who used plantation records and early nineteenth-century registration figures. In 1796 at Worthy Park, 25 percent of craftsmen were colored, although colored slaves made up only 6.6 percent of the slave population (Craton 1977, p. 149). At the Maryland coffee plantation in the early 1800s, all colored males were tradesmen (Higman 1976a, p. 197). At the Mesopotamia estate in nineteenth-century Jamaica, occupational stratification favored "mulatto and quadroon slaves who had been sired by the white staff" (Dunn 1977, p. 54). Colored slaves predominated among skilled workers in the French West Indies as well (Debien 1974, p. 103). At l'Anse-à-l'Ane in Martinique, fewer Creoles than Africans left the fields for skilled jobs in the mid-eighteenth century (Debien 1960, p. 13). In late eighteenth- and early nineteenth-century Barbados, however, Creole slaves had more opportunities for mobility than did Africans (Watson 1975, p. 134).

The advantages of work in skilled positions were many. Cash payments were made to individual skilled slaves in the British West Indies (Higman 1984, p. 203). Drivers in Trinidad sometimes had a young male servant and hired workers for their provision grounds (Carmichael 1834, vol. 1, p. 283). The internal hiring of subordinates by skilled slaves, with payment in kind or in favors, was found throughout the British West Indies. Slaves of status and authority also enjoyed deferential terms of address (M. G. Smith 1953). Artisans in nineteenth-century Martinique did not live with other slaves (Tomich 1976, p. 184). At l'Anse-à-l'Ane skilled workers were less often moved in and out of the fields than domestics (Debien 1960, p. 35). Cash payments were made to individual skilled slaves in the British West Indies (Higman 1984, p. 203).

OTHER ECONOMIC ROLES AND ACTIVITIES

Women performed other integral or lucrative tasks on the plantations. Mrs. Carmichael (1834, vol. 2, pp. 183–185) describes a woman slave of her acquaintance in Trinidad who kept grounds, marketed her crop, and sponsored dances, charging admission. This industrious bondwoman's circumstances were exceptional, for, other than through domestic work and the few skilled positions, slave women's entry to higher status, income, or authority was through healing and, in the cities, through prostitution.

Women's medical role was well established in West Indian slave societies and strongly linked to African practices. It brought slave women prestige and resources. Slaves used the services of indigenous and Western doctors as well as of women who kept and dispensed herbs and other natural healing substances. In the British West Indies at least, European doctors were often misinformed, owing to poor training and less than altruistic motives for practice in the West Indies. An unfamiliar disease environment presented them with new diseases and afflictions, exacerbated by planters' cruel treatment and poor nourishment of slaves. African "doctors" and healers had superior knowledge of diseases also found in West Africa—yaws, malaria, yellow fever (Sheridan 1985). Women healers and nurses were routinely called on to serve as midwives and attendants to new mothers and to treat reproductive diseases, problems, and maladies that seemed to plague women and children. Healers, or "weedwomen," also offered comfort to slaves who feared treatment by European physicians.[3]

Obeah men and women are discussed throughout the literature on West Indian slavery. They used herbs and potions to release the sick from supernatural forces. Generally, obeah practitioners were men, but references to women in this role are also found, for example, in Dominica (Atwood 1791, p. 269). Such examples may reflect the observer's confusion between healers and obeah people, who generally treated a wider variety of ills and understood their source in others' mischief or ill will. For women to hold this position would be an important indication of authority within the slave community, for apart from its intrinsic significance and status it was a position associated with men in the West Indies and West Africa (Sheridan 1985).

Finally, women slaves occasionally garnered income and resources through prostitution. Most white and free colored males owned female slaves. And slaveholders freely engaged in sexual relations with their slaves, as did their staffs, retainers, and guests (Stedman 1971; Moreton 1793, p. 77). Large urban centers had many nonslaveholding males and, along with nonagrarian trading centers such as Bermuda and Curaçao, fostered the formal prostitution of slaves (Higman 1984; Patterson 1969; James 1963).

Prostitution was illegal in most Caribbean slave societies but still common (Higman 1984; G. Hall 1971, p. 92). Handler (1974, p. 137) suggests that prostitution was a common way for women in the towns of Barbados to get money for freedom in the late eighteenth and early nineteenth centuries. Jamaican cities are said by Patterson (1969, p. 161) to have been full of prostitutes: "The majority of enslaved domestics in the towns were expected to support themselves in this manner." Higman (1984, pp. 231–232) agrees that prostitution in the early nineteenth-century British West Indies followed several patterns, with domestics in taverns and inns serving as prostitutes, the hiring out of individual prostitutes by masters, and independent prostitution by slave women themselves.

HIRING OUT

Throughout the Caribbean slaves were occasionally "hired out" by masters or hired themselves out to provide services for a fee to non-slave-owning whites. In nearly all parts of the region, domestics and skilled slaves worked for cash, turning over all or some portion to their masters.

French West Indian slaveholders early adopted the Brazilian system of slaves' dividing labor within the family for greater income earning. Slave men hired out their services on Saturdays, whereas women tended gardens (Debien 1974, pp. 178–182). Slaves favored this system and were dissuaded from it, finally, only when planters refused to provide supplementary food rations. There were also plantations in the French West Indies, for example, l'Anse-à-l'Ane in Martinique, where only women hired out, as laundresses and cooks (Debien 1960, p. 67).

The hiring out of plantation slaves in rural areas generally favored males. Especially on smaller farms with a smaller retinue of slaves, the usually male artisan was in demand. Women were sometimes hired out to share heavy work with men on roads and plantations (Mathurin 1974, p. 310). Servants, both male and female, were needed in urban areas in the residences of whites and free colored people (see, for example, Carmichael 1834, vol. 2, p. 20; Tannenbaum 1946, p. 57).

But the opportunity to rent out slaves' labor or for slaves to hire out their services was generally limited to particular locales and peculiar circumstances. In Bermuda, where slaves were not engaged in commodity production, they routinely hired out their services or were rented out by slave owners for shipping, sailing, and dock work as well as for the more typical artisanal and domestic work. The same was true in Curaçao, where slaves who hired out were called money-seekers. Slave societies with an urban sector generally had more rental of slaves and "self-hire" (Higman 1984, p. 246); in the towns of St. Vincent most servants were hired-out slaves (Carmichael 1834, vol. 1, p. 20). Where sugar production had ebbed or never really taken off, as in Santo Domingo, slaves were often day laborers (*jornaleros*), maintaining their own livelihoods (Silié 1976, p. 101).

MANUMISSIONS AND SLAVE ECONOMIC AUTONOMY

Rates and systems of manumission varied greatly across colonial domains and eras. The Spanish system of *coartación* was the most liberal in conception. Slaves were entitled to buy their freedom, on an installment basis if necessary (Klein 1967, p. 196). Although later altered significantly in practice, the *coartación* resulted, in the early days of sugar planting, in the region's highest rate of manumission. In 1774, 69.5 free persons of African descent resided in

Cuba for every 100 slaves. The proportion never fell below 32 per 100 (Hart 1980, pp. 136–137).[4] Where sugar planting was less intense in the eighteenth-century Spanish West Indies, the free colored population finally exceeded slaves. By the late eighteenth century Santo Domingo's free colored population, at 80,000, greatly exceeded its 15,000 slaves. In Puerto Rico the number of slaves increased from 7,000 in 1775 to 22,000 in 1820, but free people grew in number from 35,000 to 104,000 during the same period and "even outnumbered the whites" (Klein 1986, p. 222).

Other colonial systems were less open to manumission, even through purchase. Patterson (1982, p. 285) argues that Europeans in the British and French West Indies objected in the eighteenth century to the principle of manumission, as did Dutch Surinam colonists in the 1700s and early 1800s. This posture changed somewhat in the 1820s, as emancipation neared. Conservative estimates of slave manumissions in the British West Indies for 1820 are 1.2 per 1,000 slaves in Barbados, 2.4 in St. Kitts, 1.0 in Nevis, 1.7 in Antigua, 1.5 in Montserrat, 3.2 in the Virgin Islands, 1.0 in St. Vincent, 2.1 in Grenada, 1.1 in Tobago, 6.6 in Trinidad, and 0.2 in Demerara-Essequibo (Higman 1984, p. 381).[5]

In the French West Indies manumissions were initially limited to colored and elderly slaves and for elderly slaves seldom involved the transfer of cash.[6] The informally arranged *soi-disant libres* status, common after the Seven Years War, was rarely purchased. Still the freed population was relatively large in the French West Indies: 7.1 percent of the total 1802 population in Martinique, increasing to 24.9 percent in 1835; and 4 percent of the total 1784 population in Saint Domingue (Cohen and Greene 1972, p. 4). By the 1830s many manumissions were bought; from 1831 to 1847 the average annual number of manumissions in Guadeloupe was 948 (about 1 percent of the slave population) and in Martinique, 1525 (about 2 percent of the slave population) (Schnakenbourg 1980, p. 49).

Manumission rates were especially sensitive to international market transitions. Slumps created surpluses of slaves, who were sometimes easier to free than to support (Patterson 1982, p. 286). Prosperity increased manumissions where slaves had the opportunity to purchase freedom. In other circumstances intensification of sugar planting reduced manumissions. The most dramatic case of this phenomenon was Cuba, where restrictions on manumissions, increased fees, and fewer income-earning opportunities reduced the proportion of free Cubans of African descent from 20.3 percent of the total population in 1774 to 15.1 percent in 1827 (Cohen and Greene 1972, p. 11).

The practice of manumission was common during the pre-plantation era. But as the demand for labor increased toward the end of the eighteenth century and continued at a high level throughout the nineteenth century, white slaveowners became less willing and less able to grant manumissions voluntarily. At the same time, the legal route of *coartación,* by which a slave could eventually buy his freedom, was considerably restricted, partly as a result of greater and sharper discrimination against non-whites. Slaves' prospects for freedom were, then, dependent upon international trends and transitions, as well as on the largess of masters, and often, on their own initiative and economic achievements. (Knight 1972, p. 283)

Still, the subject of manumissions is pertinent to our discussion of domestic and artisanal work of slaves for two reasons related to the internal dynamics of slave societies and plantations. First, manumission was positively and strongly associated with urban residence, with high concentrations of domestics and artisans (Higman 1984; Hoetink 1972, p. 62; Cox 1984, pp. 40–41). Second, women generally outnumbered men among freed slaves and manumissions.[7]

Three women were manumitted for every two manumitted males in Jamaica (Craton 1977, p. 75).[8] Among slaves freed in Barbados between 1809 and 1829, about 62 percent were female. In Dominica and Antigua males and females had about the same chance for freedom (Handler 1974, pp. 22, 52). Women were more likely to be manumitted in St. Kitts and Grenada (Cox 1984, p. 39). Women predominated among freed slaves in the Spanish West Indies (Knight 1972, p. 286; Klein 1986, p. 227) and in the French West Indies (Debien 1974, p. 370). In Dutch Surinam twice as many women were freed as men (Hoetink 1972, p. 62). More female babies than male babies were generally freed (Cohen and Greene 1972, p. 7).

Women of mixed descent and their children had more opportunities for manumission than black slave women and children. Of a random sample of 103 slaves freed in St. Kitts from 1781 to 1826, 37 percent were colored, with slaves of mixed descent constituting less than 7 percent of the slave population. Similarly, of 586 slaves manumitted in Grenada from 1820 to 1826, 41 percent were colored, whereas colored slaves made up about 7 percent of Grenada's slave population. In the total sample of St. Kitts and Grenada more colored slaves were aged 10 and under than any other age; the manumission rate of colored slaves declined with age after age 10 (Cox 1984, pp. 47–48).

Although it is unknown how often slaves purchased their freedom and when they were freed for sentimental reasons, scattered data are suggestive. Of 455 slaves freed from 1821 to 1824 on St. Kitts, about 45 percent were freed without payment; about 80 percent of manumissions on Grenada during the same period were gratuitous (Cox 1984, p. 39). These figures are derived, however, from late in the history of these sugar-producing islands and may reflect the ameliorative measures that foreshadowed emancipation in such settings. Evidence from throughout the region consistently suggests that women were freed most often as a result of emotional or sexual ties to planters.[9] Males more often than females used income-generating activities to purchase freedom (Cohen and Greene 1972, p. 7).

Nevertheless some women purchased freedom for themselves and family members, and there was apparently a connection in the slaveholders' minds linking the entrepreneurial activities of slaves and freed men and women and manumissions. Crackdowns on the political and economic rights of free colored people throughout the 1700s in the Caribbean was accompanied by increased costs for manumissions and restrictions on marketing activities of all nonwhites (D. Hall 1972, p. 197; Handler 1974, pp. 67–82; Elisabeth 1972, pp. 135–162; Diaz Soler 1974, p. 223; Packwood 1975, p. 172).[10] Taxes on women's manumissions were increased in several settings in the 1800s, sometimes to twice that levied on men's freedom (Levy 1980, p. 11). These increases were directed to masters who paid the state for the privilege of freeing a slave. But the effect was that women's contributions to these fees increased. We can infer that whites perceived entrepreneurship and access to cash by women as an important foundation of the growing number of free colored people. It is possible, too, that women's growing value as reproducers and as agricultural laborers overwhelmed masters' sentimental inclinations to free them.

WOMEN IN FIELD LABOR

Most Caribbean plantation work was organized in a three-tiered gang system. The first tier, adult slaves, performed heavy work. The second gang, made up of older and younger slaves, did lighter labor. Children aged 5 to 12 constituted a third gang that weeded and cleared the fields of twigs and debris (Patterson 1969; Higman 1984; Lewisohn 1970; Moreno Fraginals 1978; Debien 1974). Minor exceptions formed around age and task.[11]

The pattern of age distribution on Barbados was typical, with members of the first gang aged 16 to 50 years (Levy 1980, p. 10), the second, 12 to 16 years. On weaning, children in Barbados tended animals in "hog-meat" or "pot gangs," then moved into the "little" gang for weeding and collecting grass (Dickson 1789, p. 12). At age 4 slave children on Trinidad entered the vine gang, which gathered brush and vines from the fields. At age 8 or 9 children hoed for 3 hours daily (Carmichael 1834, vol. 2, pp. 138–139). Where slaves were relatively few and labor needs substantial, for example, the Danish Virgin Islands, other groups of presumably weak slaves were also found in the second gang (Dookhan 1975, p. 79). On St. John children below age 6 or 7 did not work, but beyond that age they "carried water to the field slaves, looked after calves, and cared for smaller children" (Olwig 1985, p. 17). In the French West Indies the second gang included recently arrived slaves and new mothers (Schnakenbourg 1980; Debien 1960, p. 17). Tasks were distributed in this way: The first gang (*le grand atelier*) dug holes for sugar, generally considered to be the most demanding task in sugar cultivation. The second gang (*le petit atelier*) planted cane, bundled it, and carried it to carts, while the children covered the cane with dirt (Schnakenbourg 1980, pp. 38, 52; Tomich 1976, p. 185).

Processing of sugar involved field slaves but in less rigid form than the gang system. In Cuba about 50 women and boys were generally needed to collect cane and load it onto carts. Danish West Indian slave children and old people loaded cane onto mules and carts; young boys drove mules (Lewisohn 1970, p. 125). Sturge and Harvey (1838, p. 12) observed women and "youths" feeding cane into mills in St. Lucia.

To produce the relatively modest amount of 150 tons of sugar yearly with 200 slaves, at least 70 have to work in the fields and 27 must be in refining and milling operations, with 16 additional slaves in skilled positions and 14 domestics (Gaston Martin 1948, pp. 122–123). In fact, the fields took more workers, about 70 percent of slaves in the nineteenth-century French West Indies, whereas skilled workers constituted 20 percent of the slave force (Schnakenbourg 1980, p. 51). About one-third of total plantation slaves were in the first gang (Tomich 1976, p. 185). Where illness or age influenced the allocation of positions, the proportion was lower. At Jamaica's Worthy Park in 1792, of 355 slaves 150 were in the fields; and among Spring Garden's 528 slaves only 137 were part of the first gang (Phillips 1949, pp. 5, 8). In Cuba, of 45,000 slaves probably 15,000 performed agricultural labor (Flinter 1834, p. 263). Sheridan (1985, p. 192) reports that of 180 slaves at Rose Hall in December 1789, only 55 percent were "able and healthy" or "healthy," and 38.3 percent of the total were deemed "weak, afflicted with ulcers or sores, sick, blind, or otherwise physically impaired."

Over time the number of field laborers increased where possible, but aging, disabled populations often weakened and diminished the field labor force. Ten to fifteen percent of French West Indian slave workers were usually in the hospital, so that with the old and infirm one-third to one-quarter of slaves were unavailable for work (Debien 1974, p. 318). At l'Anse-à-l'Ane after 1763, no fewer than 20 of 92 slaves were old or sick (Debien 1960, p. 23). Invalids and superannuated slaves numbered 33 among 355 slaves at Worthy Park in 1792 (Phillips 1949, p. 5). The inactive population on Cuban estates was small until imports of Africans fell. In the period from 1845 to 1868, 19.85 percent of slaves were inactive, aged under 9 or over 60 (Moreno Fraginals 1977, p. 195).

Women, children, elderly slaves, the sick, and the disabled were increasingly called on to perform unskilled agricultural work. At the Codrington estates on Barbados in the late 1700s two-thirds of women slaves were in the fields but only about one-half of the men (Bennett 1958, p. 13). Half of the women slaves at Rose Hall on Jamaica performed field labor in the early nineteenth century, as compared to only about one-eighth of slave men (Higman 1976a, p. 194). Similar patterns were found on the Maryland coffee estate in Jamaica, where, in 1822, of 170 males aged 20 to 59, 20 were field workers, whereas only 9 of 161 females in the same age group were not (Higman 1976a, p. 197).

Women also provided more and more of the unskilled labor in the sugar fields. Women constituted 58 percent of fieldworkers at Worthy Park in the 1790s and more than 65 percent in the 1830s (Craton 1977, p. 142). Two-thirds of agricultural workers were female at Jamaica's Mesopotamia estate in the early 1800s (Dunn 1977, p. 54); and 85 percent of females became "prime field hands" in the period from 1762 to 1831, with only 55 percent of males assuming this position (Dunn 1987, p. 806). Females predominated in the first and second gangs on the Irwin sugar estate in Jamaica from at least 1821 (Higman 1976a, pp. 198–199). Women also often outnumbered males in the *grand ateliers* of the French West Indies. At l'Anse-à-l'Ane in Martinique in 1772 the first gang consisted of 20 males and 40 females, the second of 8 boys and 6 girls, and the third of 4 small boys and 4 small girls (Debien 1960, p. 18). L'Anse-à-l'Ane represented another important trend in the utilization of workers thought to be less productive: Girls entered the first gang before boys.[12] And later, as we might expect, the overall number of field slaves and those in the first gang declined and the number of free, skilled, and domestic slaves and the ill and infirm rose (Debien 1960, pp. 20–23).

Males' and females' work in the cane fields was largely the same, although some jobs, such as cane cutting, were usually assigned to males. Yet, with growing rationalization of labor organization and other dimensions of sugar production after 1780, more differences in males' and females' skilled agricultural work and processing appeared.[13] Gender division of labor in Cuba marked these technical and organizational changes. Sugar processing on *ingenios,* or sugar mills, was almost wholly male. Knight (1970, pp. 72–74) describes how the strongest men were assigned to the boiler house, as cart men, as cutters, and as workmen in the *casa de purga,* or refinery. Women and boys gathered and loaded cane and cooked and brought food and water to men in the fields. During the planting season only men dug the holes while others planted and covered the plants.

WORKING CONDITIONS

Caught up in political debates about slavery and emancipation or captives of their European hosts' influence, travelers to the West Indies described slaves' working conditions as formally set and sanctioned by slaveholders and the state. And in the early days of sugar planting, workdays were less arduous than in later times and attention to schedules greater—except during the sugar harvest, when the slaves' days belonged entirely to the masters.

Mrs. Carmichael (1834) reported that slaves in St. Vincent began work before 5:45 A.M. in the harvest months, April through June. During the rest of the year, they began after 6:00 A.M., stopping from 8:00 to 9:00 for breakfast, with a later two-hour lunch period. By 6:00 P.M. they left the fields. Slaves never worked in the rain—a doubtful observation by Carmichael. And, equally unlikely, their health actually improved during the harvest, proof that they were not overworked (Carmichael 1834, vol. 2, pp. 23–29).

Barclay (1828, pp. 306–309) noted the same schedule elsewhere in the British West Indies, although he observed that during the harvest slaves worked at night. Visiting Barbados in the still early days of sugar planting, Ligon (1657, p. 48) also saw slaves working from 6:00 A.M. to 6:00 P.M., with two hours for a midday meal. Dickson (1789, p. 8) recorded that the morning bells rang at 4:00 A.M. Danish West Indian slaves also worked from 6 A.M. to 6 P.M., with a morning break from 7:00 to 8:00 A.M. to eat and a pause at 1:00 P.M. for a midday meal. At noon and in the evenings slaves collected grass for estate animals (Olwig 1985, p. 17).

Sundays were generally free except, again, during the harvest season. Slave codes for the British Virgin Islands recognized the rights of slaves not to work on Sundays and several holy days (N. Hall 1980, p. 28). The Code Noir and Royal Ordinance of 1786 had stipulated 82 holidays for slaves in the French West Indies. Following the French Revolution and restoration of slavery in 1804, only four days were permitted (Debien 1974, p. 191), a change consistent with a general movement toward greater productivity demands of Caribbean slaves.

Workdays also increased, to 16 hours in Jamaica, 18 during the harvest (Patterson 1969, p. 69). Slaves worked increasingly in shifts, and sugar mills continued to operate through the night (Schnakenbourg 1980, p. 54). Lady Nugent (1907, p. 86), wife of Jamaica's governor and chronicler of early nineteenth-century events and social relations in Jamaica, visited a local boiling house:

> I asked the overseer how often his people were relieved. He said every twelve hours; but how dreadful to think of their standing twelve hours over a boiling cauldron, and doing the same thing; and he owned to me that sometimes they did fall asleep, and get their poor fingers into the mill; and he shewed me a hatchet, that was always ready to sever the whole limb, as the only means of saving the poor sufferer's life.

Repetitious, dangerous work patterns were characteristic of processing wherever the productivity of cane fields coincided with late eighteenth-century technical innovations in sugar refining.

Nowhere was the work regimen more brutal than in early nineteenth-century Cuba. Slaves worked up to 20 hours daily during the sugar harvest, from 15 to 16 hours daily in the coffee fields during harvest time (Turnbull 1840, pp. 293–294; Knight 1970, p. 73). Often the preparation for crop gathering and its completion lasted six or seven months of the year (Bremer 1853, vol. 2, p. 312).[14]

Bondmen and women toiled three of four daily shifts, moving from the fields to various areas of sugar processing. The exhausted work force had its greatest time losses as a result of accidents (Moreno Fraginals 1977, p. 200; G. Hall 1971, p. 18). When the harvest ended, work subsided to 14 or 15 hours a day.

Where plantation-based commodity production had peaked, working conditions were somewhat better. Goveia (1965, p. 130) contends that in the British Leewards in the late 1770s the harvest work tempo was hastened to 10 hours daily to utilize a surplus of slaves. Sturge and Harvey (1838, p. 109) observed patterns of an earlier era in Martinique, with slaves working from dawn, taking an hour for breakfast, and resting for two hours at midday.

During the amelioration periods of the nineteenth century, slave conditions were altered to increase fertility and stem mortality. Food allocations increased in some settings (Bennett 1958); incentives were offered to women, midwives, and overseers for the birth and survival of children, but few changes were made in the grueling routine of sugar planting, harvesting, and processing. In the French West Indies and Barbados work time may have decreased somewhat (Bennett 1958, p. 102; Schnakenbourg 1980, p. 56). Guadeloupe's and Martinique's planters ended some night work and more often allowed Sundays for rest (Schnakenbourg 1980, p. 58). In general, though, amelioration was restricted to those circumstances, for example, pregnancy and childbirth, that did not directly influence worker productivity.

LABOR PRODUCTIVITY IN A CHANGING LABOR FORCE

Higman (1976a) has argued that women's growing nineteenth-century contributions to Jamaican field labor had little impact on overall labor productivity. Indeed, labor productivity was higher in sugar than in other kinds of cash crop production on the 960 properties analyzed by Higman, and the ratio of 92 males to 100 females was low (Higman 1976a, p. 123). Eisner's (1961) analysis of the Jamaican economy in 1832, when women predominated in the fields and in the slave population, reveals a product per slave (£25.33) similar to Higman's for 960 properties (£23.36 per slave) (Higman 1976a, p. 215). Higman concludes that average per capita labor productivity did not drop in a discernible way in Jamaica from 1807 to 1834 despite feminization and aging of the population.

We lack comparable data and analysis for other slave-based Caribbean sugar producers. An indirect measure of women's contribution to labor productivity, gender ratio of the population and of field labor in relation to overall labor productivity, is, however, revealing. In Cuba, for example, male slaves outnumbered females by a ratio of 2 to 1 in the early part of the nineteenth century and produced an incredible 2 tons of sugar per slave annually (Sheridan 1976, p. 245; Knight 1970, p. 76). Yet, as in Jamaica, productivity did not subside as the distribution of female slaves increased.

Barbados experienced a similar phenomenon. In 1736 fewer than 75,000 slaves produced 19,800 hogsheads of sugar, the highest level of labor productivity recorded for Barbados (Edwards 1966, vol. 1, p. 347; Sheridan 1973, p. 147). The equalization of the male and female slave populations in the 1750s suggests that women's growing presence as field laborers during an economic peak did little to diminish labor productivity on Barbados.

Martinique and Guadeloupe also displayed increased productivity as women's role in the labor force increased. Both islands reached peak levels of productivity in 1835, with sugar production reaching 1.5 tons per hectare in Martinique, with about 85,000 slaves; 1.4 tons of sugar per hectare was produced in Guadeloupe by 100,000 slaves. This level of production was achieved with 79 slaves per plantation, down from an average of 112 slaves per estate in the late 1770s.[15] Slaves were highly valued at this time and still imported illegally from Africa. It is reasonable to assume that about 75 percent of these populations were Creole, with females representing a sizable population share (Schnakenbourg 1980, p. 50).

Elsewhere the relationship is quite different. In Surinam, for example, the height of sugar cultivation was in the late 1780s, with 591 plantations and 50,000 slaves (Hoetink 1972, p. 60). Males predominated, and the gender ratio was still 105.8 males to 100 females in 1830. It dropped rapidly then, to 90.8 in 1850, but only about 65 percent of slave women worked in the fields.

Shortly before the nationalist revolution and abolition of slavery in Saint Domingue, male slaves outvalued females by more than 2,000 livres, a 10 percent gap that was large in comparison with standards for the region discussed in Chapter 3 (Debien 1960, p. 37; 1962, p. 18). On some plantations female slaves were scarce, with the heavily male presence perhaps resulting in high profit rates in Saint Domingue in the 1700s, about 10 percent compared to probably 5 percent in Jamaica (Debien 1962, p. 169). But as noted earlier, Creoles may have made up as much as 59 percent of the population, and women may have been present in greater number than is generally believed. Planters may also have underestimated the number of female slaves to explain the natural population decrease; and many males, especially Africans, had joined the revolutionary forces (Geggus 1978, p. 7).

Puerto Rico presents another ambiguous relationship between gender ratio and labor productivity. The late 1700s was a time of great productivity in

Puerto Rico, and the sex ratio was high (109.7 males to 100 females), but not necessarily on the large estates (Wessman 1980, p. 279; Scarano 1984). Indeed, gender ratios are inversely associated with plantation size in Puerto Rico, suggesting that, where females were well represented (the large estates), labor productivity was high.

CONCLUSIONS

Caribbean bondmen and women endured land expropriation, increased labor exploitation, and a loss of control over other income-earning strategies or the means and conditions to make them useful. These stages in the exploitation of slave labor were more pronounced in some settings, for example, Jamaica, Trinidad, and Cuba, than in others. But they occurred with varying degrees of intensity and scope in nearly all Caribbean commodity-producing societies. Slave women more fully encountered the impact of expropriation and growing labor exploitation than did slave men. Women's social status and authority were more dependent than men's on the household economy, which declined with their greater participation in field agriculture. Women slaves were petty cultivators and marketers in the early days of Caribbean slavery; they were also domestics, healers, and prostitutes—all positions that brought cash, favors, and other items of exchange. Domestic work and other opportunities to be close to slaveholders enhanced prospects for freedom, sometimes for children that resulted from sexual contacts with whites.

The common perception that males and females were interchangeable to slaveholders derives from Caribbean slave women's unusually high level of participation in commodity export agriculture (Mathurin 1975, p. 5; Patterson 1969, p. 167; 1982, pp. 173–174). Conceptions of gender equity based on slaves' nearly gender-free identities form an elegant notion and separate slavery from all other labor systems. Slave men and women were so fully subjugated, it is argued, that all marks of individuality and comparison— except perhaps physical strength—were obliterated. In fact, there were many bases for differentiation among slaves and by slaveholders. The criteria for social hierarchy did not decrease as more men and women were absorbed into fieldwork. With most skilled agricultural and industrial positions accessible only to male slaves, intragroup stratification functioned principally for men. Females were generally subordinate to men.

These gender dynamics among Caribbean slaves have parallels to other Third World histories. Large-scale cash cropping, with its industrial patterns of labor organization, has frequently diminished women's status (Rogers 1979; Ward 1984) to that of unskilled workers, no longer entitled to a share of men's increasing resources (Boserup 1970; Rogers 1979). The historical decline in women's position in the Third World has generally been a three-stage process. First, where peasant agriculture persisted, agrarian patriarchy prevailed, with males performing heavy work and females tending gardens and animals (Blumberg 1978; Boserup 1970). Peasant economies often articulated with non-wage-based systems of production, for example, slavery and debt peonage, introduced by Western capitalists (Wolf 1982; Wallerstein 1974, 1980). In the Caribbean cash cropping and nonwage systems of labor were dominant, with peasant activities of slaves a relatively small but often important element of the social formation (Morrissey 1981). Women slaves' role in agriculture was more notable than in many other Third World settings. When wages were finally paid to workers on plantations and other systems of commodity production, males monopolized jobs (Reddock 1985). At the same time women maintained an important role in household economies, based largely on petty agriculture and trade (Rodney 1981; Beckford 1972). This period of agricultural development brought comparative prosperity to many families and households, particularly in such areas as the Caribbean, where small-scale production of export commodities was common (Morrissey 1981). But women's social status suffered, for subsistence production and petty trade could scarcely match the wages brought home by men (Rogers 1979; Reddock 1985).

A further decline in women's status has accompanied Third World industrialization and urbanization. Many women now work alongside men in wage-paying jobs (Nash and Fernández-Kelly 1983). Occasionally manufacturers and service managers prefer women workers, but in general men enjoy more opportunities for both skilled and unskilled labor (Ward 1984). Land expropriation has removed the principal basis for household economies, that is, peasant agriculture, in the Third World.

Cross-cultural comparison suggests, then, that Caribbean slave women's changing position was not unique but representative of the early stages of European commodity production in the Third World. Bondwomen's work in field labor was unusual, however; most nonwage labor systems, especially in agriculture, have not utilized female labor to the degree found in West Indian slavery. Women's earlier economic power—however limited in scope and inconsequential when part of a larger and heinous social structure such as slavery—is also rare in highly exploitive nonwage systems. On both counts, however, the study of women's position within these economic systems may reveal a more substantial contribution than has commonly been acknowledged.

CHAPTER SIX

Women and the Slave Family

The family offers the best illustration of tensions in slave studies between structuralist and class analysis of culture. Structuralists claim that totalistic systems constrain cultural expression, including family formation. Class theorists argue that slavery allowed and slaves insisted on some autonomy in constructing kinship and other forms of culture.

Research and analyses of the New World slave family have traditionally been structural in approach. Proponents of this view hold that parental, marital, and kin responsibilities and rights were prevented by the slaveholders' preemptory control over bondmen and women. Some contend that it is the slave's legal status as property and the master's as owner that finally undermined marriage and family formation (Davis 1966; Finley 1968; Elkins 1976; Tannenbaum 1946). Patterson (1982) offers a variation on this theme, proposing that the symbolic estrangement from kin and corresponding social illegitimacy of the slaves' natal ties precluded family formation.

Three dimensions of family life—parenthood, marriage, and extended kinship—are said to have been uniquely influenced by the structural obstacles and limitations of slavery. New World slavery violated the basic human right to bear children and raise them. Children could be bought and sold away from parents. Other slaves and agents of the estate cared for children separated from kin. Slaveholders recognized maternity through the first years of a child's life. Infants were generally kept with their mothers and usually nursed. Paternity was wholly disregarded by slaveholders and the society they controlled. Advocates of a structural interpretation of slavery argue that the proprietary rights of the slave master, whether legally or symbolically condoned, superseded the custodial rights of parents.

New World slaveholding societies also considered illegitimate or illegal the rights and obligations of more distant kin. Grandparents, aunts, and uncles were without customary privileges or obligations to their families. Kin selection, dowries and bride wealth, old-age security, and other prerogatives of agrarian peoples were rarely exercised. That kinship commitments were occasionally expressed in no way alters or weakens the structural viewpoint: Social ties were not respected by various authorities and could be violated at any time in an arbitrary manner.

The legitimacy and likelihood of institutionalized forms of conjugal union are intrinsic to family formation. Allowing that slave marriages were rarely legal, were they respected and preserved by custom in slave societies of the New World? Patterson (1982) argues that, wherever labor was internally supplied, for example, the U.S. South, slaveholders encouraged marriage to ensure reproduction of the labor force. In contrast, estate owners and managers actively suppressed stable conjugal unions in some areas of the West Indies, where labor was supplied through the slave trade and the expenses of childbirth and rearing of children were unwanted. But even in the pro-natalist South, husbands and wives could be sold at the will or whim of the master.

Structuralists argue further that slaveholders supplanted the rights and obligations of marriage among slaves. Planters and other whites disrupted sexual "rights" by establishing intimate unions with slave women. And neither male nor female slaves could dependably offer a spouse economic exchanges or protections. As Davis (1966, p. 104) notes:

> Probably no society has attempted to prohibit slaves from having sexual intercourse with members of their own class, or even from living in more or less monogamous or polygamous units; but marriage leads to a contractual relationship of authority and obedience, of reciprocal rights and obligations within a family, which is clearly incompatible with the concept of a master's absolute ownership of slaves.

Lacking a basis in social and economic exchange, marriages failed to form or endure.

Structuralist commentators have looked particularly at males' relatively greater economic roles in marriage in agrarian societies and their diminution in slave families. Male slaves lacked the economic assets to fulfill traditional economic obligations. Without economic strength, structuralists argue, men had *no* part to play in slave marriages or family.

> The "husband" was not an essential part of the slave family. It made little difference whether he was a free man or the slave of the same or another plantation. As long as his "wife" and children were the property of another, he had no legal rights over them, and they were not even dependent on him for their maintenance, since they received their allowances directly from the master. (Goveia 1965, p. 235)

As Goveia notes, the complement of males' economic failings was the capacity of the slaveholder to provide, through the estate, all that agrarian males traditionally bring to marriage.

This narrowly materialist foundation of structural analysis ignores emotional and sexual components of marriage, even in agrarian societies. Although lacking economic assets, some male slaves "married." Empirical analysis suggests, too, that with stratification among slaves marriage enhanced the position of many poor and less privileged slaves, although often only temporarily.

More pertinent here is the structuralists' uncritical portrait of agrarian patriarchy. Wealth traditionally entitled males in agrarian societies to property in the form of wives and children. Patterson (1969, p. 167) elaborates: Slavery destroyed males' marital "authority," leading to demoralization and continuing irresponsibility of West Indian men. Moreno Fraginals (1978, p. 44) makes a related point, arguing that the "bourgeois family and juridical structure" was incompatible with slavery and its violation of "elementary property rights."

The structuralist view of slave families is also the root of perceived gender equality among slaves. Advocates of this interpretation of slave culture argue that the slave owners' and estates' authority over male slaves rendered them equal to females: Both males and females were reduced to the property status traditionally held by agrarian females. Males' and females' equality was hence achieved by males' social decline rather than by females' social ascent. Slave women frequently capitalized on bondmen's degradation, of course, achieving relative economic strength and status.

PROMISCUITY AMONG SLAVES

The structuralists' insistence that slaves were generally "promiscuous" displays again the strong linking of economic exchange with marriage and coupling. If economic degradation precluded stable nuclear unions and equalized gender relations, it must then have made emotional commitment of any sort impossible for male or female slaves. Patterson (1969, p. 159), in his study of Jamaica, argued that the "breakdown of sexual mores and the institution of marriage among Negroes occurred all over the New World." Goveia (1965, p. 238) claimed that in the British Leewards the African custom of polygamy gave way to promiscuity, although "slavery, and not the practise of polygamy . . . accounted for the relative infrequency of lasting unions." C.L.R. James's (1963, p. 15) analysis of slaves' relationships in Saint Domingue is similar in describing casual mating and parenting. "Wives and husbands, children and parents, were separated at the will of the master, and a father and son would meet after many years and give no greeting or any sign of emotion."[1]

There can be little doubt that slavery destroyed human relationships. But today's reader of these descriptions of slaves' "decadence" and "promiscuity" may be offended by their judgmental tone. Like other social science critiques of oppressive systems, structuralist analyses of New World slavery so abhor immorality imposed from above that its victims seem to be blamed as well. The cynical denial of the slaves' capacity to fight back is best countered by the many historical examples of an integrated and morally responsible slave culture. The empirical roots of misperceptions of slaves' experience are in travelers' and slaveholders' accounts of slave mores.

Bennett (1958, p. 35) tells us, for example, that whites in Barbados often mistook polygamy for promiscuity. A male's union with several women involved emotional and other commitments that slaveholders and other whites missed, in part, because slavery prevented their full and/or visible elaboration. Jordan's (1968) research is potentially devastating of analyses built on elite accounts. His review of sixteenth- through nineteenth-century European documents about the New World shows an expectation of sexual abandon among slaves. The Western attitude was perhaps rooted in guilt or a projection of highly repressed sexuality (Jordan 1968, pp. 39, 152). Jordan (1968, p. 35) notes that "by the eighteenth century a report on the sexual aggressiveness of Negro women was virtually *de rigeur* for the African commentator." The same, it seems, can be said for observers of West Indian slave mores.[2]

Thomas Atwood (1791, p. 273) remarked, for example, that in eighteenth-century Dominica "so little are the sexes attached to each other, or constant in connubial connections, that it is common for the men to have several wives at a time, besides transient mistresses; and the women to leave their husbands for others, and to submit to the embraces of white men for money or fine clothes." Mrs. Carmichael (1834, vol. 1, p. 297) tells of how the female slaves' promiscuity allowed them to name more than one father for their children. These men then brought presents and other goods to their supposed progeny. It is no wonder, she asserts, that the slave "cares little for his father" and often does not know his identity. Janet Schaw (1939, p. 128) stressed a general emotional emptiness among slaves and a lack of warm attachments. "The husband was to be divided from the wife; the infant from the mothers; but the most perfect indifference ran through the whole. They were laughing and jumping, making faces at each other, and not caring a single farthing for their fate."

There were, of course, casual sexual unions among slaves. We have no reliable evidence that these liaisons were common, let alone the norm. Nevertheless, slavery did impose conditions, for example, sale of mates, that made coresidence and lasting unions difficult. Debien (1974, p. 262) claims that African slaves in the French West Indies, at one time polygamous, preferred free unions to more stable relationships. French West Indian slaves were apparently open to baptism by seventeenth-century missionaries, but male slaves shunned marriage, wanting the freedom to form many liaisons (Gautier 1985, p. 67). Bremer (1853, vol. 2, pp. 335–336) observed a majority of casual relationships on the intensively cultivated Cuban plantations she visited. Again, these may be cases of confusing casual and committed relationships.

Knight (1970, p. 68) asserts that, as gang size increased, slaves were ever more alienated from traditional family forms. Higman and Craton's examinations of selected British West Indian plantation records reinforce Knight's hypothesis, but these findings, reviewed in what follows, pertain only to *residence*. They do not support or refute hypotheses about the frequency of slaves' sexual liaisons.

FAMILY PATTERNS

Slaves Alone

There is some evidence that single residence was more frequent in the later stages of sugar production, when slaves resided in barracklike structures and work rhythms were hastened to increase productivity. In Trinidad in 1813 a majority of slaves 15 years and over (63.2 percent) were single; of family members 14.8 percent lived as couples, 29.1 percent as couples with children (Higman 1978, p. 171).

Slave couples were sometimes separated by sale or even plantation-directed living arrangements. They lived as single slaves or as part of maternal or extended families but considered themselves "married." Traveling in Antigua at slavery's end, Sturge and Harvey (1838, p. 76) found few married slaves residing together or even on the same estate. Slaveholders often counted as "married" only those slaves with mates on the estate. For example, the manager of Newton estate in Barbados recorded 20 women with coresident husbands and 35 with mates elsewhere. Members of the latter group were labeled single, members of extended units, or mother-child units (Higman 1984, p. 369).

Matrifocality and the Matrideme

Slaves with children lived in matrifocal or nuclear families. The structuralist view has it that mother-child families predominated. The tie between mothers and children is the building block of kinship, and where males fail to achieve economic strength or authority, mother-child units would naturally tend to prevail.

Patterson (1976, pp. 57–59) calls the West Indian family system a matrideme. With little stability and few survivals from African origins, slaves stressed the mother's attachment to the children and the influence of her kin on the family. As Patterson notes, fathers were frequently prevented from completing their role expectations, or, because of the "weakening of the husband-father role," men were not bound emotionally or economically to their children. On the other hand, the mother's relatives generally lived on the plantation, strengthening her significance in the family.[3]

Goveia argues eloquently that the mother-child family had both legal and symbolic legitimacy and was logically consistent with the slaveholder's need to own slaves in the present and future.

> It was the influence of slavery which insured that the matrifocal family would become the dominant family type among the Negro slaves and which gave slave "marriage" its typical character of informality and instability. For it was the claims of slave ownership which made the slave mother the essential link in the chain of descent and reduced marriage to the status of a personal arrangement [and] enabled the slave woman . . . to dispense with a recognized "husband and father" for herself and her children. (Goveia 1965, p. 237)

In fact, fathers and husbands were sometimes displaced through generations, as on the Bahamas, where girls tended to reside with their mothers until a second child was born (Craton 1979, p. 13).[4] In the French West Indies in the 1600s religious groups promoted marriage, assuming that birth rates would increase (DuTertre 1958, vol. 2, p. 471). By the mid-1700s plantation lists recognized only the mother-child couple. Husband-wife units were still found on estates, but the master's attention turned from the slave family to the "age, quality, [and] price" of individual slaves (Gautier 1985, p. 83). But, like other family forms, matrifocality was sometimes undermined by the exigencies of the slave trade, including intrasociety exchange of slaves and practices such as "halving," common in Bermuda, whereby a couple's first-born child was given to the mother's master, the second to the father's.

Slave women's reproduction of the matrideme in the West Indies is then questionable on empirical grounds. Were those female slaves heading families from areas of matrilineal descent? Higman finds to the contrary; for example, he notes that among African slaves in Trinidad only the matrilineal Kongo had more nuclear families than other forms of family organization. There is substantial evidence that female-headed families predominated among domestic and light-skinned urban slaves in the British West Indies in the early 1800s. "The towns also engendered occupational independence and hence the economic marginalization of the male, to a much greater extent than did the plantations (where women are concentrated into the field gangs, and men monopolized the occupations of skill and status)" (Higman 1979, p. 170). Indeed Higman's research reveals that in the British West Indies the mother-child union was the least common family type anywhere but in the cities.

Nevertheless, mother-child family units did develop in plantation areas lacking the structural foundation for nuclear family organization. Female-headed households outnumbered nuclear units in Barbados and in nineteenth-century Cuban areas of recently escalated sugar production, for example, where individualized provision grounds were few or declining (Bennett 1958; Moreno Fraginals 1978). On the late developing and highly rationalized sugar plantations of Trinidad mother-child units were numerous. In Trinidad in 1813, 22.1 percent of slaves belonged to mother-child units. However, urban areas account for a large share of these families and the proportion of nuclear families increased with the number of slaves on a plantation (Craton 1979; Higman 1978, p. 167).[5] Some matrifocal families neared nuclear family form, with males responsible for certain tasks. At l'Anse-à-l'Ane in Martinique maternal unions resembled conjugal ones, with similar patterns of child spacing and male maintenance of provision grounds (Debien 1960, p. 49).[6]

The Nuclear Family

The census, newly found plantation records, and the use of inferential statistical techniques to generalize findings to a larger slave population have revealed a more widespread tendency among slaves to form conjugal unions than was previously understood.[7] The sociological underpinnings of this research largely distinguish it from the study of single-parent families. Advocates of this viewpoint attribute to slaves an ability to override the rules and conventions of slave masters in order to build families and intimate relationships. Craton argues that nineteenth-century British West Indies slaves lived in families by choice rather than forming them to satisfy particular planters or church officials (1979, pp. 14–15). The authority of planters to break up families for sale is not denied by Craton or others, although they suggest that it has been exaggerated for some settings. Rather, new research emphasizes slaves' autonomous and courageous creation of culture under nearly impossible circumstances.[8]

Indeed, many nuclear families are found among Caribbean slaves. The most direct and extensive evidence of nuclear families is available for the British West Indies. In the early 1800s "family life—even in patterns recognizable to Europeans—was the norm for British West Indian slaves" (Craton 1979, p. 2). Registration figures from the Bahamas reveal, for example, that 54.1 percent of slaves resided in simple nuclear families. Planters there were reluctant to break up families for sale even before the 1824 law forbidding it (Craton 1979, pp. 6, 17). Analyzing a single Bahamian estate, Lord John Rolle's Great Exuma, Craton found that nearly half the slave population in 1822 lived in simple nuclear families, the most common family type (Craton 1979, p. 6).[9]

Higman studied the family status of slaves in the late eighteenth century on three Jamaican sugar estates, Old Montpelier, New Montpelier, and Shettlewood Pen. About 50 percent of slaves lived in units similar to the elementary family. Field slaves constituted half of all couples, single slaves, and groups of slaves. Domestics generally resided in female-headed families and slaves of authority in families with women and children. Only about 14 percent of Trinidad's slaves lived in nuclear families in the early nineteenth century, and as few as 4 percent of slaves lived in nuclear families in rural St. Lucia and less than 1 percent in its towns (Higman 1984, p. 366). A "fairly large proportion" of slaves lived in nuclear families during the nineteenth century on Danish St. John. In 1855, 7 years after emancipation, 117 of 387 households on St. John constituted couples or couples plus children and/or relatives. Ninety-six single men and women resided there. Of 174 kin groups 167 were headed by females (Olwig 1985, p. 69).

Marriage was most common among French West Indian slaves in the 1600s, declining thereafter. At Capesterre in Guadeloupe in 1664 about one-fourth of slaves were married. In Basse-terre one-third of mothers were single and the rest married. In the newly colonized Grand-terre marriage was rare. Most nonsingle mothers were concubines. A Jesuit missionary wrote that in his quarter of Guadeloupe 48.6 percent of adults were married, although of these unions 27.7 percent were "bad" marriages or cases of concubinage. After a year of exposure to Christian teaching 57 percent of the population was truly married (Gautier 1985, p. 73).

Slave masters sometimes forced a union to prevent a slave from marrying off the plantation (DuTertre 1958, vol. 2, pp. 471–472). In contrast to the British West Indies, stable unions were more often found among Creole than African slaves in the French islands (Debien 1960, p. 50). Slaves established conjugal families sooner in Martinique and Guadeloupe than in Saint Domingue or the British West Indies, and in the 1700s they received some incentives to do so (Debien 1974, p. 278).

In Cuba and Puerto Rico nuclear unions were common in the 1600s and 1700s and continued to form in urban areas and on small farms and *haciendas*. Indeed, the Siete Partidas permitted slaves to marry against the will of their masters, and separation of couples for sale was forbidden. The Catholic Church was to persuade slave masters to buy their bondmen's spouses from other plantations, or the church itself was to do so (Tannenbaum 1946, p. 49). Planters occasionally tried to impose marriages on the large Cuban plantations, where women were gradually introduced in the mid-1800s. In 1864 Jose Luis Alfonso arranged 29 marriages through the conversion of his slaves to Christianity and by isolation of young female slaves. But most such unions were failures because of the breakup of couples for sale (Moreno Fraginals 1978, p. 44).

European clergy occasionally sanctioned slave marriages. Spanish West Indian slaves frequently joined in religious marriage rituals. In Puerto Rico in 1830, 150 slave marriages were solemnized among 2,156 unions for all groups. In Cuba 3,684 solemnized marriages included 1,381 among slaves

(Flinter 1834, p. 223). In the British West Indies clergy from Moravian, Methodist, and other dissident religious groups sometimes performed slave marriages, but only Anglican clergy were legally permitted to carry out these rituals (Furley 1965, p. 13). Without legal standing anywhere in the region, slave "marriages" were dissolvable when partners were sold away. Clergy sometimes performed second marriage ceremonies for those who lost mates to the slave trade.

Sale of slaves and the resulting breakup of families decreased as slave plantations lost prosperity. By the 1820s there were few public sales of slaves in the British West Indies and families were rarely separated (Barclay 1828, p. 55). Occasionally an estate's economic collapse led to the sale of slaves to a more prosperous planter. In both the Bahamas and Bermuda slaves feared that sale to another island might result in a harsher work regimen and the destruction of family ties (Craton 1979, p. 19; Packwood 1975, p. 141). The threat of family dissolution may have contributed to Cuban slaves' reputed fear of sale to a large, intensely cultivated plantation. As slaveholders ameliorated conditions with the demise of sugar production in nearly all Caribbean sugar islands, colonial legislatures enacted laws to prevent the sale of family members away from one another. The Danish West Indies 1834 slave code outlawed the sale of slaves beyond the island but permitted intra-island trade (Lewisohn 1970, p. 234). The British West Indies 1824 amelioration laws permitted marriage between slaves and forbade dissolution of families in trade (Matheison 1926, pp. 126–140).

Polygamy

Some Caribbean male slaves had several wives, as some females had more than one husband. Males resided with all of their wives or kept their families in separate dwellings. Carmichael (1834, vol. 1, p. 298) reports that co-wives lived amicably in Trinidad and St. Vincent; Moreau de Saint Méry (1958, vol. 1, p. 57) reports the same for eighteenth-century Saint Domingue. Polygamy was recorded in nearly every Caribbean slave society but was usually possible only for high-status males (Goveia 1965, p. 234). These slaves, with access to income and wealth, formed polygamous unions even in settings with few females, where monogamy or other family forms dominated.[10] At the Codrington estates on Barbados, for example, polygamous unions were common, despite a predominance of males (Bennett 1958, p. 35). Women were, then, a commodity among slaves and one of the many resources available to skilled slaves and artisans.[11]

There is some suggestion that African slaves preferred polygamous unions but were not immediately able to effect them. Hence they began with nuclear families, intending to incorporate new wives and children into the unit as resources permitted (Craton 1979, pp. 25–29). This would explain the curious finding in the Bahamas, St. Kitts, Trinidad, and elsewhere that Africans more often than Creoles formed nuclear families (Craton 1979, p. 17; Nisbet 1970, p. 21). Later generations generally failed to form polygamous unions; they "either [lost] sight of these models (as part of the process of creolization) or were prevented from achieving them by the brutality of the slave regime (heavy mortality, separation by sale, miscegination, Christian proselytism, and so on)" (Higman 1978, pp. 171–172). It is also possible that Africans developed nuclear families for other reasons, for example, to establish social bonds quickly. Goveia contends, however, that the structural constraints against the reproduction of African family patterns, in particular polygamy, explain a variety of relationships found in the West Indies. "Among the field slaves polygamous marriage was most often replaced by promiscuous intercourse, or by 'keeper' relationships which were dissolved at will, or sometimes by faithful concubinage" (Goveia 1965, p. 235).

These contending hypotheses about the impact of African polygamy on slave family and mating patterns rest on little evidence. We do not know if slaves were indeed seeking polygamous unions in other types of relationships. The propensity of high-status slaves to have more than one mate is our most significant clue that polygamy was a desired family form. Nor do we know if those who sought such unions were from parts of Africa with polygamous conjugal patterns.[12]

Polygynous unions are widespread in Africa and were even more common before settled agriculture developed with European colonization (Boserup 1970, p. 37). Women often did much of the farming in the shifting agriculture of traditional Africa.[13] Diverging devolution gave women inheritance rights and encouraged males to form multiple unions and hence consolidate their wives' land and labor power. Males paid bride wealth to acquire their economically supportive wives, much as a woman's family paid a dowry in African regions where women's participation in agriculture was slight and monogamy prevalent. Population density discouraged African polygamy, as it almost certainly did in the West Indian islands where land for petty cultivation was scarce. The poor economic position of slave men made it difficult for them to amass bride wealth. Only men with resources had the means to acquire wives; only men with land in settings with the possibility of land expansion needed multiple wives. Therefore the structural conditions for polygamy were rarely present in Caribbean slave societies. Moreover, women had little incentive to join polygamous families unless a man's resources were great enough to raise his wives' standard of living well above what the estate provided. There was little exclusively female farming in the West Indies, a condition highly associated with polygamy in West Africa and suggestive again that polygamy was only occasional among Caribbean slaves.

MATERIAL ORIGINS OF FAMILIES

The structuralist and class approaches to family organization among Caribbean slaves differ over the meaning of family relationships. Both viewpoints hold that families of various types formed, but their proponents disagree about whether strong, stable families of emotional value to their members were possible. At a less abstract level there has developed another debate about the historical, demographic, and material correlates of family organization.

Demographic factors such as gender ratio, urban concentration, and plantation size have been posited (Higman 1978; Craton 1979) as key causal components of particular forms of family organization. Recent studies indicate a consistent relationship between female-headed families and urban residence. The associations between the proportion of women and family type and between unit size and families are inconsistent. Polygamous units were common in settings with few women. Although a large number of slaves would logically seem to be necessary for nuclear families to form, big estates in societies with particularly intense sugar production, for example, Cuba and Jamaica, discouraged kinship. Higman's findings to the contrary for Trinidad are exceptional.[14] Older sugar colonies in the British West Indies, for example, Barbados, Dominica, Antigua, and St. Kitts, with relatively small estates, had a higher proportion of families living apart than did estates on the newer, larger plantations of Jamaica and Trinidad. "Co-resident" households were more frequent on large estates in nineteenth-century St. John (Olwig 1985, p. 69).

Higman has also pointed to the African origins of nuclear family members. As indicated earlier, it has been hypothesized that African males from polygamous societies used the nuclear family as the first stage in polygamous family building. "Thus it must be concluded that the demographic selectivity of the slave trade determined very largely the extent to which particular groups of Africans could fulfill their familial ideals or norms" (Higman 1978, p. 174). Again, this view is at odds with the more traditional commentary on Africanisms among slaves that stressed the origins of multiple casual unions in African polygyny.[15]

Rubin (1975) has developed a provocative synthesis of the theories of Freud and Lévi-Strauss to suggest that human groups trade in women to make alliances and secure greater material security. A gender division of labor and subordination of females was the result in nearly all preindustrial societies. In African agrarian societies bride wealth secured a female's family's loyalty. Polygyny brought favor from males' kin. This exchange was highly functional in Caribbean slave societies as well, with kinship fragmented and material life poor. But, as argued earlier, multiple families were realistic only for high-status men. They alone had resources with which to bargain for women, to maintain new wives and families. Ironically the relative scarcity of women in the early stages of Caribbean slavery may have given women more substantial power in exchange than is commonly found in polygynous societies. Still, men's economic status was determinate. Even powerful women had little to gain from unions with poor men.

Family economic interests were no less important in Caribbean slave societies than in African or other polygynous settings, but their intergenerational foundations were threatened by the slave trade and lack of control over large parcels of land. Slaves bargained sexually most often as individuals rather than as members of kin groups. Caribbean slaves formed many family types—nuclear, female-headed, extended, and polygamous. Few of these groups were constructed by generations of kin. They were generally neolocal and of greater value to the newly formed family than to their forebears.

What are the economic systems and incentives associated with the creation of small neolocal families in other historical circumstances? In the West the small neolocal family developed with capitalist encroachment into agriculture and industry. As farm size shrank, fewer individuals could be supported, and the resulting peasant production of food and agricultural goods was strongly linked to nuclear families. Petty commodity production in cities also contributed to shrinking family size and separate residence from extended kin (Lasch 1977; Levine 1977; Goody 1976; Cancian et al. 1978).

Caribbean slaves had incentives to form nuclear families like those found in other agricultural settings (Morrissey 1986). Despite that slaves could not own property, their life chances were immeasurably improved by development and exploitation of the resources they could control. The growing of provisions on individualized plots and even in kitchen gardens resembled peasant agriculture, in which men's heavy labor was sometimes required but made valuable, finally, by the contributions of women and children. Craton (1982), Mintz (1974), and others have argued that the growing and perhaps marketing of provisions in the Caribbean were controlled by men, consistent with the hypothesis that nuclear families had a basis in the slaves' petty agricultural production. Some other forms of trade and income accumulation were also enhanced for adults if joined in a family. In all such cases the threat of sale and breakup of the family counteracted material incentives to family organization.

Patterson argues that, where growing of provisions was extensive, as in Jamaica, women found incentives in heading families. The equalization of male and female status and obliteration of male slaves' property rights created opportunities for females to control resources. Women used their children's labor and land to amass resources, it is argued, and were economically independent of men. This claim rests on the assumption that women could reliably depend on adult men for assistance in clearing land, constructing houses, etc. Male kin, perhaps linked to several generations of matrifocal families, were probably available for assistance. But the instability of plantation life militated against the lateral construction of kinship, particularly for more than two generations. It is doubtful that female-headed families had institutionalized links to adult male kin, although, as with female-led families in the twentieth century, informal networks of men and women probably offered support to a woman and her family.

If Patterson is incorrect in his view that heading families enhanced slave women's economic well-being, he still contributes to our understanding of slave women's experience by focusing on their economic interests. I propose, however, that women's best opportunity for acquiring income in the agricultural setting often lay with a nuclear family. Although her control of land and resources was less in this household arrangement than when heading a family, her access to male labor was greater, and, given males' opportunities in skilled and artisanal labor and other forms of income accumulation, male incorporation into the household was generally desirable. Even in Africa, where women had substantial control over subsistence agriculture, husbands and other male kin performed heavy labor and traded surpluses (Gautier 1985, p. 47). West Indian slave women probably sought many means to institutionalize male help, and, with the sale of males and high mortality, creation of co-resident ties was undoubtedly the most flexible and therefore significant strategy.

Generalizing from registration figures and plantation-specific records, we can draw some tentative conclusions about the relationship between the growing and marketing of provisions and family formation (see also Morrissey 1986). The hilly, lush environment of Jamaica, Martinique, St. Lucia, and Dominica yielded much food, individually controlled by slaves. On older estates in these areas nuclear families were numerous. On newly settled islands, such as St. Lucia, nuclear families were few. In fact, 32 percent of slaves in nineteenth-century St. Lucia lived in mother-child units (Higman 1984, p. 367). Demographic and historical factors appear to override economic ones in these settings. Women effectively utilized the opportunities offered by control of their children's labor and land, but the increase in nuclear families over time implies that women preferred a continuing male presence in the household.

In contrast, Barbados, the British Leewards, the Danish Virgin Islands, late Cuba, and Saint Domingue rationed imported or estate-grown food. There nuclear families were few. Higman attributes this pattern to creolization and to growing West Indian preference for mother-child units in Barbados and the Leewards. The continuing influx of Africans with high mortality and little likelihood of entry into any kind of family unit can be said to explain the relatively few nuclear households. While acknowledging the significance of these factors, we must also ask what economic incentives a male or female slave found to form nuclear families in these settings. That creolization accompanied the creation of female-headed families supports the point that material benefits of nuclear family formation were often few. With demographic and historical factors favoring nuclear families, mother-child families still predominated.

Women's economic interests may explain mother-child families in areas of food importation and estate cultivation and nuclear families among provision-growing slaves. With scant opportunities to earn cash or resources in kind, relatively more was available to a woman and her children if no adult man took a share. The labor that male field slaves could contribute was unnecessary where provision grounds, kitchen gardens, and marketing chances were scarce. And what men absorbed, at least in food, was generally greater than what was consumed by women and children. On the other hand, male slaves of high status must have been particularly desirable companions in those areas with few opportunities for women to enhance their economic and social position. Although there is no evidence to buttress this point, it is likely that polygamous units flourished among upper-strata males in such settings. With few alternatives in land or trade, men of prestige could effectively use women as sources of greater status and authority, although women's utility for the men's income expansion was limited if the men were landless. Powerless economically, women might gladly share with another woman the advantage of liaison with a high-status male.

Overlaying these patterns and tendencies was the history of sugar produc-tion. As productivity and output grew and family functions were collectivized, incentives to form nuclear families declined. Using data on the proportion of slaves with no living kin on plantations, Higman (1984, p. 366) cites examples that illustrate a linear relationship between the proportion of kinless slaves in a population and time of entry into large-scale sugar production. "At Newton Estate, Barbados, roughly 20 percent of slaves had no family living on the plantation in 1796, while at Montpelier, Jamaica, the proportion was about 30 percent in 1825. These proportions may be compared with the 31 percent found among rural slaves in St. Lucia in 1815 and the 44 percent in Trinidad in 1813."

There is evidence, moreover, that in Barbados and other sites of early sugar cultivation and small estates many slaves were committed to nuclear families or conjugal relationships but were forced to live apart on different plantations (Higman 1984, pp. 369–370). On Saint Domingue and Cuba nuclear families broke down with the intensification of sugar production, expansion of estates, collectivization of residence, and rationalization of estate provision of goods and services. Cuban slaves fortunate enough to remain on small farms continued to form nuclear families. Creole slaves who joined the thousands of Africans brought to mid-nineteenth-century Cuba suffered disintegration of kin relationships along with a diminution of life chances, although there is evidence that families sometimes survived in the *barracones* of the nineteenth century (Moreno Fraginals 1978; Scott 1985, pp. 17–19). Craton (1979, p. 25) summarizes the consequences of interplay between changes in sugar production and the ecological and social organizational patterns of various British slave societies. On one end of a continuum were the

> virtual peasants of the Bahamas, Barbuda and, perhaps, the Grenadines, with locational stability, a small proportion of African slaves, natural increase and a relatively high incidence of nuclear and stable families. At the opposite pole were the overworked slaves of new plantations such as those of Trinidad, Guyana, and St. Vincent, with a high rate of natural decrease, a majority of slaves living alone or in ''barrack'' like conditions, and a high proportion of ''denuded,'' female-headed families.

Similar trends occurred in the French islands, with slaves on small, less productive Martinique and Guadeloupe developing more nuclear families than eighteenth-century Saint Domingue. Puerto Rico produced peasant agriculture and corresponding nuclear family patterns to a greater degree than Cuba. And the Dutch and Danish Virgin Islands exhibited more nuclear family organization than the late-developing Surinam. Still, in many settings reliable kinship and affective networks were impossible because of the shifting population and excruciating labor demands. We may conclude, finally, with Craton and Higman, that, where nuclear families were possible, they were often the building blocks of other kinds of kinship organization and family structure (see also Morrissey 1986). Female-headed families were adequate or simply viable vehicles for economic survival elsewhere.

Materialist explanations for the frequency of nuclear family organization on the small, less intensively cultivated Caribbean islands are confounded by the physical support available from large, stable kinship networks. Olwig (1985, p. 75) presents evidence of slaves assisting one another with food preparation and child care. She questions whether spouses were the principal sources of economic support for slaves, noting that ''family life among the St. Johnian slaves does not seem to have centered on the household or a nuclear-type residential family, but rather on networks of relationships involving various relatives and spouses.'' Larger estates, particularly in more recent sugar-producing societies, lacked the population consistency and stability found on St. John. But Olwig's work raises the significant question of how Caribbean slaves formed and utilized kinship networks. The idea of neolocal self-sufficiency was almost certainly foreign to African women who had large support networks through matrilineal kinship and polygamy (Gautier 1985, pp. 43–45).[16]

Domestic workers, especially in cities and towns, were the only female slaves able to *improve* their economic position autonomously. These female slaves had independent access to income and little need for male labor or contributions to overall resources. Their houses and household belongings were arranged for them. Moreover, the presence of a slave "husband" may have discouraged white male advances, the most important potential source of income and freedom for slave women. Lewis (1834, pp. 122–132) reports having heard that colored slave women could have sexual relationships with white males of status only if accorded the position of housekeeper. Although generally improbable, the assertion suggests that women recognized opportunities in liaisons with Europeans or were perceived by whites as shrewd sexual bargainers.

FAMILIES AND RESISTANCE

In 1959 Stanley Elkins (see Elkins 1976) published the essay "Slave and Personality" in which he analyzed the personality and culture of slaves in the U.S. South. Elkins argued, on the basis of the scattered information about slaves' psychological and emotional expressions, that bondmen and women resembled Nazi concentration camp victims. Both were, according to Elkins, benumbed and childlike, passively enduring the horrors of life in totalistic institutions. Elkins's portrait of slaves and victims of Nazi oppression has brought considerable critical commentary. It at once rings true—as victims of social oppression and life's tragedies, all humans sometimes feel despair, hopelessness, and identification with oppressors.[17] Yet Elkins seems to blame the victims for their plight, confusing passive reactions to slavery with passive personalities and cultures that allowed slavery to happen. Human pain breeds active responses and reactions that Elkins overlooks among nineteenth- and twentieth-century slaves. In every historical setting slaves have rebelled and occasionally prevailed, most dramatically in the Caribbean with Saint Domingue's revolution. As James (1963, p. 25) comments: "Men make their own history, and the black Jacobins of San Domingo were to make history which would alter the fate of millions of men and shift the economic current of three continents."

Stress on the courage of slaves as the basis of analysis fails as well, creating overstatements and errors. Not all slaves were revolutionaries or rebels. Not all social action was rebellious or insurgent. Borrowing from other literature on the Nazi slave regime, we can hypothesize instead that Caribbean slaves reacted to slavery in a variety of ways, as humans do in all settings.[18] Bettelheim (1943, 1960), for example, observed a range of responses as an inmate of German concentration camps. He concludes that the militant but "informed" prisoners fought when winning was possible and withdrew when rebellion brought unnecessary or unproductive danger to themselves, their family, or their friends. Bettelheim's analysis is also pertinent to our discussion of culture as a vehicle of conformity and reaction to totalistic regimes. If passivity is generally politically useless in an authoritarian environment, he asks, why are ideological or cultural preservation and reconstruction from the past any less so? Devotion to a cultural ideal, like a particular family form, is finally retreatist, argues Bettelheim, no more seriously threatening the system than does conformity. To express one's needs to kin is to fail to express them more directly or rebelliously.

It is perplexing that creation of nuclear families in particular is perceived as a form of political opposition among New World slaves (Genovese 1976; Craton 1978, 1979). If it was the inflexible and contrived cultural preservation that some have claimed, then family formation must have been counterproductive to slave resistance. This was especially true of the nuclear family, more often than the female-headed family, that fulfilled the occasional hopes of slaveholders for the reproduction of the work force. But Caribbean slaves' female-headed families were intrinsically no less retreatist than nuclear ones. Mother-led households did not seriously threaten the slave system, except insofar as fertility was relatively diminished and women heads of households reacted to the pressure to both bear children and produce sugar with malingering or feigned illnesses. Neither of these patterns is consistently associated with female-headed families. And even if infertility and low productivity were common correlates of female-headed households, they would not necessarily constitute rebellious behavior.

Family life, especially in nuclear form, also appears to contemporary observers to buffer the individual from the cruelties of work. Industrial society has infused in home a sense of shelter, "a haven from a heartless world" (Lasch 1977). The modern example has been uncritically applied to New World slaves, it seems, and the family described as a therapeutic institution. Those who see slave families as politically effective institutions are in fact equating their therapeutic value with rebellion. The family filled slaves with the comfort to stay alive—exactly what slaveholders wanted.

The equation of slave insurgency with family formation is, then, grounded in bourgeois assumptions about family and not in serious consideration of what cultural opposition and resistance entail. For female slaves the link between resistance and family is especially troubling, for their household responsibilities were greater than men's. It has in fact been proposed that family creation and maintenance were common vehicles for bondwomen's opposition to slavery. Bush (1986, p. 128) suggests, for example, that in the British Caribbean "the family was the crucible of resistance. Women slaves, strengthened by traditional African culture, were the backbone of the slave family and community" (see also Jones 1986; White 1985).

Yet, as I suggest in Chapter Nine, women were both visible and invisible partners in more active forms of West Indian slave insurgency than is commonly recognized. More important, slave women's strong affective ties toward friends and kin, often discounted by contemporary observers, are not necessarily rebellious or insurgent, even in a hostile and emotionally sterile environment. A simpler view is that women's contributions to family life were substantial, as in many other cultures. A more critical perspective is that slave women's affection and love for their families was functional to slavery.

Yet there were slave enterprises and activities closely tied to kinship that had a potentially disruptive effect on slavery. Families' control of household economies—petty agricultural production and marketing—was sometimes the basis of authority and status for women. Mintz and others have suggested that household economies were an integral part of New World slavery: By achieving economic self-sufficiency, slaves relieved masters of responsibility for food and other resources. Nevertheless the slaves' household economies were potential sources of contradiction in Caribbean slavery. They offered status, authority, and economic power to women and families and provided incentives for men and women to reduce their labor commitments to slave masters and increase time and resource investments in their own petty industries. In this sense home production and trade sabotaged the plantation structure. Although difficult to measure, the influence of household economies on slavery does not require judgments about slaves' political intentions and goals.

Families performed another, similarly disruptive task. As a primary institution within the slave community, they formed vehicles for slave conspiracies (Bush 1986; Mathurin 1974). Women may have been especially important communicators, given their more frequent presence in slave owners' homes as domestics. And, as principal socializers of slave children, they passed on knowledge about communication lines and channels. We can verify slave rebellions and acts of sabotage and assume with confidence that they were possible only with the support of kin and informal slave networks.

In summary, the structuralist and class views of family formation among Caribbean slaves are echoed in debates about the contributions of family types to slave insurgency. Structuralists deny the existence of families or their potential incompatibility with slavery, a notion that history does not support. Nor can the class hypothesis that slave families were numerous and intrinsically rebellious be upheld. The emerging portrait is one of synthesis: Families sometimes formed and in specific ways contributed to tensions and contradictions in slavery. Two means by which families were at odds with Caribbean slave systems are suggested: through household economies and by supporting insurgency. The latter may have involved women's full participation and leadership. Household resources were accumulated by many family members, sometimes under women's guidance and supervision.

CONCLUSIONS

Family organization varied among Caribbean slaves. Nuclear families developed where provision growing was extensive, suggesting a structural basis for nuclear family formation among slaves such as that found in peasant societies. Many slaves lived alone, especially in areas of late and intense sugar cultivation. Mother-child family units were perhaps less common than previously thought. High-status slaves formed polygamous families. Organization of nuclear families among African slaves is thought by some to be the basis of polygamy, although in the British West Indies later generations were less likely than Africans to live in nuclear or polygamous units.

Structuralist interpretations, particularly popular in the 1960s, expressed doubt that stable nuclear families could form among slaves because households were vulnerable to sale of members. Moreover, the father's economic role in nuclear families was usurped by slave masters. More recent scholarship has revealed many nuclear families among Caribbean slaves. It can be inferred that slaves bravely created families despite structural constraints.

I have argued that the material bases of slave societies provided incentives for the formation of nuclear families in settings where household economies were possible. Land and income accumulation in the rural setting were enhanced by contributions of many family members. Males' physical strength was often needed in households involved in food production and marketing and was most reliably provided through the nuclear family. Men's greater access to skilled and artisanal jobs contributed further to women's and children's resources. There was little incentive for women to head households except in urban areas, where their access to income through domestic work was comparable to men's.

In both cases we are referring to neolocal families with relative estrangement from extended kin. The economic advantages of household and family relations accrue to individuals in this kind of familial arrangement, not to several generations of kin. Wrested from African kinship systems of depth and breadth, Caribbean slaves appear to be shorn of kin, much as the structuralists suggest. The class approach sensitizes us to the continuing formation of slave families, no less valuable or meaningful to family members than the creation of extensive kinship networks. Women's economic interests were expressed in all resulting neolocal family forms and reflect the complex mix of modes and systems of production that generally resulted in bondwomen's loss of economic power and the rising social equality of male and female slaves.

CHAPTER SEVEN

Fertility

Women's interests and intentions in both the biological and social reproduction of the work force have been recognized by feminist theorists (Mitchell 1972; Benston 1969; Leacock 1983). There may be many material and social benefits to females from childbearing and rearing, including physical protection by males, access to food and other resources, and the security attained by incorporation into one or more lineages. On the other hand, incentives to reproduce may also be few or insignificant, given the risks of pregnancy, reduction of income-earning opportunities for pregnant women, and the sometimes small likelihood of infant survival. The capacity to bear children may also be destroyed or reduced by overwork and undernourishment or by uterine infections and venereal and other diseases.

Caribbean slave women had few children compared to U.S. female slaves and women in other comparable settings. Research has generally focused on low birth rates and hence on low sex ratios, skewed age distributions, and high infant mortality. Low fertility itself has received little attention, although occasionally the class view on family formation has been echoed in fertility research, with different implications. Class theorists have held that slaves organized stable families in response to oppressive conditions, but they have also suggested that women failed to have children to protest their subjugation as slaves.

The continuing natural decrease of Caribbean slaves intrigues scholars, in part because revisionist research has uncovered both high birth rates and high levels of fertility in the U.S. South (Fogel and Engerman 1974; Klein and Engerman 1978). Demographic conditions explain much about low birth rates. Yet women's choice not to bear children and their incapacity to do so remain important and largely unexplored explanations for low fertility. Even less is known about slaves' feelings about children. A materialist analysis suggests few economic incentives for Caribbean slave women to bear children, compared to societies in which children's labor is valued by spouses or kin and women's workload is less than men's. But like materialistic reasons to form families, the reasons for bearing children varied among slaveholding societies of the region, with differing opportunities for slaves to utilize their children's labor to economic advantage and divergent and shifting demands for women's labor in agriculture.

LOW BIRTH AND FERTILITY RATES AND CARIBBEAN SLAVES

New World slave societies present a major challenge to our understanding of fertility in conditions of low individual and family autonomy. It has generally been thought that slaves in the United States and in the West Indies had little reason to bear children, lacking control of their offsprings' labor. Conditions conducive to high fertility, in particular, stable conjugal unions, were presumed to be absent among New World slaves. Recent scholarship has revealed high levels of nuclear family formation in the United States, along with greater intergenerational familial stability than was previously recognized or thought possible (Blassingame 1972; Fogel and Engerman 1974; Gutman 1977). Studies of Caribbean slaves have also revealed more nuclear families and historical endurance of kinship than was understood by earlier scholars (Higman 1976a; Craton 1978). Nevertheless there seems little doubt that family organization among slaves was more often nuclear in the U.S. South than in the Caribbean and that southern conditions were more encouraging to family continuity.

The difference in fertility between U.S. and Caribbean slaves is more dramatic than that found between styles of family organization in the two regions. The birth rate in the United States in the early 1800s was from 50 to 55 per 1,000 slaves, with a death rate of from 25 to 35 per 1,000. At the same time Jamaican slaves experienced a crude birth rate of 23 per 1,000; the crude death rate among Jamaican slaves was 26 per 1,000. About four-fifths of slave women bore children in the United States, but only two-thirds of potential female childbearers did so in the British West Indies (Klein and Engerman 1978, p. 366).[1]

Hence Caribbean slaves experienced a continuous natural decrease. Figures from the post-1816 British West Indian registration of slaves (Table 3.1) show that, even with the amelioration of conditions, natural decreases continued. Craton (1971, p. 5) estimates a natural population decrease in Jamaica of 4 percent during the early 1700s, dropping to 2 percent around 1790, 1 percent in 1808, and less than 0.5 percent in 1834. A natural increase was not achieved in Jamaica until 1845, nine years after the emancipation of British West Indian slaves, although slaves were probably reproducing themselves and the population growing on one-third of the estates by the 1830s (Craton 1971, p. 18). Records from individual estates indicate the problem: At Jamaica's Worthy Park deaths outnumbered births by 2 percent annually from 1730 to 1780 (Craton 1977, p. 54).

Planters on Barbados purchased 75,893 Africans from 1712 to 1734 to increase the population from 41,970 to 46,362 (Bennett 1958, p. 44). During the 1770s the 2 percent birth rate at Codrington was less than the 2.5 percent annual death rate. Yet Barbados provided the major exception to British West Indian patterns of natural population decrease. Watson (1975, p. 139) contends that as early as 1760 slaves reproduced themselves. The Codrington estate achieved a natural increase later. From 1712 to 1761, 450 slaves were bought by the Society for the Propagation of the Gospel for Codrington, yet its population fell by more than one-third. In 1795 a net gain of 3 slaves was recorded, 11 in 1800, 5 in 1804, and 7 in 1805 (Bennett 1958, pp. 52, 96, 112).

French West Indian slaves also experienced natural population decreases. The general mortality rate for the region has been estimated at 5–6 percent and the natality rate at 3 percent (Debien 1974, p. 348). Imports of 258,300 slaves to Martinique from 1701 to 1818 expanded the slave population from about 14,000 in 1700 to 75,584 in 1802 (Tomich 1976, p. 41; Elisabeth 1972, pp. 148–151). Curtin (1969, p. 80) estimates the rate of natural decrease from 1664 to 1735 at 5.4 percent, dropping to a loss of 4.2 percent from 1736 to 1787 (see Table 7.1).

At the Case-Pilote estate in Martinique the slave population fell by 573 from 1806 to 1861, despite 1,349 baptisms (performed on nearly all French West Indian slave babies) (David 1973, p. 351). Debien (1962, p. 50) reports a Saint Domingue plantation that replaced its total work force of 133 slaves from 1765 to 1778. In Saint Domingue as a whole the purchase of slaves raised the population by 85,000 between 1763 and 1776, but deaths outnumbered births by 50,000 (Fouchard 1981, p. 68). On selected indigo and coffee plantations in Saint Domingue, Siguret (1968, p. 223) found a 20 per 1,000 birth rate from 1778 to 1788 offset by a 60 percent mortality rate for the 10-year period, suggesting no marked demographic difference on coffee, indigo, and sugar estates.

Jesuit and Dominican estates in the French West Indies traditionally achieved population increases. On some other estates, generally in Guadeloupe and Martinique, births gradually outnumbered deaths by late in the eighteenth century. At l'Anse-à-l'Ane in Martinique a small natural increase

Table 7.1. Estimated Slave Imports into Martinique

Date	Slaves Imported	Annual Averages	Growth Rate Slave Population	Assumed Rate Net Natural Decrease (%)
To 1663	4,000	—	—	—
1664–1735	121,600	1,690	4.3	5.4
1736–1787	182,200	3,500	0.8	4.2
1788–1831	48,900	1,110	0.0	1.3
1852–1861	9,100	910	—	—
	365,800			

Source: Curtin 1969, p. 80.

developed after 1763 (Debien 1960, p. 78). From 1753 to 1773, 60 to 98 children under age 11 resided at l'Anse-à-l'Ane for every 100 women over age 17, suggesting a still low fertility rate if the distribution of children is roughly equal among women under age 55.

The ample demographic data from the Catharina Sophia estate on Dutch Surinam support trends found elsewhere. The average annual birth rate of 26.8 per 1,000 from 1851 to 1861 was significantly less than the death rate, which rose from 38.9 per 1,000 between 1852 and 1856 to 47.7 per 1,000 between 1857 and 1861 (Lamur 1977, p. 168).

The Spanish West Indies present shifting patterns of mortality and fertility. Deaths increased and the birth rate fell in new areas of cultivation that opened up on southern Cuba. Table 7.2 offers demographic figures for nineteenth-century Cuban slaves. The mortality rate fell slightly from 63 deaths per 1,000 from 1835 to 1841 to 61 deaths per 1,000 from 1856 to 1860. At the same time the crude birth rate increased, from 19 to 28 births per 1,000. The rate of natural decrease was dramatic, worsening from a loss of 44 per 1,000 from 1835 to 1841 to a population decline of 33 per 1,000 from 1856 to 1860.

The mortality rate was higher in rural Cuba than in urban Cuba and higher on larger estates than on smaller coffee and sugar estates. Even in the eighteenth century, however, when semipatriarchal labor relations were characteristic of Cuban cash crop production, the slave mortality rate was about 4 percent, comparable to that in the British islands (Knight 1970, p. 182). Turnbull (1840, pp. 288–289) visited La Pita estate, finding 5 deaths in a year among 161 slaves but only 1 birth. He also found mortality higher on sugar than coffee estates, a relationship Higman (1984, p. 325) confirms for the nineteenth-century British West Indies. Slaves on nineteenth-century Cuban sugar plantations generally endured no more than 10 years of agricultural work, but on coffee estates as many as 30 (Turnbull 1840, p. 294).

In Puerto Rico, on the other hand, birth rates were consistently high, even after sugar planting intensifed in the mid-1800s. Census figures from 1838 for Ponce, a *municipio* of widespread sugar cultivation, reveal 319 children for

Table 7.2. Demographic Indicators for Cuba, 1835–1841 and 1856–1860

Indicator	1835–1841	1856–1860
Crude Death Rate	63	61
Infant Mortality Rate	575	283
Crude Birth Rate	19	28
Fertility *(Tasa global de fecundidad)*	87	132
Natural Decrease	−44	−33

Source: Moreno Fraginals 1977, vol. 2, p. 88 (translation mine).

every 100 Creole slave women, and 132 children for every 100 women in the slave population as a whole (Scarano 1984, p. 142). The latter comparatively high fertility rate prevailed despite a heavily male and African population. The birth rate for 4,667 slaves in Ponce was 43 per 1,000 population in 1864, with mortality at 32 deaths per 1,000 (Curet 1985, p. 137). Although slavery was not as "mild" in Puerto Rico as once thought (Curet 1985; Nistal Moret 1980; Scarano 1984), better living conditions may have endured in the eighteenth and early nineteenth centuries and influenced demographic change after the revival of the sugar industry.

CAUSES OF NATURAL DECREASE

High slave mortality contributed substantially to natural decreases in population among Caribbean slaves, as Moreno Fraginals's and Higman's data reveal (see Tables 7.2 and 3.1). The death rates of slaves varied with time, place, and period in the creolization process. Early commentators and contemporary analysts agree that many slaves died in their journey to the Americas. Craton (1971, p. 26) speculates that at least one in ten slaves perished in the Middle Passage en route to the British West Indies and every third slave died during the next three years. Survivors had a 30-year life expectancy in 1730, 40 years in 1830. Ortiz (1975, p. 249) cites the observations of the slave trader Captain Trench Townsend that an agricultural slave could live no more than five years. Posing the problem in different terms, Dirks (1978, p. 148) suggests that 50 percent of African slaves were lost from passage through the first two or three years in the Caribbean.

The mortality rates of slaves during passage to the New World and through the trauma of settlement differed along the dimensions of place and time. Craton (1974, p. 195) estimates, for example, that for Barbados, with a 6 percent importation rate in 1670, annual mortality was probably more than 70 deaths per 1,000 slaves, slightly lower than his judgment for the British West Indies as a whole. If a newly arrived slave endured another 10 years in the West Indies, he or she lasted 16 in Barbados (Ortiz 1975, p. 249). However, at the Codrington estate on Barbados mortality was higher: From 1712 to 1748 six slaves died for every one born. Forty-three percent of new slaves soon perished (Bennett 1958, pp. 53, 60), in contrast to Barbados as a whole, where only one-quarter of newly arrived slaves died (Watson 1975, p. 139).

Some discrepancies in mortality rates reflect likely overestimations by early observers, along with the real tendency of Europeans to treat slaves as though they were abundant and cheap. Charles Leslie (1740, p. 326) observed, for example, that half of slaves perished during the seasoning period in Jamaica.

In St. Kitts two-fifths of slaves were said to have been lost during the seasoning period early in the 1700s (Sheridan 1985, p. 326). Humboldt (1960, p. 168) concluded, however, that only 7 percent of new Africans (*bozales*) fell to the rigors of initiation in nineteenth-century Cuba, the lower numbers reflecting his greater care in judgment and the better treatment accorded new slave imports as they became scarce with the constriction of the international slave trade in the nineteenth century [see also Kiple (1976, p. 53) and Dirks (1987, p. 92)].

It is widely claimed that at least one-third of slaves were lost in transport to the French West Indies and the first years of plantation work. The remaining slaves then survived no more than 15 years (Hilliard d'Auberteuil 1776, vol. 2, p. 62; Labat 1930, vol. 2, pp. 46–47; Debien 1974). On the Case-Pilote estate a life expectancy of 23 years was reported for the period from 1783 to 1848 (David 1973, p. 351). At Bisdary in Guadeloupe, men survived to 32.8 years in the 1770s, women to 30.8 years, considerably less than the life expectancy in France at the time (46 years for males, 45.6 years for females) (Gautier 1985, p. 122; Mathieson 1926, p. 53). On Catharina Sophia in Dutch Surinam the life expectancy of slaves was 23 years during the period 1852 to 1861. Only half of children reached the ages of 15 to 24. Mortality later rose even higher.

Throughout the region predial slaves generally experienced greater mortality than nonpredial slaves; rural slaves had higher mortality rates than urban slaves (Dirks 1978, p. 149; Knight 1970, p. 82). Mortality was generally higher for seasoned Africans than for locally born slaves (Higman 1984, p. 324; Craton 1971, pp. 13–14), but often differences in mortality rates and life expectancies were marginal; once conditioned to their new surroundings, Africans sometimes outlived Creole slaves (Dunn 1987; see also Dirks 1987, p. 92; Siguret 1968).

High levels of infant mortality raised the rate of natural decrease and reduced the recorded birth rate because slave owners failed to log many early infant deaths. The infant mortality rate is estimated at 15 percent for early nineteenth-century Cuba (Moreno Fraginals 1978, p. 39). The mortality of slave children through the first year of life at Jamaica's Worthy Park estate is judged to have been 200 per 1,000, counting stillbirths and miscarriages. Fifty-two per thousand children under age 5 died there annually (Craton 1977, p. 87). The latter figure has also been cited for the nineteenth-century British West Indies as a whole (Bennett 1958, p. 55; Goveia 1965, p. 124). Abénon (1973, p. 315) found that for two parishes in eighteenth-century Guadeloupe child mortality fluctuated between 30 percent and 50 percent.[2] At the Seguineau au Fonds-Baptiste coffee estate in Saint Domingue, all 11 births recorded in 1778 were followed by death, an indication of the continuing dramatic loss of infant life there (Gautier 1985, p. 120).

SOURCES OF MORTALITY

Slaves died from physical abuse, exposure, malnutrition, overwork, and disease. Conditions contributing to these afflictions varied in time and place, but poor food supplies and the incidence of infectious diseases and other illnesses are consistent across plantations and societies. Recent research suggests that West Indian slaves were especially susceptible to particular diseases because of inadequate consumption of specific nutrients and unsanitary living conditions.[3]

Early observers found many cases of yaws, dropsy, cacabay, fevers, dysentery, and eye inflammation among Caribbean slaves. Other afflictions, such as pica (dirt eating), were not recognized as disease. Yaws (frambesia), a disfiguring skin condition, was highly contagious but rarely fatal (Edwards 1966, vol. 2, p. 166). Africans and male children disproportionately contracted yaws; half of the sick children on one Saint Domingue estate suffered from this debilitating disease (Geggus 1978, p. 26).[4] Ophthmalia, an eye inflammation that often leads to blindness, originated in West Africa. Dropsy, fevers, and dysentery frequently ended in death (Kiple and Kiple 1980, p. 210).

The leading causes of adult death varied with intensity of sugar planting, generally a consequence of the period of entry into cash crop production. On the new British sugar colonies, Trinidad, Tobago, and St. Lucia, diarrhea killed more slaves than other diseases, and it is linked by Higman (1984) to work demands and unit size. Cuban plantation records for the period from 1837 to 1853 also reveal that dysentery was the most common illness among slaves (Moreno Fraginals 1977, p. 200). Deaths resulting from diarrhea are common among modern people in poor countries; the diarrhea is usually caused by bacterial and viral infections and is intensified by dehydration. Lack of potable water contributed to and worsened diarrhea and dysentery among slaves as well (Dirks 1987, p. 85).

Dropsy, or edema (swelling), was the leading cause of death in some older areas of sugar cultivation. At the Newton and Colleton plantations in Barbados from 1811 to 1825 and from 1819 to 1834, dropsy accounted for 14.3 percent of deaths, followed by tuberculosis (12.2 percent), diarrhea (9.0 percent), marasmus (9.0 percent), nervous system diseases (7.9 percent), scarlet fever (6.9 percent), and leprosy (5.8 percent) (Higman 1984, p. 341). At Jamaica's Worthy Park from 1811 to 1834 dropsy caused 10 percent of 222 deaths, ranking behind old age (53 percent) and fever (23 percent). From 1817 to 1820 in St. James Parish 11 percent of slave deaths were from dropsy. In 1843 Havana's death rate from dropsy among blacks was three times that of whites (Kiple and Kiple 1980, pp. 210–211; Koplan 1983, p. 318).

The causes of dropsy remain unclear. Schaw (1939, p. 128) observed that boilers in late eighteenth-century St. Kitts often died from dropsy, apparently resulting from exposure to heat. Boiling sites were hence raised to permit more air circulation. Recent research by Kiple and King (1981) suggests that Caribbean slaves suffered thiamine deficiencies, leading to beriberi. A low-fat, high-carbohydrate diet and the boiling of food and consequent leaching out of nutrients robbed slaves of thiamine. Dirks (1987, pp. 88–90) speculates that a niacin deficiency may have caused pellagra that combined with beriberi to produce a number of closely related syndromes among slaves.[5]

At least one white physician attributed dropsy to pica. Dr. Caddell, of Barbados, believed that in 1812 pica caused 75 percent of adult deaths (Higman 1984, p. 295; Dirks 1987, p. 87). Pica is now generally associated with malnutrition, in particular, iron and calcium deficiencies, or with hookworm (Higman 1984, p. 296). Kiple and Kiple (1980, p. 208) point out, however, that hookworm was both known and resisted by blacks.[6] They hypothesize that beriberi caused dirt eating and dropsy. A cultural component may also have contributed to pica. Higman (1984, p. 296) reminds us that dirt cakes were manufactured and sold by slaves, a practice that has continued in areas of West Africa (see also Dirks 1987, p. 87). And indeed Africans were everywhere in the Caribbean more likely to practice dirt eating, suggesting cultural continuities, stronger nutritional deficiencies among Africans than Creoles, or different ways of assuaging the hunger for thiamine and other as yet unidentified nutrients (Geggus 1978, p. 29).

Child Mortality

Children suffered high mortality rates in Caribbean slave societies. They died from yaws, worms, and dropsy; from marasmus and hookworm related to poor nutrition; from dirt eating; and from teething ailments (Higman 1984, p. 344; Sheridan 1985, p. 201). In the British West Indies in 1830 whooping cough killed more children under age 10 than any other disease (Sheridan 1985, p. 235). Another major killer of the same population was "worm fever" (Barclay 1828, p. 333).

Tetanus was the scourge of West Indian slave children. It killed perhaps one-fourth of infants before they reached nine days old,[7] yet was unknown among whites and freed populations. Babies stricken with the tetanus bacillus suffered from "spasms and muscular rigidity" and finally died (Sheridan 1985, p. 238). Tetanus was called the sickness of seven days by the Spanish and may have taken the lives of one-third of infants born to Cuban slave women (Ortiz 1975, p. 258). Moreno Fraginals (1977, p. 200) claims that newborn tetanus accounted for 20 percent of annual child mortality. Of 134 slave child deaths in Grenada 20 resulted from tetanus in 1820; 24 of 288 children died of tetanus in 1830 (Sheridan 1985, p. 236). Higman (1984, p. 29) speculates that more than 25 percent of births were unrecorded in the British West Indies because of rapid infant death, frequently from tetanus.

The cause of tetanus among slaves has long been a mystery. It is now suspected that mothers and midwives packed the severed umbilicus with mud contaminated by animal feces. The use of rusty or dirty instruments or muddied stones to cut the cord also contributed to infection. Animal waste was applied as fertilizer in the cane fields and may well have been used by slaves to improve productivity in their kitchen gardens. Slaves' quarters were near livestock pens, making it likely that dirt or tools taken from slaves' yards would be lethal to newborns.

Planters were frustrated by the loss of infant lives to tetanus, and some believed that mothers themselves caused the deaths. Saint Domingue planters occasionally punished women whose babies died from tetanus and the midwives who attended the birth (Debien 1974, p. 297; 1962, p. 129). At the large Foache estate in Saint Domingue both mothers and midwives encountered sanctions at the death of a child in the eighteenth century, the owner stating that this abusive course was known among slaveholders to prolong infant life (Debien 1962, p. 129).

Tetanus was most common in the Spanish West Indies from November through February. Ortiz (1975, p. 259) suggests that there were two forms of infant tetanus, one contracted from foreign objects and the second caused by cold dry weather. The cool atmosphere may have worsened infections contracted from dirty tools or dressings. The high incidence of tetanus during the winter months suggests that some children actually died from tetany. Caused by deficiencies in calcium, magnesium, and vitamin D, tetany is a "hyperirritability of the neuromuscular system, whose symptoms include convulsions and spasms of the voluntary muscles" (Kiple and Kiple 1980, p. 291).[8] Thus winter's little sunshine meant vitamin D shortages for those with poor diets and convulsive infant deaths. Tetany also caused teething problems, which killed many Caribbean slave children (Ortiz 1975, pp. 258, 260–261; Higman 1984, p. 344). Some infants simply died following convulsions and fever unassociated with tetanus or tetany (Kiple and Kiple 1980, p. 213).

Similar infant disease and mortality patterns were found on U.S. plantations. In the 7 southern states with 75 percent of the black population from 1849 to 1850, children accounted for 51 percent of deaths, whereas white children made up only 38 percent of white deaths (Kiple and King 1981, p. 290). Of deaths among U.S. slave children 9 years and younger, 23 percent can be accounted for by convulsions, teething, tetanus, lockjaw, suffocation, and worms (Kiple and King 1981, p. 290).[9]

Fertility

The continuing natural decrease of West Indian slave populations was attributable to both high mortality and low fertility. It is difficult to discern which variable had a larger impact on population change, but British West Indian registration figures suggest that changing mortality was generally the major determinant of population growth and decline in the early nineteenth century, with low fertility levels remaining constant (Higman 1984, p. 374).[10] A planter and trader claimed before the Privy Council that low slave birth rates had many causes, some of which pertained specifically to fertility: early and frequent sexual unions, male and female venereal diseases, abortion, menstrual disorders, long-term suckling of infants, and lack of interest of slave women in their children (Sheridan 1985, pp. 226–227). These factors have continued to interest scholars, although virtually no research has been conducted on fertility control or subfecundity among Caribbean slaves.

Demographic Correlates of High Fertility

There were areas and eras within the history of Caribbean slavery that generated fertility increases. For example, the amelioration of the living conditions of slaves during the early 1800s led to some modest rises in fertility. An adequate number of females was required to achieve population increase; in the British West Indies natural increases occurred generally after the population was disproportionately female (Higman 1976b, p. 65). Although Caribbean male slaves sometimes outnumbered females by 3 to 1 in the eighteenth century, sex ratios in the United States were nearly even. Eighteenth- and nineteenth-century U.S. slaveholders purchased women to allow for family creation, whereas Caribbean planters preferred males or were able to purchase only males (Klein and Engerman 1978, p. 365). During the last years of U.S. slavery women were present in the following proportions: In 1820 there were 95.1 female slaves for every 100 males; in 1830, 98.3; in 1840, 99.5; in 1850, 99.9; and in 1860, 99.3 (Blassingame 1972, p. 78).[11]

Selected groups largely accounted for fertility increases in the Caribbean. Higman (1984, p. 357) summarizes the situation in the British West Indies after 1807, when their participation in the international slave trade ended and slave owners and colonial governments sought to preserve slave lives.

Thus, it is apparent that in general, the level of fertility was highest in colonies where the slaves lived most often in small units, producing crops other than sugar or, to a lesser degree, coffee or cotton. But the proportion living in towns seems not to have mattered. Of the demographic variables, high fertility was more commonly associated with relatively large proportions of creoles than with low sex ratios. High fertility also tended to occur where there were large proportions of colored slaves.[12]

It has been argued further that African slaves accounted for much lower fertility throughout the region (Higman 1976b, 1978; Craton 1979). As the female slave population grew and became creolized, their fertility increased. African women were more vulnerable than second-generation slaves to a variety of ills that reduced fertility, and they were perhaps less willing to build sexual liaisons in a new and strange environment. There is also increasing evidence that the West African diet was poor and fertility low. Curtin (1985, pp. 181–182) reports that African "famines may have been a major source of slaves." Starving people in drought-stricken areas were surely sold as slaves, Curtin argues, although the dimensions of this phenomenon are unknown. Hence North American slavery, especially in the U.S. South, represented an improvement in the nutrition of many Africans and thus their prospects for bearing children. Advances were greater in the second generation, of course, when the trauma of forced emigration, enslavement, and absorption into a new "disease environment" had passed (Sheridan 1985).

Slaves in the United States were mostly locally born before those in the Caribbean. There was a native-born black majority in the American mainland colonies as early as 1680, but only 25 percent of the Caribbean slave population was African in 1800 (Fogel and Engerman 1974, p. 23).[13] This difference in creolization rates is thought to explain much of the high level of slave fertility in the U.S. South. Evidence of greater Creole fertility is found, for example, at Jamaica's Worthy Park, where African slave women had only half the fertility of Creoles (Craton 1977, p. 96). A similar contrast was found at Jamaica's Mesopotamia, where from 1774 to 1831 African women had an average of 2.4 births and Creole women, 4.2 (Dunn 1987, p. 815; 1977, pp. 60–61). Creole slaves were also more fertile on the 197 absentee plantations held by the British from 1796 to 1797, although they were also younger than their African counterparts (Geggus 1978, p. 13). Yet some slaveholders, particularly in the French West Indies, believed that African women were more fertile than Creoles (Debien 1974, p. 348). Creole women were no more fertile than Africans on the Saint Domingue coffee and indigo plantations studied by Siguret (1968, p. 225).[14] In the eighteenth century at Nippes in Saint Domingue, however, African women had fewer surviving children than did Creoles (Gautier 1985, p. 84).

In the early days of Caribbean slavery, with more women than in the eighteenth century but a majority of Africans, fertility was often high. On early eighteenth-century French islands, for example, Labat and DuTertre found high fertility levels (Labat 1930; DuTertre 1958, vol. 2, p. 472; see also Jesse 1961, p. 148). Gautier (1985, p. 75) surmises that early French West Indian plantations exhibited high fertility if large and if males outnumbered females, stabilizing marriage and increasing fecundity. Childlessness and few births per mother then increased to levels considerably more than those found among U.S. slaves. At the Mt. Airy estate in Virginia, for example, at least two-thirds of slave women of childbearing age listed in estate records from 1809 to 1828 were mothers; perhaps 90 percent of all females on the estate during that period bore children or would eventually do so. Of families, 86 percent had 4 or more children. In contrast, from 1799 to 1818 at Jamaica's larger Mesopotamia plantation, of 200 potential mothers, half bore no children, with only 37 percent of mothers bearing 4 or more children, and as few as 55 percent of all women ever becoming mothers (Dunn 1977, pp. 58–59).

A similar situation occurred in the French West Indies. At la Sucrerie du Comte Pasquet de Lugé in Saint Domingue, for example, 36 of 111 women from 17 to 60 years old became mothers from 1723 to 1788, and 53 percent had only 1 child (Gautier 1985, pp. 112, 120). The age of first birth of a surviving child may also have risen, as it did at Nippes in Saint Domingue, from 20 years in 1721–1730, to 23½ years in 1731–1750, to 25 years in 1761–1770 (Gautier 1985, p. 83).

Debien (1974, p. 359) observed many births of few women on the sugar plantations of Saint Domingue that left records. At l'Anse-à-l'Ane in Martinique the 52 conjugal families each had an average of four children, with the fertility of maternal families (with a nonresident but continuing male presence) nearly as high (Debien 1960, pp. 51–58). Creole females generally had four or five children on the indigo and coffee plantations of Saint Domingue (Siguret 1968, p. 225). Geggus (1978, pp. 12–13) estimates a lower fertility rate for 197 Saint Domingue estates occupied by British troops in the early 1800s, with an average of 321 children under 5 years present per 1,000 women aged 15–44 on *sucreries,* and 439 on *caféières* (see also Geggus 1982, pp. 290–294).

FERTILITY CONTROL

It is commonly assumed that Caribbean women exercised considerable choice in fertility. Knowing the physical risks and hazards of pregnancy and the economic and political benefits of rearing children, women—sometimes in consultation with lovers and kin—decided whether or not to conceive and bear children. Demographic research generally attributes high levels of authority and control to families in fertility decisions. Caribbean slave women, so often family heads, are thus credited with rational calculation of costs and opportunities.

The focus on women's power in fertility is perplexing, given the meager attention to women's intentionality in other areas of slave studies. Moreover, some commentators seem to believe that preindustrial peoples, such as West Indian slaves, were in control of effective contraceptive and abortion technology, when these resources vary greatly cross-culturally, even in the contemporary world. Caribbean bondwomen were dependent on African women healers and midwives for assistance and information in birth control. With poor sanitation, lack of medical supplies, and little support from planters and other whites, neither slave women nor indigenous healers can be expected to have controlled fertility effectively.

Low fertility in human populations is generally attributable to contraceptive use and abortion, the physical inability of women and/or men to reproduce, and few occasions for sexual intercourse (McFalls and McFalls 1984). Caribbean slave women have been variously described as frequent contraceptive users, skilled practitioners of abortion, and sexual abstainers. Fertility control by Caribbean slaves may well be overestimated in explaining the low birth rate. A review of the evidence for women and family discretion and choice in fertility reveals little substantiation of the voluntary control hypothesis. Subfecundity and women's frequent single status seemingly have as much significance in explaining slave fertility.

It is likely that slave women throughout the New World abstained from sexual intercourse when the likelihood of marriage and stable family life were slim. Or women may simply have feared pregnancy. There were grave dangers of maternal mortality, a strong likelihood of the newborn's death, and little lessening of the mother's workload during pregnancy or after birth. Moreover, in the eighteenth century, after Caribbean plantations increased in size and profitability, slaveholders strongly expressed their wish to keep plantations free of children and the expenses they incurred.

> Indeed, to the masters and the slaves alike high-fertility patterns were unacceptable. The function of the female slave as a "work unit" was heavily stressed; in this capacity she was as essential to the plantation as a male slave, being required for domestic service and for the lighter operations connected with field and factory. It was even claimed by Governor Parry of Barbados, "the labour of the females . . . in the works of the fields is the same as that of men." The rearing of children impaired her function as a labourer and thus was not countenanced by the master. The position of the pregnant slaves, it seems, was not a happy one. In the words of Ramsay, they were "wretches who are upbraided, cursed and ill-treated . . . for being found in the condition to become mothers." A witness before the Select Committee of 1790–1 declared that "a female slave is punished for being found pregnant." (Roberts 1957, pp. 225–226)

Some have argued that women's failure to contribute to the slave labor force was their greatest act of political resistance (Hine 1979; Reddock 1985; White 1985, pp. 84–85; Brathwaite 1971; Bush 1986). "The low fertility was a reflection of the slave condition; it amounted to a class stand on the part of women'' (Moreno Fraginals 1977, p. 196). The hypothesis that women resisted pregnancy on political grounds runs counter to the notion discussed in Chapter Six, that New World slaves formed families in cultural opposition to slavery. It is possible, too, that women wished to have children but were often unable to conceive them or carry them to term because of malnutrition, disease, overwork, or lack of sexual opportunity.[15]

Hence it has also been posited that women robbed slave owners of interest and effort by attending to their children. Jones (1982, p. 237) succinctly states this position in reference to U.S. black women, whose "full attention to the duties of motherhood deprived whites of their power over these women as field laborers and domestic servants." And, given slaveholders' early attitudes toward slave childbearing, the birth of slave children did oppose slave owners' goals. Evidence of collectivized child care conditions on many West Indian estates and women's heavy work in the fields and in food cultivation in parts of the region implies that many nineteenth-century slave women were in fact able to devote little time or concentration to nurturing children (Gautier 1985, p. 115).

Slave owners and observers of the era thought slave women were promiscuous, likely to contract venereal disease and thus become sterile (Moreno Fraginals 1978, p. 51). It is politically tantalizing to suggest that slave women actually resisted sexual relations, whether to oppose the system or to preclude the rigors and sadness of bearing and rearing children as slaves. More interesting, however, are the ideological and cultural factors implicit in Europeans' understanding of African mores and slave women's position within the slave and plantation communities. It is clear, for example, that the portrayal of slave women as sexually free was in part wishful thinking for white men. Even if not willing or able to enjoy slave women's favors, masters could imagine sexual abandon in slave quarters and envy the slaves' presumed amorality (Jordan 1968). Even the idea that promiscuity led to childlessness reinforces the planters' illusions of guilt-free sexuality among slaves.

There is little dependable evidence that Caribbean slaves had multiple unions, simultaneously or over time. That unions were so easily broken up suggests, however, that many people had more than one enduring or short-term union in their lives and several casual ones. The situation for Caribbean slaves, then, is not unlike that of other migrating peoples. Among such groups multiple sexual partners are common and have little apparent impact on fertility. Migratory people often exhibit high rates of birth and fertility. With meager historical evidence we can conclude little about Caribbean slave promiscuity, female sexual abstinence, or associations with population change. At most we can speculate that the rigid and closed social relations of blacks and whites in the Caribbean and the United States are reflected in the popular white notion that female sexuality was strong and fully expressed and that low fertility ensued.[16]

Contraception

West Indian slave women probably used intrauterine devices and herbal mixes to prevent conception or implantation of a fertilized egg. The frequent indication of uterine and vaginal infections suggests that irritation to the reproductive organs was common and could well have been caused by intrauterine contraception and abortions (Sheridan 1985, p. 227).

Slave women nursed their newborn children, reducing the risks of another pregnancy. Slaves on some British West Indian plantations nursed their infants for two years, whereas slaves in the United States generally suckled their infants for only one year (Klein and Engerman 1978, pp. 360, 366; Fogel and Engerman 1979, p. 568; Dirks 1987, pp. 111, 201). Variations occurred even in British West Indian nursing practices, of course: Mrs. Carmichael (1834, vol. 1, p. 191) reports that weaning seldom occurred before the infant reached 15 or 16 months. Plantation managers on Barbados generally allowed slave women to nurse their babies for only one year (Bennett 1958, p. 13). Dr. Kuhn, practicing in Surinam in the 1850s, asserted that slave women nursed infants for two to three years and refrained from intercourse (Lamur 1977, p. 168).

Sheridan (1985, p. 245) argues that slaves in the British West Indies suckled their babies in order to prevent births. Yet nursing is an ineffective contraceptive if not used as the exclusive source of infant food (Scott and Johnston 1985). By the second year of life, babies are generally eating enough solid food that breast feeding has dubious contraceptive value. And West Indian slaves apparently fed infants solid foods, sometimes as early as the first week of life (Ortiz 1975, p. 284; Carmichael 1834, vol. 2, p. 189).[17]

Higman claims that the long breast feeding period among slaves carried over from Africa and nourished babies better than weaning and transition to the limited Caribbean slave diet.[18] He finds little evidence of its use as a contraceptive or as a means for women to resist full-time return to agricultural labor. He suggests that, although planters protested long breast feeding, they often did little to prevent it (Higman 1984, p. 354). On the other hand, few accommodations were made for nursing mothers, as Dickson's observations of a Barbados sugar plantation reveal: "When I first went to Barbados, I was particularly astonished to see some women far gone in their pregnancy, toiling in the field; and others, whose naked infants lay exposed to the weather, sprawling on a goat-skin, or in a wooden tray. I have heard, with indignation, drivers curse both them and their squalling brats, when they were suckling them" (Dickson 1789, p. 12). Combined with other physiological factors and social conditions, however, extended breast feeding may have influenced Caribbean slave fertility. There is increasing indirect evidence, for example, that malnutrition can prolong amenorrhea, the absence of menstruation, and perhaps ovulation among nursing mothers, even when they provide only food supplements to the child (Lunn et al. 1984).[19] Also significant was the West

African taboo on intercourse during the breast feeding period, apparently reproduced in the Caribbean (Kiple 1984, pp. 110–111).

Infanticide and Abortion

Abortion and infanticide are both frequently reported by planters and others (Roberts 1957, p. 226; Moreno Fraginals 1978, pp. 52, 53; Brathwaite 1971, p. 213; Debien 1974, p. 363; Fouchard 1981, p. 73; Ortiz 1975, p. 283; Deerr 1949–1950; Moreau de Saint Méry 1958; Hilliard d'Auberteuil 1776; Labat 1930, vol. 2, pp. 216–217). Dunn (1977, p. 63) suggests that slave women practiced abortion to retain their attractiveness to white men, an alternative to the hypothesis that abortion was a means of political resistance for slave women and in keeping with the idea that slave women's unions with white men were their greatest source of status and income. Schaw (1939, pp. 112–113) reinforces this point in claiming that black women aborted their children by European men: "They have certain herbs and medicines that free them from such an incumbrance, but which seldom fails to cut short their own lives, as well as that of their offspring." Peytraud (1973, p. 235) offered another motive for French West Indian women's abortions—to avoid punishment if their newborns died. Gautier (1985, pp. 113–114, 120) speculates that planters' efforts to save infant lives during the amelioration period by punishing mothers at the death of their children failed to bring about population increases in part because of the resulting rise in abortions.

The actual incidence of abortion and infanticide cannot be determined. The argument that these practices were widespread is bolstered by the misery of slave life: One can legitimately ask why bondwomen would want to bear children, particularly if doing so stood in the way of other social rewards, as Dunn suggests. In the French West Indies abortion was severely punished and, with marronage, was a major concern of nineteenth-century planters (Gautier 1985, p. 137). We lack the history of enduring and frequent nuclear families and songs and oral traditions of parental devotion for the West Indies that Genovese (1976, p. 497) cites for the U.S. South, claiming that the incidence of infanticide and abortion is overstated. Nevertheless, three characteristics of interaction between whites and blacks suggest that the frequency of these practices has been exaggerated for West Indian slavery as well.

First, colonial officials often blamed low slave fertility on planters: their neglect of slaves' health, mistreatment of infants, and overworking of women slaves. Hence it was in the interest of plantation owners to argue that conditions were sufficient for the reproduction of slave labor but that the slaves themselves did not want children (Gautier 1985; Bush 1986; Sheridan 1985). Indeed some early commentators seem to have attributed miscarriages to slave women's neglect, failing to differentiate this passive behavior from abortion

(Gautier 1985, p. 134; Dirks 1987, p. 105). Moreau de Saint Méry (1958, vol. 1, p. 61) believed that slave midwives and healers were responsible for many aborted pregnancies, stillbirths, and cases of tetanus. The loss of their children caused dramatic cases of *mal de mère* among bondwomen, worsened by midwives' cures.

Second, planters feared and respected slave healers and may have attributed to them more than they could actually achieve. Reproductive medicine was largely controlled by Africans, and herbal abortifacients were used in West Africa (Bush 1986, p. 127). Although Bush is surely correct that local knowledge of means to induce abortions is "universal, transcending chronological and cultural barriers," it did not always lead to effective application by healers and midwives, particularly without causing death or illness to mothers, as Moreau de Saint Méry's comments on the eighteenth-century French West Indies suggest.

Why are there not more female deaths recorded from bleeding or fever if abortions were common, especially with the highly unsanitary conditions in slave quarters and in light of Schaw's comment that abortion was often fatal to the mother? White doctors eventually saw most fatally ill slaves and would have been able to detect the sad results of badly performed abortions. Sheridan (1985, p. 244) notes, for example, that Michael Clare, a physician in Jamaica, described to a House of Lords select committee the administration by a midwife of the abortifacient "wild cassava" to a pregnant slave woman who then miscarried (see also Mathurin 1974). "Unexplained" deaths, common to every plantation, probably included fatalities from abortions, but the failure of contemporary observers to speculate on this, given the general conviction that abortion was common, is at least curious.[20]

A similar inconsistency arises when infanticide is considered. Most immediate infant deaths were accounted for by various forms of tetany and tetanus. European doctors left us their discussions of infant diseases, yet they were generally silent about means or patterns of infanticide despite its presumed frequency. This is in contrast to the United States, where white doctors and slave owners wrote often about slaves killing infants by smothering them (Kiple and King 1981; White 1985, pp. 87–89).[21]

CONCLUSIONS

Caribbean slaves experienced high mortality and low fertility, accounted for in part by the skewed sex ratios and a large proportion of African slaves of middle age. The brutal lifestyle endured by slaves on Caribbean sugar plantations and the voyage from Africa took many lives through accidents and disease. Quantitative evidence from British plantations indicates that slaves suffered from yaws, pica, dropsy, fevers, and tuberculosis. These patterns are found as well in plantation records from other islands. Infant mortality was extremely high, with tetanus and other forms of tetany the major causes of infant death.

Slaves controlled their fertility but perhaps to a lesser degree than is generally assumed. The use of contraceptives and the practice of abortion, infanticide, and sexual abstinence are documented, but inconsistencies and omissions in the historical record suggest that Europeans may have overstated efforts by slaves to prevent childbearing and rearing. Our discussion of infertility in Chapter Eight reveals that subfecundity, along with common lack of continuous opportunity for sexual contact because of the sale of slaves and frequent reconstitution of plantation populations, may contribute new understanding of low Caribbean slave fertility.

The discussion of population change in West Indian slave societies is informed in part by events and transitions in U.S. southern slave communities. With a younger, creolized population and low gender ratios, southern bondmen and women achieved a natural population increase early in the eighteenth century. If age and place of birth are held constant, Caribbean slaves experienced greater mortality and lower fertility than U.S. slaves. Women apparently wanted fewer children and may have been less often able to conceive, carry, and deliver children than bondwomen in the United States.

Slaves in the United States had more reasons to have children, given the economic conditions of southern plantations. With a stricter gender division of labor, males controlled much of the income-generating potential of household economies. Women had both a measure of economic security and material incentives to bear children to provide assistance in enhancing household incomes. The construction and maintenance of kin connections were also supported by child rearing, although slaveholders broke up families and kinship systems with frequency, frustrating slaves' efforts to keep family ties strong. United States slave owners encouraged childbirth to reproduce the slave population, adopting measures to ease birth and preserve infant life. Still, life on southern plantations was short and cruel for many slaves, and amenities were a function of smaller-scale production and smaller slave populations.

In contrast, eighteenth-century Caribbean slave owners did not welcome slave children and did little to conserve their health and welfare. Conditions of pregnancy, birth, and early infant life contributed to maternal and child mortality. Under these circumstances women had little reason to value children. Whether they could successfully control fertility, however, is questionable.

Although seldom considered, it is likely that many Caribbean slaves wanted children for both emotional and economic reasons. Household economies based on the growing of provisions and artisanal activities could, after all, usefully incorporate children, as they did in the United States. In some Caribbean settings the birth rate actually rose among women responsible for households and among women with limited opportunities for cash accumulation. Yet, even for many Caribbean slave families in conjugal families and incorporated into extensive household economies, childbearing was relatively infrequent.

CHAPTER EIGHT

Fecundity

With the poor living conditions of West Indian slaves and their introduction into a new and hence threatening disease environment, it is intriguing that ill health has not been invoked more often to explain slaves' low fertility rates. We see instead a strong analytical preference for understanding low fertility as a result of Caribbean slave women's control of births through contraception, abortion, and infanticide. As argued in the preceding chapter, evidence of these practices by slave women is actually slender. I have suggested ideological reasons for popular and scholarly acceptance of the hypothesis that West Indian slave women controlled births: European and North American fascination with African women's reputed sexual and healing powers. In this chapter I review the evidence that disease, malnutrition, and illness resulting from overwork were important contributors to male and female subfecundity.

Fertility is an important indicator of women's economic position and intentions (Ward 1984). Yet in ignoring the evidence of male and female physical incapacity for conception and birth, we may falsely assume that women's economic interests were opposed to childbirth. In fact, women's often powerful position within households created an incentive for large families, particularly when men were continuously present. I propose that the bondwoman considered economic and other factors in assessing the costs and benefits of childbirth and child rearing. The more frequent her presence in field labor and the more limited her access to income, the less her material interest in having children. These same economic conditions, in turn, promoted disease, malnutrition, and the illnesses of overwork. Thus subfecundity and voluntary fertility control must *together* account for low birth rates among Caribbean slaves.

In other settings slaves controlled small-scale agricultural production and trade. In these cases men and women worked in field labor but had the time and opportunities to earn income through the growing and trade of provisions, artisan activities, and hiring out. Women had economic incentives to rear children *whether or not alone* and regardless of levels of infant mortality. Such conditions generally accompanied low productivity in the production of commodities for export, less likelihood of disease, and better slave nutrition. The slaves in these circumstances also had more access to food and more control over health care and housing. As with other groups in historically similar circumstances, Caribbean slaves presumably found large families an

119

asset in household economies. Thus slaves' inability to conceive and bear children is an important factor in explaining low fertility.

I review these arguments in light of comparative examples from Caribbean slave societies. The cases suggest again that both voluntary fertility control and subfecundity contributed to low fertility in the region.

Subfecundity

If voluntary fertility control by Caribbean slaves has been overstated, in what other ways can we account for slaves' low fertility? The possibility that women slaves were subfecund has been explored little but may suggest as much about the low fertility of bondwomen as sexual abstinence, contraception, abortion, and infanticide do. Cross-culturally and historically the most common causes of population subfecundity are coital inability (individuals cannot perform "normal heterosexual intercourse"), infertility and sterility, involuntary pregnancy loss, and perinatal mortality (late fetal and neonatal mortality) (McFalls and McFalls 1984, p. xix).

Infant mortality was high among Caribbean slaves. It is commonly assumed that miscarriages were frequent (Dirks 1987, p. 105), although direct evidence is slight. Craton (1971, p. 12; 1977, p. 87) found that among once-pregnant slaves at Jamaica's Worthy Park in 1793, as many as one-third suffered miscarriages and stillbirths. His estimate of 1 miscarriage for every 4.6 births at Worthy Park is not, however, especially high.[1] Some thought that colored women were more likely to have miscarriages and other related problems (Nugent 1907, p. 94).[2] We perhaps encounter again whites' belief that African women were strong and fertile and African medicine powerful.

Coital inability has not been considered a source of slave subfecundity in the literature. Yet there were some slave diseases, for example, yaws, that surely made intercourse painful or difficult. Moreover, the large number of slaves with diseases and ailments on nearly all Caribbean plantations reduced fertility by decreasing opportunities for sexual intimacy.

Illness was more frequent among males than females. "Comparative mortality suggests that female diseases were less lethal than those that affected males" (Sheridan 1985, p. 186). Men's coital inability and ill health may therefore have contributed as much or more substantially to low fertility as female abstinence. An observer on St. Lucia reported to Sturge and Harvey (1838, p. 118) that from 1815 to 1834, a period of intensive sugar cultivation, half of the males but only a third of the females died before the age of 20. Male infant mortality, too, was greater than that of females in the British West Indies (Higman 1984, p. 196). French West Indian women were also healthier than men. Siguret (1968, p. 223) notes in her sample of *caféières* and *indigoteries* one coffee plantation where the female population renewed itself but the male population did not. On the British-occupied plantations of Saint Domingue, women, especially Creoles, were less often ill than men (Geggus 1978, pp. 29-30).

It was not unusual, however, for bondwomen to be ill. On William Beckford's Clarendon estates in 1780, for example, of 604 females 188 (31 percent) were ill or ailing, and 30 women were labeled "superannuated" or "useless" (Mathurin 1974, p. 313). Of 274 women aged 15 to 50, 78 (28 percent) were in poor shape; of 284 field women 65 (22 percent) were unwell. Perhaps most telling in plantation-specific material about women's health and its relationship to fertility is Dunn's finding (1977, p. 59) that at Jamaica's Mesopotamia half of childless women but only one-third of mothers died in their twenties and thirties. Presumably, healthier women bore children, although it is possible that childbearing had a salutary effect on some slave women's health. Roberts (1977, p. 156) points out further that slaves' low life expectancies reduced childbearing years. Using the 22-year life expectancy derived from registration figures for Demerera and Essequibo and assuming a childbearing span from ages 12 to 42, Roberts concludes that bondwomen could expect to survive for only 75 percent of their fertile years.

Did slaves' illnesses reduce fecundity and opportunities for intercourse? That is, were slaves who engaged in sexual intercourse unable to conceive children because of disease? Two common slave disabilities, venereal disease and tuberculosis, are known to cause subfecundity. In the West Indies, "with tuberculosis, venereal disease was the greatest cause of sterility among the women and, no doubt, of illnesses among children" (Debien 1974, p. 307; see also Lowenthal and Clarke 1977; Roberts 1977; Moreton 1793, pp. 28-31; Dickson 1789, p. 153). Venereal diseases reduce fertility but in fact rarely render population segments sterile. From their analysis of the black fertility drop after emancipation in the United States, McFalls and McFalls (1984, pp. 469-477) contend that venereal disease accounted for no more than 0.5 percent of fertility decline despite the popular assumption that syphilis and gonorrhea were the major sources of postbellum black subfecundity.

Neither syphilis nor gonorrhea impairs male fertility. Women with syphilis generally suffer two years of subfecundity shortly after contracting the disease. McFalls and McFalls (1984, p. 470) speculate that 2-4 percent of newly emancipated black slaves in the United States had syphilis.[3] Assuming a dramatic increase, to an infection rate of 20-30 percent to the end of the nineteenth century, fertility would have dropped by only 1 percent. Caribbean slaves probably had more sexual partners than slaves in the United States, resulting in higher syphilis rates. But it is unlikely that syphilis had the impact on fertility that is generally assumed.

Gonorrhea has more serious consequences for fecundity than syphilis, with about 20 percent of female gonorrhea victims contracting salpingitis. From 60 percent to 70 percent of that 20 percent are generally rendered sterile (McFalls and McFalls 1984, p. 476; see also Bongaarts and Potter 1983, p. 41; Keller et al. 1984, pp. 181–182).[4] Working again with data on U.S. blacks, McFalls and McFalls assume that, even if as many as 6.4 percent of women had gonorrhea in 1880, only 1.2 percent would become sterile, even with repeated reinfections. There seems little question, then, that gonorrhea contributed to the low West Indian birth rate but that its influence is overstated.

Tuberculosis, on the other hand, has a powerful effect on fertility and may have been responsible for much of the fertility loss of black Americans in the late 1800s and early part of this century (McFalls and McFalls 1984; Kiple and King 1981). Tuberculosis was common among New World slaves and underestimated because of its common misdiagnosis as dropsy and other diseases (Kiple 1984, pp. 141–142). Africans lacked immunity to tuberculosis and lived in crowded conditions conducive to the spread of the disease. On many West Indian estates tuberculosis was a leading recorded cause of death (Ortiz 1975, p. 282; Debien 1974, p. 307; Dirks 1987, p. 85). At the Newton plantation in Barbados, for example, one in twelve slaves died from tuberculosis between 1790 and 1810. Adding deaths from scrofula, a commonly misdiagnosed form of tuberculosis, the death rate was at least one in eight (Kiple 1984, p. 142). Among black soldiers in the British West Indies studied in 1838, "diseases of the lungs" led other causes of death (whereas white troops died principally from fevers) (Tulloch and Marshall 1977, p. 156).[5]

Tuberculosis can cause sterility, particularly when it spreads in women from the lungs to the fallopian tubes (McFalls and McFalls 1984, p. 484; Keller et al. 1984, p. 184; Bongaarts and Potter 1983, p. 41). Amenorrhea (cessation of menstruation) results from endometrial destruction in up to 50 percent of infected women (Keller et al. 1984, p. 184). Tuberculosis often strikes young people before they have had children; primary amenorrhea (failure to begin menstruation in adolescence) occurs in probably one-third of tubercular females. The effect of tuberculosis on the fertility of New World blacks has been underrated, it is now argued, in part because of overestimation of the contribution of venereal disease to infertility (McFalls and McFalls 1984; Kiple and King 1981).

Subfecundity has also been associated historically with African sleeping sickness, schistosomiasis, leprosy, and smallpox. Occasional epidemics of these diseases occurred in West Indian slave populations. Whooping cough, pneumonia, and dysentery can cause subfecundity, and all were common among West Indian slaves. In the absence of clinical evidence, of course, it cannot be proven that diseases caused subfecundity. Because such data are rarely available for population aggregates, "it is not known what diseases are actually capable of materially affecting population fecundity" (McFalls and McFalls 1984, p. 65). Still, the broad incidence of diseases linked to subfecundity in Caribbean slave populations is suggestive and supplements hypotheses about material incentives for and prohibitions against bearing children. It should be noted as well, though, that U.S. slaves suffered from many of the same diseases as slaves in the West Indies but had a growing number of children. In general, however, U.S. slaves were much healthier than their Caribbean counterparts (Fogel and Engerman 1974).

Two other factors associated in the historical record with West Indian slave subfecundity are poor nutrition and overwork. In both cases it is assumed that slave women's physiological stress prevented ovulation and hence conception. Does available evidence support these assertions?

Nutrition appears to have little direct impact on fertility, contrary to the generally held assumption (Debien 1974, p. 360; Schnakenbourg 1980; Turner 1982). Kiple and Kiple (1980, p. 200) estimate that West Indian slaves consumed on average about 3,000 calories daily and less than half a pint of animal protein. This is one-third the generally accepted daily requirement of protein but twice what is now recommended to the relatively sedentary adults of industrial countries. Others estimate a more meager slave diet. Schnakenbourg (1980, p. 54) claims, for instance, that French West Indian slaves ate fewer than the 1,500 to 2,500 calories daily prescribed by the Code Noir. Dirks argues that slaves in British West Indian first gangs needed 3,500 calories daily and probably got 1,500 to 2,000.[6] Slaves generally required 45 grams of protein daily, he suggests, and consumed 41 to 63 (Dirks 1978, p. 139). In Cuba slaves ate an average of 200 grams of jerked beef daily, containing 70 grams of vegetable protein, 13 grams of fat, and 382 calories, plus 500 grams of cornmeal or its equivalent, providing 15 grams of vegetable protein. These were, says Moreno Fraginals (1977, pp. 198–199), sufficient calories for a day's work. It has been argued that the diet of New World slaves was in fact superior to that of their contemporaries in Africa (Fogel and Engerman 1974; Moreno Fraginals 1977, p. 62).

Whatever the caloric and protein consumption of Caribbean slaves, however, there is little evidence that poor nutrition alone reduces fertility.[7] Experts agree that "moderate chronic malnutrition" has little impact on births (Bongaarts 1980; see also Scott and Johnston 1985). Indeed, contemporary malnourished populations often have extremely high fertility. Age of menarche is slightly delayed among malnourished women, and length of amenorrhea associated with lactation is increased (Kleinman 1980, p. 138; Bongaarts and Potter 1983). Watkins and van de Walle (1985, p. 15) conclude, however, that "short of extreme deprivation . . . the available evidence suggests that neither the period of post-partum amenorrhea nor the length of the waiting period [for resumption of menstruation] vary substantially among women of different nutritional status."

Severe weight loss, specifically a decline in fat below 12–13 percent of body mass, can cause amenorrhea, however. Slave women probably retained sufficient levels of body fat to allow ovulation, based on slave diets and despite the low levels of fat consumed. Combined with overwork, however, malnutrition manifested in weight loss is likely to have inhibited conception. This association may be reflected in extensive eighteenth- and nineteenth-century commentary on land and labor productivity in relation to fertility. British abolitionists believed, for instance, that the slave population dropped or increased with the ratio of sugar exported to the total number of slaves (Mathieson 1926, p. 104). Pitman asserted that, where sugar production exceeded 2,000 pounds produced by three slaves, births fell. Soil fertility was also believed to be negatively associated with natality, suggesting that, the harder slaves had to work, the fewer children they bore (Dirks 1978, p. 150). Long (1774, vol. 2, pp. 437–439) asserted that hard work damaged pregnant slave women in Jamaica; cane hole digging, although rarely done by women, was believed to cause infertility (Sheridan 1985, pp. 150, 242).

In fact, Trinidad's population fell by 2.75 percent when productivity reached 11.80 hundredweight per slave (Mathieson 1926, p. 105). Slaves from the Rolle plantation in the Bahamas had fewer children when sold to a Trinidad plantation where they were forced to work much harder (Craton 1979, p. 23). In many parts of the British West Indies domestics bore more children than did female field slaves (Dirks 1978, p. 149). In the United States similar relationships are found. For example, slave fertility in South Carolina fell with increased rice production and productivity (Wood 1974, p. 164). Fogel and Engerman (1979, p. 575) found that, in general, U.S. slave childlessness increased with plantation size and presumably with productivity.

These cases of decline in fertility in association with women's apparent work increases can be explained by reference to declining material incentives for fertility and increased infant mortality. The hypothesized relationship between work and rising female incapacity for conception and birth is, however, sufficiently common in early commentary to warrant further consideration. It *is* likely that women's work in the field impeded menstruation and ovulation (Dirks 1978, p. 149), as strenuous exercise often does (Keller et al. 1984, p. 50). Amenorrhea is uncommon, found historically among concentration camp victims and others suffering from starvation and more generally among athletes (especially runners), all of whom resumed menstruation when adequate food had been consumed or vigorous training ended (Kleinman 1980, p. 138; Bongaarts and Potter 1983, p. 16).[8] But combined with weight loss from malnutrition, intensive field labor probably reduced body fat to perilously low levels among Caribbean bondwomen, causing amenorrhea and anovulation. This was likely a temporary condition, developing with the harvest and subsiding later, as strenuous work ended and daily diets improved. This hypothesized pattern is consistent with the increased number of slave illnesses immediately after the start of the harvest, dropping and then rising again later (Higman 1984, p. 300).

Finally, infections in female reproductive organs can reduce fertility. Many types of bacteria and viruses cause vaginal, tubal, and other infections. They can be introduced by abortions and intrauterine devices or spread from the intestines, bladder, and kidneys (Keller et al. 1984, p. 182). Deficiencies in vitamin A and other nutrients can also foster pelvic disease. The impact of infections on infertility is, like most other physical causes of natural decrease among Caribbean slaves, incalculable because reproductive diseases were poorly documented by Europeans and the influence of poor health on fertility was mediated by environmental and social circumstances.

Sexual Opportunities

Caribbean planters eventually wanted slaves to reproduce, reversing their earlier attitude of disapproval of pregnancy and children. By the late eighteenth century slave owners and colonial governments tried various means to increase fertility, including promoting lasting slave conjugal unions (Roberts 1977, p. 159; Carmichael 1834, vol. 2, p. 19). It had long been believed that marriage encouraged fertility, increasing opportunities for intercourse and incentives to have children. For women in particular the continuing presence of a male partner lessened the material risks of childbearing and allowed children to be a vehicle for kin creation and consolidation.

The relative absence of lasting slave unions, especially in comparison to slaves in the U.S. South, contributed to low fertility. Indeed, demographers measure subfecundity by the number of noncontracepting, *continuously married* women. The individual's inability to reproduce or tendency to control fertility assumes maximum opportunity to conceive children (McFalls and McFalls 1984, p. 10).[9] Access to sexual opportunities were few for many Caribbean slaves (Dirks 1987, pp. 118-120, 201).

Sexual opportunity should be distinguished from marital frequency as a structural precondition for fertility but is not entirely independent of a group's tendency to marry or establish kinship networks. The strong economic position of some slave women as producers of food and other goods made children an economic asset. But the sale of male slaves and their illnesses and injuries shrank the pool of potential partners to young, strong males, many of whom were already committed to other women and families. Moreover, the slave regimen, especially the long workdays and the separation of males and females into barracks housing, further reduced the chances for sexual union and contributed to subfecundity.[10]

Amelioration

From the late eighteenth to the early nineteenth century colonial governments and slave owners improved slaves' conditions, especially those associated with pregnancy, childbirth, and early infant life. These changed attitudes and policies were meant to preserve slaves' lives, including infants' and childrens', to maintain pregnancies and to provide incentives to bear and successfully rear more children.

In the seventeenth and eighteenth centuries work demands on slave women varied in the Caribbean. Richard Ligon reported, for example, that in Barbados new mothers usually had only two weeks relief from work. "If the overseer be discreet, shee is suffer'd to rest her selfe a little more than ordinary; but if not, shee is compelled to doe as others doe" (Ligon 1657, p. 48). Jamaican slave women worked in the fields until the last six weeks of their pregnancies, according to Lady Nugent (1907, p. 94), and returned two weeks after birth, three in unusual circumstances. In Bermuda a slave mother could "lay in" for six weeks (Packwood 1975, p. 98). Bryan Edwards (1966, vol. 3, p. 253) visited an estate where a women who reared children received five yards of cotton. Jamaican estate bookkeeper J. B. Moreton (1793, p. 152) wrote that the pregnant woman worked in the fields until a few days before birth. The overseer then sent her salt beef, some flour, rum, and sugar. A few days later she and her infant returned to the fields. The baby was laid on a sheep skin in a clearing and watched over by an "invalid woman."

French West Indian slave mothers with five or six children were exempted from field labor; nursing mothers were generally able to avoid heavy tasks (Debien 1974, p. 355; Raynal 1981, p. 181). Tomich (1976, p. 188) reports a more generous planter attitude toward pregnant and new mothers in Martinique. Women were moved to the *petit atelier,* or second gang, on reporting their pregnancies to the overseer. After 7 months they stopped work, returning to the second gang 40 days after birth, and the *grand atelier,* or first gang, after 75 days. New mothers worked half-days until the child was 15 or 16 months old. Similar patterns were observed in St. Croix (Lewisohn 1970, p. 240). In St. John after 1843 pregnant women were relieved from the heaviest physical labor, spared harsh punishment, and allowed to recover for five to six weeks after birth. New mothers were permitted a break at 11:00 A.M. to nurse their babies and could stop work at 5:00 P.M. for a year following birth (Olwig 1985, p. 32). In Cuba, however, women were hurried back to work, unable to nurse their children or provide adequate care. Ortiz (1975, pp. 284, 287) reports that a contemporary commentator found newborns cold and uncovered and lying in their own excrement.

By the 1820s conditions had changed in the British West Indies. Women were permitted to cease work three months before giving birth and did not have to return for two months after (Barclay 1828, p. 308). Higman (1976a, pp. 206–207) suggests that planters exempted women from regular fieldwork with their first missed menstrual period. New mothers remained in the second field gang as long as they nursed their infants, even if the child was 2 years old. In Jamaica overseers were rewarded £3 for each birth, and a tax exemption was offered to slave owners whose bondwomen reproduced (Roberts 1957, pp. 235–236). A women with six living children was exempt from work in Jamaica according to a 1792 law (Higman 1984, p. 350). In Trinidad, Mrs. Carmichael's planter husband offered two "joes" (each equal to 1 pound, 25 shillings, 6 pence) to mothers with healthy babies of at least 2 years of age, although only three or four slaves received this award, as others "preferred work, and the nurse to take care of their babies" (Carmichael 1834, vol. 2, pp. 187, 200). At Codrington estate in Barbados mothers received prizes at their children's births; the attorney for the Newton estate reported that mothers with children surviving to 1 month were given 6 shillings, 3 pence (Higman 1984, p. 349; Bennett 1958).[11] Child care also improved on British West Indian estates. Slave masters built nurseries with sleeping platforms and yards for play (Barclay 1828, p. 312). Mothers of a prescribed number of children born in wedlock were freed in 1826 by the Slave Laws of Barbados (Riland 1828). Incentives were occasionally offered for marriage. A 1798 British Leewards law mandated cash payments to couples who had lived together for a long time (Higman 1984, p. 351). Couples also received assistance in house building (Higman 1984, p. 355).

Cuban planters moved children into nurseries (*criollas*) under the care of elderly women slaves. Overseers became better educated about birth and early infancy in the 1860s and 1870s. Women waited 45 days after giving birth to return to the field, and their workdays were shorter (Knight 1970, pp. 75–76; Ortiz 1975). Mothers and overseers were rewarded for the survival of babies to 2 years of age (Ortiz 1975, pp. 56–57).

Yet the results of amelioration programs were disappointing throughout the region, in part because their application was haphazard (Gautier 1985, p. 129).[12] Most areas mirrored French West Indian patterns with only an *"insensible"* change in birth rate with amelioration (Debien 1974, p. 356; see also Higman 1984, p. 355). Dutch Surinam, for example, began its pro-natalist policies before the slave trade ended but with poor results. As in Jamaica and Cuba, creolization and improving age and gender ratios can account for recorded fertility changes in Surinam (Lamur 1977, pp. 164, 166–167; see Tables 3.1, 7.2, 8.1, and 8.2). On some estates, such as Jamaica's Worthy Park, the fertility rate fell during the amelioration period (Craton 1978, p. 331). Trinidad, at the height of sugar production and productivity in the early nineteenth century, experienced a similar decline (Higman 1984, p. 355). Only in Barbados did population increase occur independent of demographic preconditions and as an apparent result of amelioration.

What do these generally negative results of amelioration programs suggest about the causes of low fertility among Caribbean slaves? Amelioration programs assume that slave women voluntarily controlled their fertility and that slave women suffered from overwork during and immediately after

Table 8.1. Population and Population Decrease of Slaves in Catharina Sophia

Year ending December 31	Population (in 1,000s)	Birth Rate per 1,000	Death Rate per 1,000	Natural Decrease
1833 (May)	286			
1839	239			
1841	347			
1845 (Nov.)	281			
1846	263			
1847	264			
1848	258			
1849	251			
1850	498			
1851	548			
1852	534	25.8	42.5	16.7
1853 (Sept.)	531	20.6	33.8	13.2
1854	516	28.6	53.4	24.8
1855 (Sept.)	511	23.3	35.0	11.7
1856	485	24.0	30.1	6.1
1857	465	25.2	50.5	25.3
1858	460	32.4	34.5	2.1
1859	444	24.3	55.3	31.0
1860	434	34.1	56.9	22.8
1861	429	30.1	41.7	11.6

Source: Lamur 1977, p. 166.

pregnancy. Let us consider these assumptions in turn. First, did amelioration programs give women reasons to have children? Higman (1984, p. 355) contends that incentives were too few, and time, more valuable to slaves than cash, was not directed to the satisfaction of planter and colonial government goals of population reproduction and infant survival. Many slave women used newly extended confinement periods to tend their grounds or engage in other money-making ventures (Debien 1974, p. 356; Sturge and Harvey 1838, p. 64). Higman argues further that, by flaunting their own economic interests and placing them before the needs of slave masters, women revealed little interest in their children, whose survival chances were at best slim.

Pregnant women's use of extra time to their own economic advantage may be more myth than fact, promulgated by planters to explain low birth rates. The self-serving perspective of Europeans is repeated by abolitionists Sturge and Harvey (1838, p. 64):

During slavery the people declined in numbers; especially on the estates near town. This was partly, we are told, to be attributed to the fact, that women, in an advanced state of pregnancy, after discontinuing estate labor, would employ themselves in bringing heavy loads of sticks and

Table 8.2. General Fertility and Related Factors among Slaves in Catharina Sophia

Year	General Fertility Rate	Women Aged 15–44 as % of Female Population[a]	Women Aged 20–29 as % of Females Aged 15–44[b]	General Fertility Rate		Gross Reproduction Rate	Sex Ratio	
				Nonstandard	Standard		Total Population	Fertility Group
1852	96.6	42.9					92.7	99.1
1853	85.8	41.4					93.0	99.1
1854	118.6	45.5	27.1	100.0		1.4	92.5	86.0
1855	90.1	46.7					95.7	90.1
1856	93.6	44.8					92.4	82.3
1857	108.5	44.4					91.3	77.7
1858	117.1	47.8					93.2	77.1
1859	89.6	46.5	33.0	107.0	98.4	1.3	89.7	83.4
1860	121.4	46.0					90.3	84.7
1861	94.7	47.7					93.2	83.9

Source: Lamur 1977, p. 167.

a The absolute number of women aged 15–44 was about 115 annually.

b For the whole period 1852–1856 the number of women aged 15–44 was approximately 160; for 1857–1861 the figure was 179.

grass to market, for their own benefit. On certain estates . . . the slaves declined in numbers from twelve hundred to eight hundred; dating from the abolition of the slave trade. In such cases, it was often impossible to contract the cultivation proportionately . . . so that the diminished number was compelled to perform an increased amount of labor, and thus the destructive ratio of decrease was accelerated.

If true, it can be argued that petty agricultural production and trade were more compatible with late pregnancy than field labor, and they were not usually detrimental to the health of women or the children they carried. This judgment can be made based on both historical example and the degree of self-pacing and autonomy intrinsic to horticulture and petty trade. More to the point, high rates of infant and child death are a constant for most preindustrial peoples, and women work in food and subsistence provision through pregnancy to compensate economically for anticipated familial deaths. They also often generate high fertility to counteract the loss of economically productive children. The incentive to produce children as valued laborers must be qualified, of course, for settings such as the Caribbean in the era of slavery, where neither extended kin nor enduring nuclear families were available to help bear the costs of pregnancy or childbearing or to contribute to income accumulation. But there is also little reason to assume that the use of free time by slave women to tend gardens or engage in related activities indicated a lack of material interest in or emotional commitment to their children.

Finally, the impact of amelioration on voluntary fertility cannot be fully assessed so long as subfecundity remains a probable cause of infertility. The likelihood that disease, malnutrition, and overwork kept women from bearing children means that the degree of fertility control is unknown. And what impact did amelioration have on subfecundity? Very little that I can discern, except perhaps in circumstances such as those in Barbados, where production and productivity had ebbed sufficiently to lessen physical stress and its likely manifestation in disease. Future research like Kiple's (1984) and Sheridan's (1985) on the physical conditions and diseases of Caribbean slaves will answer this question more satisfactorily, especially if biological and environmental determinants of subfecundity receive fuller attention.

COMPARING SOCIAL STRUCTURE AND FERTILITY

A comparative analysis of Caribbean slave societies can show more clearly how ameliorative efforts were hamstrung by concurrent planter programs to increase productivity, resulting in subfecundity and fertility control among slaves. There appears to be an association between styles and stages of Caribbean production and fertility. This relationship is independent of family form but corresponds to access of a woman and her family to income.

Higman's work (1976b, 1984) suggests a historical sequence for the analysis. He divides British West Indian slave societies into three stages, similar to those offered by Mintz. Stage 1 sugar producers achieved their highest levels of sugar production in the seventeenth and early eighteenth centuries. They are exemplified in the following discussion by Barbados, the Bahamas, and the Leeward Islands. Stage 2 areas peaked later as sugar producers. They include Jamaica, Martinique, and Saint Domingue. Extensive sugar production began in the stage 3 producers in the early nineteenth century, a pattern found in Trinidad, Cuba, Puerto Rico, and Surinam.

Higman separates the sugar-producing islands from the non-sugar-producing islands to determine population dynamics, that is, fertility and mortality rates. This simple equation yields the expected results, with sugar producers manifesting low birth and high death rates. It masks, however, the complexity of the relationship and the many variables that contribute to population change. Several factors that are obscured in schemas of stages of sugar production are relevant to demographic trends.

1. Labor productivity indicates whether men and women could benefit from children's labor and whether subfecundity—occasioned by malnutrition, overwork, and disease—was a factor in low fertility.

2. Women's agricultural labor force participation, specifically the proportion of women engaged in field labor, influenced women's material incentives to bear children and their physical capacity to do so.

3. Slaves' access to provision gardens and other means of acquiring cash reveals whether children would be well employed as laborers and aids to their families.

4. An increase in the number of conjugal units among slaves generally raised fertility. Two subfactors are pertinent to family organization and its effect on fertility: sexual opportunity and the incentive for women to have children in order to construct kinship networks and thus increase their material security.

5. Demographic characteristics, including the proportions of women, Creole, and youthful slaves, constricted and created opportunities for population change.

Only those cases with ample information about productivity and work patterns and birth and death rates are considered. None is entirely representative of the era, but all are sufficiently typical to allow comparison with other cases from the same general stage.

Stage 1 Sugar Producers: The Bahamas, the Leewards, and Barbados

Bahamian slaves produced cotton on a large scale, but "conditions did not exist which led . . . to the development of a fully fashioned slave society of the plantation type" (Lewis 1968, p. 309). Slightly more than half of the 10,000 Bahamian slaves registered from 1821 to 1822 lived in "simple nuclear families" (Craton 1979, p. 6). Planters were "Eurocentric, pro-natalist, or publicity-conscious" and encouraged the formation of nuclear families, even on large estates, where infrequent movement and sale of slaves fostered family stability. Gender ratios were even by the 1825–1828 period (see Table 3.1). The birth rate climbed to 31.0 births per 1,000 by the 1825–1828 period, with a natural increase of 16.1 per 1,000.

In 1791 Bahamian cotton production fell and profits dropped. Low labor productivity and work intensity is apparent from the health of older males, not yet outnumbered by female slaves, as in most declining West Indian commodity-producing societies. "Aging and wasting" of females and related drops in fertility did not occur. There is no evidence that women were absent from field labor, only that men and women appear to have enjoyed comparative physical well-being, a prerequisite for population fecundity.

In contrast, the British Leewards experienced few increases in births or high levels of natural increase. The highest recorded rate of natural increase was in Montserrat, where 6.0 people per 1,000 were added from 1824 to 1827 (see Table 3.1). What distinguishes the Leewards from the Bahamas, and what can account for these population trends? Both areas settled and began export production in the 1600s, but the Leewards became major sugar producers, with the smaller Antigua surpassing Barbados in sugar production in the mid-eighteenth century (Sheridan 1973, p. 150).[13] By the end of the eighteenth century sugar production in the Leewards had peaked. Yet birth rates remained lower than those in neighboring Barbados, with its generally greater level of sugar production. Gender ratios were more nearly equal in St. Kitts and Nevis, presumably contributing to births.[14]

Fewer nuclear families formed in the Leewards than in the Bahamas. The Leewards resemble Barbados in this regard, however, and births in Barbados were more numerous. Two factors appear to separate the experiences of Leewards slaves from those in Barbados and point to both the lack of economic incentives for childbearing and to subfecundity in explaining low fertility. First, the Leewards slaves had little or no land for the growing of provisions and depended on food imports and collectively grown food. Slaves barely survived periods of drought and poor production (Mathieson 1926, p. 772; Fergus, 1975, p. 15; Frucht 1977, p. 3). Slaves on Barbados were similarly dependent on plantation- and foreign-grown foods, but repeated droughts and the boycott of Barbados by U.S. food producers during the American Revolution led to greater local food production (Dickson 1789, p. 13). Indeed by 1815 some proprietors were devoting two-thirds of estate land to the cultivation of provisions (Levy 1980, p. 9). A similar if less extensive transition was eventually made in Montserrat. With perhaps the best developed cash economy in the Leewards, 27 percent of Montserrat's slaves were domestic servants, tradesmen, or fishermen (Goveia 1965, p. 146), but these activities could not reverse the effect of the poorly developed system of food growing on fertility.[15]

Two factors, then, stand out among stage 1 producers and may help to explain population change. First, cultivation of food, even carried out collectively, generated opportunities for trade and incentives for privatized production on small plots of land. These activities reinforced and extended other income-generating efforts in trade and crafts. If sufficiently extensive, such economic opportunities created motives for the formation of nuclear families; but single women could also benefit economically, especially by having children. Women apparently had children in Barbados through the amelioration period but failed to do so in the Leewards, where entrepreneurial opportunities were few. It is likely that continuing food shortages also contributed to subfecundity in the Leewards. Amelioration was powerless there against long-term impediments to population reproduction.

Stage 2: Martinique, Jamaica, and Saint Domingue

The French islands of Martinique and Saint Domingue are hilly, humid lands with great potential for indigenous cultivation of food crops. Saint Domingue's food production, on individual plots and estates, ebbed and flowed with the intensity of sugar production. Martinique and French Guadeloupe had more consistent and continuous histories of local food production.

Low fertility in Saint Domingue is easily explained by the continually high proportion of males and Africans (Debien 1962). Estimates of the ratio of males to females in eighteenth-century Saint Domingue range from virtually no women to a gender ratio approaching equality, with 1.39 males for every female in 1754.[16] Many other factors contributed to natural decreases, in particular the intense working conditions of Saint Domingue's slaves, manifested in unparalleled labor productivity (and assisted by rich soils). Moreau de Saint-Méry (1958) estimated in the late 1700s that only 200 slaves (100 effective workers) were required to produce 150 tons of sugar. As a result, from 1680 to 1776, 800,000 slaves were imported to Saint Domingue and 290,000 survived. From 1763 to 1776 the population increased by 85,000, with deaths exceeding births by 50,000 (Hilliard d'Auberteuil 1776, vol. 2, p. 63).[17]

Creolization and feminization of the population were forestalled by continued planter commitment to replacement of slaves by purchase. Economic decline and the abolition of the slave trade might have brought demographic changes and related if slight population increases, as in Jamaica and

Martinique. But the Revolution of 1791 came first, bringing marked improvements in fertility along with mortality declines.

French settlers occupied Martinique in 1653 and quickly established plantation agriculture. On the eve of the French Revolution, Martinique exported more than 8,000 tons of sugar annually, surpassing Barbados. The abolition of the slave trade along with European wars and changes in French domestic and colonial governments brought a decline in the fortunes of sugar producers that never fully reversed itself (Deerr 1949–1950, p. 233; Schnakenbourg 1980).

Jamaica, the Caribbean's second great nineteenth-century sugar island, surpassed Martinique and other competitors except Saint Domingue. In 1780, 200,000 slaves produced 500 pounds of sugar each. By 1808, 300,000 slaves produced more than 650 pounds of sugar per capita annually. Production per slave remained roughly the same from 1800 to 1834 (Higman 1976a, p. 213). In 1753, at the height of Martinique's sugar production, 80,000 slaves there produced 20,544 tons of sugar, about 500 pounds per capita (Deerr 1949–1950, p. 233).

The traditional extent of provision growing, hiring out, and petty trade contributed to a large proportion of conjugal families among slaves in Martinique and Jamaica. The rate of natural decrease fell in Martinique. Curtin estimates that from 1664 to 1735 5.4 individuals were lost per 1,000, improving to a loss of 4.2 per 1,000 from 1736 to 1787 and 1.3 from 1788 to 1831 (see Table 7.2). Gautier (1985, p. 123, 136) concludes that Martinique's slaves generally sustained an annual natural loss higher than 0.15 in the late eighteenth century, improving to a slight population increase by the 1840s. The natural decrease in Jamaica worsened continuously from the start of the registration period of 1817–1820 through 1829–1832 (see Table 3.1).

Selected estates in Martinique and Jamaica exhibited high rates of conjugal family formation. By reviewing Debien's (1960) survey of documents from l'Anse-à-l'Ane in Martinique, we find a predominance of conjugal units among Creole slaves, although in other groups maternal units generally prevailed.[18] Analysis of records from three plantations suggests that conjugal units became important at some locations in Jamaica (Higman 1976a). At l'Anse-à-l'Ane fertility was higher in conjugal than in other families, but we see little evidence of the same phenomenon in the Jamaican cases (Higman 1976a, p. 175). Nor does access to provision gardening, extensive in both settings, explain fertility differences. Amelioration efforts had increased in both Martinique and Jamaica, of course, but to little apparent effect.

A single factor emerges as significant: Jamaica's sugar productivity remained high during the early nineteenth century, and women's participation in plantation labor actually intensified (Higman 1976; Craton 1977). Either women's incentives to profit from income-generating activities by increased fertility were reduced or their fecundity waned. Registration figures from the amelioration period in Jamaica reveal that the death rate increased. We can reasonably infer that women's health suffered and that the physical limits on fertility did not abate and may have increased.

Stage 3: Cuba, Puerto Rico, Trinidad, and Surinam

Cuban sugar production exceeded that of other Caribbean producers by 1838, the small-scale cultivation of the eighteenth century having given way to greater unit size and productivity. By the early 1800s four-fifths of Cuban slaves were on plantations and rural farms (Knight 1970, p. 48). Age and sex distributions changed, with young males predominating over females and other age groups. By 1822, 55 percent of slaves were from 20 to 45 years of age (Moreno Fraginals 1978, p. 86).

The birth rate increased from about 19 per 1,000 from 1834 to 1841 to 28 per 1,000 from 1856 to 1860 (Moreno Fraginals 1978, p. 88; 1977, pp. 193–195). From 1823 to 1844 children 5 years of age and younger commonly constituted up to 8.19 percent of an estate's population. The influx of women slaves accounts in large part for fertility increases. From 1790 to 1822 women aged 15 to 40 years made up nearly 16 percent of the slave population, and children aged 15 and under only 2.9 percent. Finally, by the 1845–1868 period children made up 29 percent of the population and women of 15 to 40 years of age, 22 percent, suggesting rising fertility during the nineteenth century. But if from 1845 to 1868, as a result of the growing purchase of young slaves, the ratio of imported to locally born children approached that of slaves gen-erally—53 Africans for every 47 Creoles—fertility remained low, with perhaps only half of women aged 18 to 40 years bearing a surviving child (Moreno Fraginals 1977, p. 192). Still, this projected fertility rate surpassed that of earlier eras, implying that in Cuba amelioration had a slightly positive impact on reproduction.

The productivity of Cuban slave women was unprecedented in the history of Caribbean sugar planting, although per capita productivity dropped with the gender ratio (Moreno Fraginals 1977). Women worked with men in nearly all areas of sugar production and labored the extended harvest days, longer and more arduous than elsewhere in the region. Major technological refine-ments contributed to a dramatic production increase and to increased labor demands in planting and cane harvesting. Mid-nineteenth century "eco-nomic pressures forced proprietors to work slaves harder and this, too, accentuated the depletion of the labor force" (Corwin 1967, p. 135). Cuban slaves numbered at most about 400,000, comparable to Jamaica's peak figure of 350,000 slaves. Yet Cuban sugar production, at the mid-nineteenth-century height of more than 200,000 tons, far surpassed Jamaica's highest annual production of over 90,000 tons (Aimes 1967, p. 158; Moreno Fraginals 1978, p. 106).

As remarkable as Cuban slave women's rising workloads was their rapid loss of control over income-generating activities, in particular, provision growing and hiring out. Subsistence cultivation on *conucos* ended in many plantation areas during the sugar boom (Knight 1970, p. 68; Scott 1985, pp. 15–19). Hiring-out opportunities also diminished. These restrictions are reflected in the decline of the free colored population, dropping from nearly 20 percent of the total Cuban population at the end of the eighteenth century to 15 percent in the 1820s and 1840s (Knight 1970, p. 21).

Trinidad's experience closely resembles that of Cuba. Britain seized Trinidad from Spain in 1797. In 1782 there were only 310 slaves in Trinidad; 4,500 slaves were imported annually from 1797 to 1803 (Millette 1970, pp. 7, 17). Slaves numbered 18,302 by 1809 (Brereton 1981, p. 47). Sugar production increased from nearly 6 million pounds in 1798 to over 14 million pounds in 1802; the number of estates rose from 159 in 1796 to 739 in 1809 (Millette 1970, pp. 19, 122; Brereton 1981, p. 47).

Alone among British West Indian colonies, Trinidad failed to generate rising fertility during the registration period after 1813, although the birth rate increased modestly from 1813 to 1825 (see Table 8.3). Its slave population was heavily African, male, and young, all characteristics contributing to low fertility and birth rates in the region. Although mother-child units predominated in towns, nuclear families were commonly associated with plantations of more than 50 slaves with relatively large African populations. The low birth rate on Trinidad's sugar estates does not, then, reflect women's isolation from kin but other factors.

Work requirements and related diseases and malnutrition may have discouraged higher fertility levels. Few provisions were grown in Trinidad; foodstuffs were imported from Venezuela, the United States, and the British North American colonies. The interruption of Venezuelan shipments by

Table 8.3. Basic Demographic Indicators for Trinidad, 1813–1834

Dates	Males per 100 Females	(Adjusted) Births per 1,000	(Adjusted) Deaths per 1,000			Registered Natural Increase per 1,000
			Male	Female	Total	
1813–16	123.1	44.1	47.2	40.9	44.4	−6.6
1816–19	125.2	31.8	46.3	55.3	50.3	−18.5
1819–22	126.5	35.1	44.3	47.4	45.7	−13.0
1822–25	124.0	37.9	35.8	28.9	32.7	−1.7
1825–28	117.2	33.7	37.0	30.8	34.1	−5.2
1828–31	110.0	34.0	37.4	31.5	34.6	−5.4
1831–34	104.4	31.0	39.4	35.2	37.4	−9.4

Source: Higman 1984, p. 310.

British and Spanish ships led to frequent food shortages for Trinidad's slaves, which probably reduced fertility. The apparent low fertility of urban slaves can also be linked to food shortages. Mrs. Carmichael (1834, vol. 2, p. 103) complained that domestics, lacking access to provision grounds, stole food.[19] Higman's (1984, p. 329) discovery that urban slaves, particularly women and children, had higher mortality levels than rural slaves in the newer colonies, including Trinidad, reflects the urban slaves' lack of provision grounds.

Dutch Surinam differed from Cuba, Trinidad, and Puerto Rico in the continuing intensity and scope of sugar production from the late seventeenth century to the early nineteenth century. From 1715 to 1735 the slave population increased from perhaps 3,000 to 50,000, where it remained until the early 1800s; yet 300,000 to 325,000 Africans were imported from 1668 to 1823, indicating a greater rate of loss than Jamaica or Saint Domingue experienced (Price 1976, p. 9). And the slave population remained skewed in favor of young African males longer than in most Caribbean slave societies: "Until 1735, more than 70 percent of the total imports to Surinam were male, and children constituted under 7 percent even after the planters began more seriously to encourage breeding as a replacement strategy in the period after 1735, the proportion of female imports did not rise above 40 percent, nor that of children above 22 percent" (Price 1976, p. 12). Slaves generally worked on large plantations, even where cash crops other than sugar were grown. The average eighteenth-century sugar estate had about 228 slaves, with even smaller estates averaging 137 bondmen and women (Price 1976, p. 16). The treatment of slaves was reputedly harsh and manumissions rare, with freed men and women constituting only 7 percent of the nonwhite population as late as 1787 (Price 1976, p. 22).

Lamur estimates the rate of natural decrease before 1814 at 40.0 per 1,000. This figure declined steadily, however, to between 25.0 and 30.0 per 1,000 from 1814 to 1826, to 12.5 per 1,000 from 1826 to 1848, and finally to about 3.1 per 1,000 from 1848 to 1862 (Lamur 1977, p. 163). Demographic factors clearly favored an improving rate of natural decrease. The gender ratio changed rapidly in the nineteenth century, with males outnumbering females in 1830 (105.8 males for every 100 females) but with females outnumbering males by 1850, when the gender ratio was 90.8 males for every 100 females. The female population continued to grow faster than the male population, apparently because of higher male mortality rates.

Slaveholders and colonial officials adopted ameliorative measures early in the 1800s. Lamur's analysis of the model 500-slave, government-controlled Catharina Sophia estates may be revealing about the effects of amelioration on population change. The rates of natural decrease at Catharina Sophia were 14.5 per 1,000 for the 1851–1861 period and 18.5 per 1,000 for 1857–1861, despite an increase in fertility from 100.0 births per 1,000 women in

1852–1856 to 107.0 in 1857–1861 (Lamur 1977, p. 165). These changes came in part because of a modified adult female age distribution.[20] The gender ratio changed especially quickly in fertile age groups, suggesting the significance of an increased number of women on births. Lamur (1977, pp. 166–167) cautions, however, that "the average number of live births per fertile woman . . . remained virtually constant . . . at an estimated level of far less than 3.0 children." Mortality rose on Catharina Sophia in the 1850s, although less dramatically than if the age structure had remained unchanged. Life expectancy for slaves born between 1852 and 1861 was only 23.0 years. "Of the 10,000 newborn persons in the life table [covering all age cohorts and estimated life expectancies from 1852 to 1861] only half reached the 15–24 age groups" (Lamur 1977, p. 170).

Lamur concludes (1977, p. 171) that slave women in Surinam wished to have few children, presumably using contraception and abortion as means to limit population. The constantly high death rate implies that women's health may have inhibited fertility as well. Lamur points to the possible influences on fertility of nutrition, noting that in 1840 the colonial government mandated more food for slaves. This action was consistent with amelioration measures throughout the region, however, and does not in itself indicate relative hunger or subnutrition in Surinam. The death rate at Catharina Sophia increased markedly in 1859 and 1860, perhaps as a result of epidemic diseases (Lamur 1977, pp. 166–167). The birth rate also fell dramatically in 1859, implying that the factors that influenced deaths also affected births. Time inconsistencies are displayed, however, with deaths increasing in the same year that births fell but continuing to rise for another year, while births again increased the next year to earlier levels. Disease thus seems an unlikely explanation for population shifts. An alternative hypothesis is that a particularly brutal harvest diminished female fecundity by reducing opportunities for intercourse. Similar isolated events may have increased deaths, particularly of Catharina Sophia's older male slaves, who probably contributed little to fertility.

Puerto Rico's situation as a stage 3 producer contrasts with that of other cases. As with Trinidad and Cuba, Puerto Rico was not initially a large-scale eighteenth-century sugar producer. A sugar boom then occurred. From 1828 to 1852 the expansion in production of sugar and sugar products was dramatic, with sugar exports growing from 14,595 tons to 52,622 tons and molasses exports increasing from 5,869 hogsheads to 39,407. Meanwhile, coffee production fell from 6,259 tons in 1828–1832 to 5,350 tons in 1845–1852 (see Table 8.4).[21]

Research has generally concluded that Puerto Rico's labor and land productivity was much less than that of Cuba and other stage 3 islands. Scarano has argued recently, however, that, although slaves never constituted more than 12 percent of the Puerto Rican population, they were the main

Table 8.4. Puerto Rican Sugar, Molasses, and Coffee Exports, 1828–52 (five-year annual averages)

Years	Sugar (Tons)[a]	Molasses (Hogsheads)	Coffee (Tons)
1828–32	14,595	5,869	6,259
1833–37	20,757	13,308	4,890
1838–42	39,664	28,608	5,234
1843–47	43,702	30,941	5,059
1848–52	52,622	39,407	5,350

Source: Scarano 1984, p. 8.
[a]   Moscovado (unrefined or raw sugar).

sugar workers in the principal sugar areas (Scarano 1984, p. xxii). Moreover, "on a comparable scale [Puerto Rican estates] were at least as efficient as the Cuban plantations." Puerto Rico produced 23 percent as much sugar as Cuba in 1838–1842, and 16 percent as much in 1848–1852, with far fewer slaves, on much smaller estates (Scarano 1984, p. 6; see also Klein 1986, p. 105).

Flinter's journal of his sojourn to Puerto Rico introduced the idea that the slave population was small and quickly replaced by free labor. He also described the stable family life of Puerto Rican slaves and their tendency to reproduce themselves. In contrast, French abolitionist Victor Schoelcher believed that Puerto Rican slaves were exceptionally productive and owners very cruel. He argued that Puerto Rico's 4,000 slaves produced two-thirds as much sugar as Martinique's 78,000 slaves, although no comparison of soil fertility or technique was offered (cited in Scarano 1984, p. 29).

Still, reproduction rates were high, even with many male Africans. "The Ponce fertility level was about 15 percent greater than the average for the Jamaican parishes [nine analyzed by Higman (1976a)], despite the fact that the proportion of Africans in the Puerto Rican district was higher, and despite an enormous difference in the sex ratio, which was almost 175 males:100 females in Ponce, but only 98:100 in the Jamaican sample" (Scarano 1984, p. 142). Slaves in the U.S. South, the sugar-producing region, had no access to provision grounds, and food crops were seldom grown collectively, given planters' wish to devote all available land to sugar (Flinter 1834, p. 193). The relatively high birth rate may then be a function of plantation size, with related better slave health and fertility. In contrast, Trinidad, also a stage 3 sugar producer with small estates, exhibited low fertility. But other, related factors may help to explain the differences between Trinidad's and Puerto Rico's demographic experiences: The sugar revolution in Puerto Rico was both less extensive and shorter in duration than that of Trinidad and other stage 3 producers, although it is also clear that earlier commentary underestimated the scope and intensity of Puerto Rico's production of commodities for export.

AFTER THE REVOLUTION

What can we conclude from the comparative analysis of fertility and birth rates in Caribbean slave societies? First, the stage of participation in the international sugar market is strongly associated with birth rates and fertility. The utility of children for household income earning appears to be significant as well, along with widespread and effective slave amelioration, seen only in Barbados. In order for children and amelioration to influence fertility, the population must display fecundity, determined by demographic characteristics, in particular suitable age and gender ratios, and physical health and capacity for reproduction.

What emerges most meaningfully from this comparative review, however, is a continuing pattern of population loss or stagnation despite amelioration. Two notable exceptions emerge. In the Bahamas conditions were optimal for increased fertility and rapidly diminishing deaths. In stage 1 societies, with a preponderance of young Creole women, "entrepreneurial encouragement, and virtual self-sufficiency" (Lowenthal and Clarke 1977, p. 516), births were comparable to U.S. slave levels, yet conditions were less favorable to natural increase in the United States at its productive heights. Likewise for Barbados: Demographic conditions, decreased productivity, and amelioration contributed to increased fertility and decreasing mortality. Still, these conditions led to lower levels of natural increase (0.4 percent annually from 1816 to 1834) than among slaves in the U.S. South (3 percent in the early nineteenth century), where working conditions were generally worse (Roberts 1977, pp. 149, 158).

Even under relatively good circumstances, birth rates in Caribbean slave societies were low, suggesting that fertility was somehow impaired. Two additional cases support this inference. Barbuda is a Caribbean island where the production of commodities for export failed. Several hundred slaves remained.

> Barbudian slaves enjoyed an abundance of provisions from their large garden plots, from hunting game in the forests, and from fishing. Moreover, they lived virtually on their own, little supervised by the solitary (and often absent) Codrington manager and one or two overseers. Independent and largely self- sufficient, the Barbudian community was all the more close-knit owing to its demographic isolation: no Africans were brought into the island after the mid-eighteenth century, and the Creole inhabitants became essentially one community. (Lowenthal and Clarke 1977, p. 515)

An astonishing natural increase occurred. From 1817 to 1832 the birth rate varied from 26 to 43 per 1,000, with the remarkable death rate of only 10 per 1,000 (Lowenthal and Clarke 1977, p. 518).[22] Visitors noted the relatively robust appearance of Barbudian slaves.

How significant were children to slave economies? Availability of work on the Codrington estates and a plentitude of food and game suggest little economic incentive to have offspring. Plentiful resources inhibited the development of a highly stratified slave society, reducing the potential value of childbirth as a means to compete for scarce goods. Rather it appears that a demographically and physically healthy African population in the Caribbean was capable of rapid reproduction, even in the absence of economic need.[23]

Population trends after emancipation seem to reinforce the significance of slaves' health as a variable in explaining population change. Debien (1974, p. 360) contends that the greatest sources of subfecundity among French West Indian slave women were malnutrition and overwork (see also Deerr 1949-1950, p. 277). The ultimate proof of this proposition, he argues, was the enormous increase in birth rates among slaves after their revolutionary emancipation in 1803, when sugar production declined and slaves retreated to small-scale production of food crops (Deerr 1949-1950, p. 240). Former estate owners were shocked to find their once childless slaves the parents of many children. At la sucrerie Foache à Jean-Rabel, for example, the number of children remained nearly constant from 1779 to 1797, although it had dropped during earlier years when the estate failed to renew its youthful slave population through purchase (Debien 1962, p. 153).[24]

Slave emancipation offered improvements in material life and physical well-being (Debien 1962), and peasant control of means of production marked a major structural change conducive to population reproduction. Transitions in slaves' health were necessary to increase fertility, whereas political and economic transformations were barely sufficient, as the case of U.S. slaves following emancipation illustrates. Their previously high birth rate fell after the Civil War until the mid-1930s.[25] Access to land by newly emancipated U.S. slaves was curtailed in many areas; regional migration occurred, and nuclear families became less common. All of these factors contributed to lowered birth rates. But further evidence suggests that subfecundity among U.S. slaves was a major cause of their declining fertility (McFalls and McFalls 1984; Kiple and King 1981).

Caribbean bondwomen's health in particular had to improve for social factors to have a positive impact on fertility. Sheridan (1985, p. 340) notes the dramatic change: ''Perhaps the most marked difference between slavery and freedom was in the condition of black women.'' And their economic position shifted drastically as well. Women moved out of field labor into household work, horticulture, and marketing; men remained in sugar production, now as wage workers. As with Barbuda's slaves, West Indian emancipated populations generally lived in relatively open resource situations. It appears that children were often of limited utility. Much like hunter-gatherer groups, postemancipation Caribbean populations had relatively easy access to food and cash that children could little enhance. Still, their numbers increased.

Ex-slaves in some Caribbean societies enjoyed no more household prosperity than during slavery, impeding health improvements and fertility growth. Sturge and Harvey (1838, p. 45) note, for example, that in the Leewards, estate provisions were broken up after emancipation, as it was thought cheaper to import food. Some estates sold provisions to slaves. Of Antigua, Sturge and Harvey (1838, p. 45) remark, "There are no independent villages whatever, and though the people have the strongest desire to acquire what they call 'a pot of land,' meaning about an acre, yet great obstacles exist." Some slaves, then, lacked resources for accumulating income or ensuring their own health and nutrition, suggesting once more two overlapping causes of population stagnation or decrease.

The sugar industry sustained itself nowhere in the region throughout the late nineteenth century. Internal and international economic pressures reduced estate control of rural land, increasing physical capacity and material incentives for children. By the turn of the century, corporate land control increased, with encroachment on peasant farms. But fertility generally increased also, as in other Third World societies where social structures do not enhance quality of life but do not impede fertility either.[26]

Conclusions

Voluntary fertility control by Caribbean bondwomen has been overstated in explaining low birth rates. Physical causes of subfecundity are offered here as a complementary explanation along with the relatively few opportunities many slaves had for sexual intercourse. A variety of diseases common to Caribbean slave societies can cause subfecundity. The most significant, tuberculosis, caused many deaths among West Indian bondmen and often led to sterility. Others, including syphilis, gonorrhea, and whooping cough rarely caused sterility but probably reduced births by temporarily impairing the capacity of males and/or females to engage in intercourse and conceive children and by impeding women's ability to carry and deliver infants. The instability of sexual unions among slaves not only reduced material incentives to bear children in order to create kinship networks but also contributed to subfecundity by reducing opportunities for sexual intimacy.

A comparative analysis of Caribbean slave productivity, demographic patterns, and fertility delineates more clearly the probable impact of amelioration on population change. The progression of Caribbean sugar cultivation suggested by Higman and Mintz offers a framework for comparison. Early, stage 1 cultivators had declining production and productivity levels by the early nineteenth century, improving demographic profiles but not necessarily birth and death rates, which were apparently a function of the availability of food and material incentives to have children. For stage 2 producers continuing high levels of sugar production and trade and enduring importation of male Africans also discouraged fertility. Even where children could contribute to household economies, births were relatively few—inhibited, I propose, by the physical demands on men and women as fieldworkers and by subfecundity resulting from disease, overwork, and malnutrition. The final group of sugar colonies was intensively cultivated. Slaves' lives were brutal. Natural decreases fell slightly as demographic conditions improved and amelioration enacted. Both voluntary fertility control and subfecundity lowered birth rates in these difficult circumstances.

Finally, the postemancipation period marked a demographic transformation in much of the region. Births increased dramatically where resources were plentiful, suggesting that the health of ex-slaves had improved. In contrast, the fertility of former slaves in the United States fell, a result of land loss, conjugal instability, and increased subfecundity.

CHAPTER NINE

Sex, Punishment, and Protest

Students of gender in slave societies have noted the significance of personal ties between Europeans and slave women in expressing the complex dynamics of gender and race in New World slavery. Caribbean slave women's relationships with European men strained the social structure of slavery, violating laws and drawing the region's relatively few European women into tension with bondwomen (Bush 1981; Mathurin 1974). Intimate bonds are but one kind of personal relationship between slaves and masters. Slave owners' authority to inflict physical punishment on their slaves created another personal tie. Punishment in the period from the seventeenth to the early nineteenth century was at once public and personal. Torture and execution were public responses of authorities to personal transgressions. Yet state authorities could not intervene in the elite's response to their slaves, servants, or subjects. The personal relationship underlying physical punishment, combined with its public visibility, kept its victims in terror.

Both sexual intimacy and physical abuse manifested forms of power perhaps unique to New World slavery, in one instance to control males' and females' sexuality, in another to end their lives (Foucault 1977, 1978).[1] And in both cases the values of an earlier agrarian era are recalled. European slave masters, like feudal lords, had personal relations with slaves that could be publicly displayed. Agrarian societies sanctioned the same type of relationship between husband and wife: A male valued, honored, and finally owned his wife and children. He could express affection or great brutality. Objections by civil authorities or women's kin to the violation of law or standards of human dignity were of limited legitimacy and effect.

The patriarchal nature of the master-slave relationship seems to explain much about the contradictions of the master-slave tie. Yet some dimensions of this link and its expressions in sexuality and physical punishment are not consistent with the analogy to agrarian society. Few other agrarian regimes had the sexually free character of Caribbean slavery, at least as manifested in relationships between white men and black and colored women. Although white males were at liberty to establish personal ties with slaves, these ties were not sanctioned by law or religion after the seventeenth century. Indeed, many white males had formal and legally protected primary relationships with white women. On the other hand, punishment of slaves was under increased colonial scrutiny, particularly in the nineteenth century when public pressure created by disputes among advocates of the continuation of slavery and the slave trade over the treatment of slaves influenced state policies.

The peculiar mix of agrarian and industrial, capitalist and noncapitalist elements that define Caribbean social formations and have many ideological expressions is manifested again in personal associations between slave owner and bondwoman in New World slavery. Relationships between European men and slave women were sexually free, increasingly so over time. Yet punishments appear to have become more routinized and regulated, consistent with changing patterns of justice in Europe and its direct manifestation in the abolition movement (Davis 1966; Foucault 1977). Sparse data make it difficult to document trends in sexual and physical relationships between Europeans and slaves. What can be observed are the continuing contradictions and paradoxes of these encounters.

In this chapter I examine the treatment of slave women by white men in privatized sexual liaisons. I also look at the physical abuse of slave women by masters and mistresses. Finally, I trace the responses of slave women who were often drawn into complex social relationships in the slave and European communities. Conventional analysis holds that revolt and flight were the most significant sources of slave rebellion. In neither instance were slave women's numbers or authority equal to men's. I consider briefly both constraints on protest by women and forms of rebellion that were more compatible with their social position and commitments.

WHITE AND BLACK SEXUALITY

Women's sexuality is often considered dangerous to the community. Taboos associated with menstruation, childbirth, and lactation remind us of women's mythic power and their frequent cultural association with the forces of creation and destruction (Sanday 1981; Douglas 1966). Black women in the New World had such cosmic power when they fulfilled the roles of healers and practitioners of witchcraft (Debbasch 1963; Sheridan 1985). Women field and domestic slaves were culturally imbued with great sexual attraction and licentiousness (Davis 1966; Jordan 1968; Peytraud 1973, pp. 194–195; Gautier 1985, p. 151). Davis suggests that the nakedness and greater sexual pleasure apparently enjoyed by Africans, in contrast to European reserve, confused whites.

Such a mixture of freedom and restraint was, of course, incomprehensible to Europeans. It was inconceivable that nakedness should be taken as a sign of virginity in a girl, or that purity could coexist with what seemed the most obscene rites and ceremonies. Travelers faithfully reported that Negroes valued chastity and punished adultery; but this information could not be reconciled with the obvious and shocking fact that Africans enjoyed sex and were unashamed. (Davis 1966, p. 470)

Jordan (1968, p. 39) concurs that travelers' accounts of journeys to Africa routinely included reference to women's sexuality. "It may be that Englishmen found Negroes free in a primitive way and found this freedom somehow provocative; many chroniclers made a point of discussing the Negro women's long breasts and ease of childbearing." When they arrived in the Caribbean, other factors intensified European perceptions of African sexual license. Kinship relations were destroyed and "promiscuous" nonmarital ties formed. The act of enslavement and social subjugation may have stimulated the sexual imagination of some highly repressed Europeans.[2]

A demographic factor finally affected the formation of relationships between white European males and darker-skinned slave and free women: the scarcity of white women. Sex between master and slave was best tolerated where white women were most scarce (Davis 1966, p. 262).[3] The physical terrain, climate, and lack of indigenous European culture discouraged white women's residence in much of the region. Those who endured to establish grand estate households complained of the ambience, the lack of local cultural activity, and the manners and mores of other Europeans (see, for example, Lady Nugent 1907 and Mrs. Carmichael 1834). Sympathetic visitors found their lives monotonous and difficult. Bremer (1853, vol. 2, p. 351) observed that in Cuba "the life of the ladies is not cheerful and scarcely active at all." Disease was often rife and childbearing and pregnancy apparently more perilous than in urban Europe among the upper classes (Bremer 1853; Stedman 1971; Nugent 1907; Bush 1981).

If women do indeed bear the culture of a community, as some have argued, West Indian white women had little success or assistance from their male companions (Patterson 1973). Contemporary observers found the local European males loutish (Bush 1981). Young males had little apparent interest in building an expatriate community. They hoped to make money quickly and return home. Patterson suggests that absenteeism and the related scarcity of white women led to violent and abusive treatment of slaves by slaveholders. There were no shared values; there was a "nearly complete absence of a cohesive set of collective sentiments among the masters" (Patterson 1973, p. 285).

European males regularly sought liaisons with slave women (Patterson 1976; Stedman 1971; Nugent 1907; Atwood 1791, p. 273; Edwards 1966, vol. 1, p. 273; Labat 1930, vol. 1, p. 215). "Every unmarried adult man, and of every class, has his black or his brown mistress, with whom he lives openly" (Stewart 1823, p. 178). James (1963, p. 32) claims that in Saint Domingue in 1789, of 7,000 mulatto women 5,000 were either prostitutes or the "kept mistresses" of white men. The West Indies were occasionally presented as a land of sexual opportunity for young European males. J.B. Moreton (1793), a former estate bookkeeper, warned men to restrain themselves, for venereal disease was common in the British West Indies and not easily cured. Atwood (1791, p. 209) lamented that "in the English West Indian islands in general, there prevails a great aversion to forming matrimonial connections." Edwards reassured his readers that free women of color, "universally maintained by white men of all ranks and conditions, are not prostitutes, as flourished in Europe at the time" (Edwards 1966, vol. 2, pp. 25–26).[4]

Under what circumstances did slave women enter into sexual relationships with European men? Forced sexual relations were common (Westergaard 1917, p. 141; Sheridan 1985, p. 243). Slave women had legal protection against sexual violence in some settings, but these proscriptions had little apparent influence on behavior.[5] Stedman (1971, p. 370) attributed many murders of whites in Dutch Surinam to the rage of male slaves over European exploitation of slave women. Slave masters and their agents in the British West Indies procured women for visiting Europeans (Moreton 1793, p. 77). The use of authority to force women into sexual encounters was also adopted by blacks of status. Stedman (1971, pp. 177–178) recounted, for example, the story of a young slave woman who was punished for resisting the sexual advances of a black overseer.

Slave women learned the value of sexual ties with European men and sometimes aggressively sought them. Stedman (1971, p. 17), Pinckard (1970, vol. 2, p. 383), Atwood (1791, p. 273), and Schoelcher (1842, p. 73) related that they or other Europeans were approached by slave families who offered young women for sexual intimacy in exchange for money or gifts. Lewis (1834, p. 78) described an incident from one of his Jamaican estates, Cornwall, in 1816, in which a slave woman left a black man for a white bookkeeper "because he had a good salary, and could afford to give her more presents than a slave could."[6] Economic motives and dealings might be rewarded, then, by a slave woman's freedom or by food, clothing, and petty luxuries for herself and her kin.

Such ties between slave women and white members of the plantation staff were common. At Blandine estate in Guadeloupe from 1764 to 1772, five of thirteen single mothers had mulatto children (Gautier 1985, p. 163). At the Mesopotamia estate in Jamaica at the turn of the nineteenth century, sexual relations between no more than six white overseers and bookkeepers and slave women accounted for 11 percent of slave births. This ratio is high, given that 90 black males between the ages of 17 and 50 lived on the estates. Data from Mesopotamia reveal as well that "whites preferred their mistresses to be young: of the nine women who bore mulatto or quadroon infants [between 1799 and 1818], one was only fifteen years old and four others were under twenty. The whites also preferred light-complexioned women" (Dunn 1977, pp. 48–49).

Free colored women were in a better position to seek the attention of European men. They frequently formed a society of dances, balls, and other social rituals where European men came for entertainment (Moreton 1793; Fouchard 1981; James 1963; Moreau de Saint Méry 1958, vol. 1, pp. 104–107; Wynter 1967, p. 29). For the mostly French free colored women of Dominica, "dancing is the chief part of their amusements, their preparation for which are commonly very expensive; their ladies being usually dressed in silks, silk stockings and shoes; buckles, bracelets and rings of gold and silver, to a considerable value" (Atwood 1791, p. 220). With their "insatiable passion for showy dresses and jewels," they "ensnare" young white men (Carmichael 1834, vol. 1, pp. 75, 71). Fouchard (1981, p. 43) comments that slave women in Saint Domingue imitated the mores of free women: "How could the slave avoid being drawn to . . . that intermediary class whose insolent ostentation gave birth to the war of lace and clothing that involved the entire colony in an all-out competition?" In a phenomenological sense, however, the brown or black woman was finally passive, Wynter argues (1967, p. 29). She could make demands only in a covert and manipulative way, lest she lose her coveted position.

Pinckard (1970, vol. 3, p. 252) claimed that slave women understood freedom to mean an intimate relationship with a white man (see also Hilliard d'Aubert euil 1776, vol. 2, p. 83). Certainly prospects for manumission were enhanced by intimate contact with Europeans. Sio (1976) warns, however, against confusing the incidence of miscegination, apparently high in the British West Indies, with manumission, rare there in the eighteenth and nineteenth centuries. Daughters of Europeans and slave women were, for example, often given to other Europeans as mistresses (Pinckard 1970, p. 204).[7] In fact, manumissions were generally few, even in the French and Spanish West Indies where freed men constituted a greater proportion of the population than elsewhere in the Caribbean. In Saint Domingue in 1785 only 845 slaves were freed, but as many as 8,490 concubines were estimated among slaves in 1780. One-hundred slaves were freed in 1776 in Martinique, with concubines numbering 3,150 (Peytraud 1973, p. 419).

Some slave women and their racially mixed offspring were freed, of course. Light-skinned slave women occasionally attained considerable status as the mistresses of prominent white males. John Stedman's mistress, Joanna, had a long and apparently loving relationship with him during his sojourn in Surinam when Dutch troops were fighting the Bush Negroes. Joanna refused to leave Surinam when he returned to Europe, instead remaining with a "humane" slave mistress. She was later poisoned by "persons envious of her privileged position" (van Lier, in Stedman 1971, pp. x-xi).

Free women of color were more likely than slaves to develop beneficial relationships. Many prominent West Indian officials were known to have free colored mistresses (N. Hall 1976). Anna Heegaard was the companion of

Peter von Scholten, the Governor-General of the Danish West Indies at the time of abolition in 1848. In Barbados several colored women, freed by white lovers, became wealthy tavern owners (Handler 1974, pp. 133–134; Pinckard 1970, vol. 1, p. 249).

European women are said to have reacted with anger to affairs between European men and slave women. "The jealousy of the [white] creole ladies is intense. The easy availability of other women reduces their status. They are intended to breed legitimate heirs and little else" (Wynter 1967, p. 28). Handler (1974, p. 199) expresses a perhaps more realistic view, that "white females condoned or were indifferent" to concubinage between Europeans and women of color.

A lore has also developed that European women, bored and jealous, were more cruel to the slaves than white men (Brathwaite 1971; Bush 1981, p. 258; Gautier 1985). Journals of visitors and plantation personnel have contributed to this impression. Stedman (1971, p. 179), for example, tells a tale that serves an an archetype for stories of white women's cruelty. A European woman was disturbed by the cries of a slave infant. She tore the child from her mother's arms and drowned it. The bondwoman was then severely punished for trying to save the dying child. That children were abused underlines the anger European women felt about sexual relations between European men and dark-skinned women and the resulting children.

Eighteenth- and nineteenth-century travelers relate other incidents in which white women punished slaves or were insensitive to other whites' cruelties (see, for example, Pinckard 1970; see also Brathwaite 1971, p. 305; Nistal Moret 1980, p. 89; Gisler 1965, p. 48).[8] Turnbull's account of a Cuban *criolla*'s attitude toward her domestic servants is telling.

> The mistress of many a great family in Havana will not scruple to tell you that such is the proneness of her people [domestics] to vice and idleness, she finds it necessary to send one or more of them once a month to the whipping post, not so much on account of any positive delinquency, as because without these periodical advertisements the whole family would become unmanageable, and the master and mistress would lose their authority. (Turnbull 1840, p. 53)

The "cruel and capricious" Marquesa de Prado Ameno thus terrorized the family of the nineteenth-century Cuban slave Juan Francisco Manzano (Mullen 1981, p. 14).[9]

The underlying theme in all of these situations is the mercurial nature of European women. It is not that they punished slaves more often than did European men—impossible given that most slaves were in the fields, exposed primarily to white male authorities. Rather, some European women defied observers' expectations by punishing slaves excessively and with pleasure, as many European men did. Visitors to the West Indies undoubtedly expected more of women, a tenderness toward the slaves and ambivalence about the institution perhaps. This expectation is consistent with popular images of U.S. southern slave mistresses.

Clinton (1982) has recently reinforced this vision, describing the sad and lonely white plantation mistress in the U.S. South. The southern estate owner's wife often had personal ties to slaves, caring for them at times of illness and intervening on their behalf when slave owners threatened punishment or the breakup of their families. White women considered themselves the conscience of the South. They were often hard workers as well, organizing and managing large farm or estate households. Most observers of Caribbean white women have been less kind, claiming that they contributed little to their communities and benefited shamelessly from slave labor.

James (1963, p. 30) repeats a common perception of European women in the West Indies.[10] "Passion was their chief occupation, stimulated by overfeeding, idleness, and an undying jealousy of the black and Mulatto women who competed so successfully for the favours of their husbands and fathers." European males may have preferred slave women and free women of color; they were more attractive than the European women who ventured to the New World (Bush 1981). Atwood (1791, p. 211) found white females a pale but pleasing group. They were pure and not possessed of the "inordinate desires" one would expect of white women in the tropics. Edwards (1966, p. 13) also noted their languid appearance. Moreau de Saint Méry (1958, p. 10) describes Saint Domingue's white Creole women as lively but not strong, disabled by the warm climate and idleness. Marrying on average four years before their contemporaries in France, they acquiesced to social pressure to fulfill their most valued role, that of mother (Gautier 1985, p. 34; see also Hilliard d'Auberteuil 1776, pp. 31–32). Bremer (1853, vol. 2, pp. 343–344) suggests that the white woman in Cuba found it difficult to "maintain herself in an honorable way." She notes further that "it frequently happens that marriage does not follow love and betrothal." Ely (1963, pp. 748–751) cites contemporary observers who generally found Cuban women beautiful but flirtatious and coy.[11]

The West Indian plantation mistress's life, then, was boring and debilitating and surely produced behavior not in keeping with European upper-class norms for females. One can also infer from contemporary writings an anger at European women for failing to erect a mantle of gentility on slave society. Contact with a refined and gracious European coterie would have allowed visitors to deny the oppressive nature of slavery.

Another indication of white women's projected status of decorum and purity is the colonial attitude toward sexual encounters between European women and black slaves. White women were not free to engage in intimate relationships with black men, particularly after the mid-1700s (Bush 1981, p.

252). There was little expectation, of course, that these conservative women would seek such unions. The degree of white women's desexualization and the dehumanization of black slaves is perhaps best indicated by the European acceptance of the slaves' nudity. Little or no clothing was allowed most slaves. Domestics served in the homes of people who would never tolerate undress among their peers.[12]

Nevertheless, white women and darker-skinned males occasionally developed emotional and physical relationships. Westergaard (1917, p. 162) reports one such encounter between a planter's daughter and a slave in the Danish West Indies. Colonial officials recommended corporal punishment and life imprisonment for the woman; the slave was to be burned to death. He escaped, however; the woman's fate was not recorded. In a similar situation in late eighteenth-century Surinam, the European woman was "reviled" and the slave killed (Stedman 1971, p. 162). Labat (1930, vol. 1, pp. 215–220) reported several such incidents in the seventeenth-century French West Indies, resulting in social ostracism of the white woman. Even Lady Nugent, wife of a Jamaican governor, was criticized by her Creole companions for dancing with an old black man (Nugent 1907; see also Brathwaite 1971, p. 305).

Sympathy has sometimes been accorded to black males for the loss of wives and lovers to white men (Moreton 1793; Patterson 1969, p. 168). It appears, however, that in some settings slave women retained sexual ties with black men while becoming Europeans' lovers (Gautier 1985, p. 175). Modern observers have explored the social implications of miscegenation for bondmen in racially stratified slavery. Jordan (1968, p. 141) argues that, where slaves greatly outnumbered whites in the United States, symbolic acts of oppression reinforced whites' superior social status. "White men extended their dominion over their Negroes to the bed, where the sex act itself served as ritualistic reenactment of the daily pattern of sexual dominance." Patterson, too, notes emasculation of male slaves, who had little recourse but to tolerate the sexual exploitation of their female kin and companions.

PHYSICAL ABUSE OF SLAVE WOMEN

If European males related to individual slave women in a particular way, they were still the masters of many women. Slave owners generally treated bondwomen like bondmen, subject to the same punishments. Eighteenth- and nineteenth-century literature on the Caribbean is replete with references to the brutalization of slave women and free women of color. There appears to be little difference in the severity with which men and women were punished, although men may have been brutalized more frequently. Mathurin (1974, p. 343) notes, however, that in the last years of Jamaican slavery bondwomen were frequently victimized in the many well-known cases of brutality against slaves (Mathurin 1975).

Women were occasionally executed. For example, Stedman (1971, p. 33) observed 11 rebel captives killed. "One man was hanged alive upon a gibbet, by an iron hook stuck through his ribs; two others were chained to stakes, and burnt to death by a slow fire. Six women were broken alive upon the rack, and two girls were decapitated." Women, along with young children and elderly slaves, were frequently whipped and flogged (Knibb 1832, p. 17). Cuban slave writer and poet Juan Francisco Manzano told, for example, that his mother was held down by two slaves and beaten for asking about her son's fate as he was about to be punished (Mullen 1981, p. 87). Laws were enacted in the amelioration period in the French, Danish, and British West Indies to limit the punishment of women but to little apparent effect.

The abuse of pregnant women is notable in eighteenth- and nineteenth-century accounts of plantation life. French West Indian slave owners followed the custom of whipping the pregnant woman by staking her to the ground, hollowing an area in the ground for her unborn child. The same practice was observed in Cuba (Ortiz 1975, p. 231; Ely 1963, p. 486). Lewis (1834, p. 390) offers a similar example from Jamaica: "I have not passed six months in Jamaica, and I have already found on one of my estates a woman who had been kicked in the womb by a white book-keeper, by which she was crippled herself, and on another of my estates another woman who had been kicked in the womb by another white book-keeper, by which he had crippled the child." Olwig (1985, p. 34) reports that three women on Cinnamonbay plantation in St. John complained that, although pregnant, they were beaten for insufficient work. Sturge and Harvey (1838, p. 5) visited a prison in Bridgetown, Barbados, where guards insisted that a woman in late pregnancy shatter stones at the same pace as other women. Similar incidents are noted in the British West Indies and Puerto Rico (Moreton 1793, p. 153; Curet 1985, p. 129). Gisler (1965, p. 49) repeats the 1845 complaint against the brothers Jaham, planters in Martinique, charged with twice beating the pregnant slave Rosette.

The abuse of pregnant slaves seems to run counter to slave owners' intentions to reproduce the labor force. In the U.S. South slave masters monitored pregnancies and punished women who aborted (Clinton 1982). The latter policy was enacted during the amelioration period in parts of the Caribbean. In the French West Indies, for example, women thought to have aborted or contributed to the death of a newborn were whipped or made to wear an iron collar, sometimes until pregnant again. The mothers of children who died of tetanus were often killed (Gautier 1985, p. 113). But even when childbirths were encouraged in Caribbean slavery, slave owners and their agents abused pregnant women, meaning, it seems, to inflict special pain on women slaves by threatening the lives they carried.[13]

WOMEN'S PROTESTS

Women seldom exercised active leadership in Caribbean slave revolts. We have tended lately, therefore, to focus on their participation in indirect forms of protest. I have argued against understanding family formation as a means of rebellion. I have also questioned whether abortion, infanticide, and sexual abstinence, all hypothesized to be rebellious behavior by Caribbean slaves, were as common as sometimes claimed. Women are also said to have joined men in withholding productivity through a variety of evasions and deceptions of the slave master and his managers. Women were apparently adept at fooling slaveholders through complaints of illness, the need to nurse their children, and other behaviors that were defined as malingering by whites (Hine 1979; Patterson 1969). Mathurin (1975, p. 12) captures one implication for Caribbean slavery of this response:

> One of the crucial factors that eventually helped to put an end to black bondage in the British Caribbean in 1838 was the fact that slavery, as a system of labour, became more and more expensive; it was expensive because it was unproductive; it was impossible to get maximum work output from forced labour. An important element in this low productivity was the unwillingness of the slave woman to work.

Women are once again here portrayed as sentient beings capable of anger and response and acting in the tradition of other "prepolitical" groups constrained by circumstance and custom from more direct forms of protest (Hobsbawm 1959).

The larger political message is a needed antidote against the tendency to conflate the experiences of male and female slaves and then focus only on the males and the kinds of protest, for example, revolts, in which they were prominent. Yet, in the absence of a written record and with only a fragmented oral tradition handed down from slaves, we have little ground for inferences about indirect forms of slave protest. As for women's proclivity for illness as an excuse for absence from work, there is no consistent evidence that women slaves were more frequently ill or absent from work because of illness than men. The nature of slaves' maladies is of course often vague in the historical record (Mathurin 1974, p. 314). They may appear to be contrived because research has focused so little on the epidemiology of Caribbean slavery and the entry of two population groups into a new disease environment (Sheridan 1985, pp. 1–41).

Protests against work and slavery varied in form with what was possible and effective. Some productivity lapses annoyed the slave master, for example, on Lewis's Jamaican estates. There slaves bore less likelihood of violent retribution than in the brutal sugar factories of more successful producers. Still, the sadism of some slaveholders was extreme and their reactions to insubordination unpredictable, making it difficult for slaves or modern observers to gauge the political advances brought by insurgency.

How, then, did slave women protest the awesome burdens inflicted on them by slavery, especially in its highly rationalized and intense nineteenth-century forms? Women took part in some revolts and rebellions, if not overtly then as conspirators (Gautier 1985; Craton 1982, pp. 122, 132–133; Westergaard 1917, p. 176). Women sometimes served ritual roles, such as "queen" of a band of rebels (Craton 1982, p. 235; Mathurin 1974, pp. 91–92). Others appear to have been at the heart of plotting and planning: Nanny Grigg, a domestic slave, participated in the 1816 Barbados slave rebellion (Craton 1982, pp. 260–261). Certainly women and children were killed by whites in generalized acts of retribution against communities suspected of aiding insurgents (Craton 1982, pp. 315, 328; Schnakenbourg 1980, p. 108; Ortiz 1975, p. 151; Gautier 1985, p. 243). If captured, rebel women were subject to torture and execution alongside men (Price 1976, 1979; Stedman 1971; Gisler 1965, p. 54). Their knowledge of "le Vaudou" fortified slave troops in the Saint Domingue revolution. Women also served as spies and nurses and traded themselves for weapons in French West Indian slave revolts (Gautier 1985, p. 242).

Women became Maroons, although everywhere less frequently than men (Westergaard 1917, p. 176; Kopytoff 1976; Silié 1976, p. 78; Gautier 1985, pp. 227–238; Franco 1979; Price 1976, p. 26; Debien 1979).[14] Women were occasionally taken from estates by Maroon leaders to serve as companions and workers (Edwards 1966). Women also fled to join lovers and kin. Lewis (1834, p. 91) writes of the escaped slave Pluto, whose generosity led women to join him in flight. Manigat (1977, p. 430) suggests that sexual and emotional motives often influenced slaves' inclination to flee.

> "Courrir les filles" ("girl-hunting") was a natural urge that could not always be met within the plantation. Given the hard work and scarcity of leisure for the slaves, womanizing was a favorite diversion for which it was worth taking the risk of a "fugue" to another plantation or a more serious flight. Sometimes the slave became a maroon after a love grievance or conflict on the plantation with a luckier fellow-slave or even an enterprising master. A whole chapter could be written on *marronage-sexuality*, the slave running away because of girl-hunting, or running away because of girls who wanted to elope with them, or abducting girls after having fled and lived as maroons.

Polygyny among some Jamaican Maroons suggests that stratification within the band at times intensified the competition for women.

The peasant and hunter-gatherer communities established by the Maroons offered freedom to women but difficult circumstances. Women did nearly all the farming in Jamaican Maroon communities, claims Edwards (1966, vol. 1, p. 504).[15] Mathurin (1974, p. 95) asserts that, without women's contributions to "the resistance movement in the area of agriculture," Maroons would have been a far less potent and pervasive political force in Jamaica. Maroon women ground millet and carried out domestic chores in Saint Dominigue (Fouchard 1981, p. 180). They performed domestic tasks while men farmed among the *cimarrones* of Capo Beata in the Dominican Republic (Silié 1976, p. 78).

Maroon communities probably had a higher birth rate than estates (Mathurin 1974, p. 93) but may have lacked a large population of children. Gautier (1985, p. 237) suggests that women fled less often than men, resisting separation from children and considering it too risky to include them in escape plans (see also White 1985). She offers a periodization of patterns of flight by women in the French West Indies that may have application elsewhere in the region. In the seventeenth century women fled with families, even newborns. By the eighteenth century, "with the dissolution of families and increased difficulties associated with marronage," they fled alone.[16]

The Jamaican Windward Maroon obeah woman Nanny was an important political presence in the group and an able warrior (Kopytoff 1976; Tuelon 1973; Patterson 1973, p. 262). Her feats are legendary in Jamaica, but her origins are unknown. She may have been an escaped slave who, with five brothers, took leadership of a Maroon band (Tuelon 1973, pp. 20–21). Her status is apparently anomalous, however, as no other comparable female Maroon leader has been identified and other evidence suggests that the Maroons were male dominated in number and in their frequent militancy.

"Insolence" was a frequent female offense, often resulting in punishment (Mathurin 1975, p. 13; Craton 1984). Arson and poisoning involved women (Debien 1974; Debbasch 1963). On many occasions these acts of insurgency required networks of conspirators and remind us that the often hidden support of women and children buttressed revolt.[17] Whole households of domestic slaves conspired to poison masters, their families, and guests in nineteenth-century Saint Domingue. Larger networks poisoned significant segments of masters' slave work forces as well (Gisler 1965, p. 54; Hilliard d'Auberteuil 1776, vol. 1, p. 137). To the extent that abortion and infanticide were practiced, largely female groups worked together to conceal these events from the white plantation staff (Mathurin 1974, pp. 358–363; Hine 1979, p. 125).

It has been argued that suicide and self-mutilation also constituted "political acts" (Geggus 1983; Ely 1963; Ortiz 1975). Again the historical literature offers examples of women engaging in these forms of resistance. On the British Virgin Islands in 1793, for example, a well-known case involved "eight slaves, two of them women, who cut off their arms with their bills, as a protest against plantation labour'' (Dookhan 1975, p. 83).

Caribbean slave women's heavy involvement in subsistence and household tasks reinforced their biological ties to the family. A woman's range of protests was generally limited to those that would not endanger her family or her ties to it. The peculiar sadistic need of white male authorities to abuse pregnant females is a reminder of the emotional and physical commitments women brought to interaction with slave masters and their agents and the reactions that they could elicit.

This interpretation of females' comparative reticence to revolt openly or in a militant way puts the emphasis firmly on intentionality—on women protecting their households. It is more consistent with our increased knowledge about women's major roles in production. It also calls our attention to women's tendency to flee to lovers and kin on other plantations and in Maroon communities and to work together, invisibly, to defy and destroy slave owners.

Efforts to establish the humanity of slaves and their ''class consciousness'' are sometimes at odds with information about the successful exploitation by masters of slaves' labor power. Their pursuit of ''political acts'' did not mean that slaves had ''cultural autonomy'' or a full range of options for protest (Geggus 1983). Women slaves did not generally fulfill prominent leadership roles in traditionally understood vehicles for revolt, that is, Maroon communities and rebel movements. They did, however, fill subsidiary positions and give many kinds of support to male rebels. Female insurgency may have sometimes been expressed in malingering and in the refusal to conceive and bear children. But evidence of these practices is limited, and their incidence is at odds with other more fully documented tendencies, including physiologically based female subfecundity and high levels of work productivity.

CONCLUSIONS

Sexual relationships between European males and slaves and the severity with which female slaves were physically abused are not entirely separate phenomena. For some sadistic slave owners sexuality and punishment were perversely linked. For all, it is a contradictory and puzzling relationship that black female sexuality could be valued and black women's bodies mutilated and destroyed.

A conceptual break existed for slave masters between the slave woman as sexual being and as worker. It is a profound separation, unusual even for other slave societies.[18] Labor shortages and the failure of European women to settle in the region combined to make white men completely utilitarian in their treatment of slave women, untroubled by the degraded social status of their sexual partners.[19] The bondwomen's economistic pursuit of white men was also a means to control their situation. The colored and black mistresses of Europeans rarely achieved real security, but they remained ahead of field-workers, largely avoiding the physical abuses and difficult work lives those slaves endured.

The social autonomy of slave women underlay their vulnerability to sexual exploitation and physical abuse. A lack of economic power made their social position even more precarious and unstable. It is likely that whites' personal power over black women grew more totalistic during the course of sugar cultivation in the region.[20] The frequent marginality of slave women to their own community is thus clear. The refuge provided by marronage further highlights slave women's marginal social status. Treated as the spoils of war, pawns in males' ranking systems, and the principal agricultural workers in Maroon communities, women's status was low and subordination to their male comrades pronounced.

CHAPTER TEN

Conclusions

Gender Stratification and Economic Change

This examination of the experience of slave women in the Caribbean has revealed that the progressive spread and intensification of the production of commodity crops in the Americas hurt bondwomen. Traditional gender-based divisions of labor—whether influenced by African or Western agrarian patterns and gender role differentiation—were subverted to the demands of large-scale cash cropping. Slave women's field labor increased, and gender became a salient issue in the distribution of workers in skilled plantation occupations.

A growing body of historical and comparative literature concludes that, although economic evolution created some new socioeconomic opportunities for women, in many simple societies women experienced greater gender equality and status (Sanday 1981; Leacock 1983; Chafetz 1984; Safilios-Rothschild 1977; Blumberg 1978). Proponents of this view concur further that, even though males and females occasionally had relatively equal socioeconomic status and females sometimes enjoyed more access to particular social resources than males, females rarely enjoyed a broadly superior position to males (Chafetz 1984, p. 1).[1] Finally, students of gender and social change agree that kinship ties have progressively broken down through history and that the separation of private and public spheres of life have become more marked (Nicholson 1986).

The simplest set of hypotheses on gender stratification and economic change is presented by Sanday (1981), who argues that the material base of society influences "sexual scripts," with hunting and agricultural societies generating male dominance. Threats to a society's material base (war, colonialism, natural disasters) likewise bring men into powerful positions. Boserup (1970) and Goody (1976) agree that advanced agriculture gives men a dominant social role. Male authority in production, along with the development of a complex polity, encourages diverging devolution, or inheritance by both sons and daughters. The system is reinforced by homogamy, monogamy, and prohibition of premarital sex, all of which contribute finally to the formation of nuclear families and the subordination of women.

Other theorists link women's subordination less to social types than to social characteristics. Chafetz (1984) contends that eight factors finally determine the degree of what she terms "sex stratification":

1. Average percentage of female life cycle spent in childbearing and nurturance.
2. Degree of separation of home and work sites.
3. Relative importance of physical strength/mobility in production.
4. Relative societal emphasis on sustenance versus surplus production.
5. *Degree* of environmental threat/harshness.
6. Level/type of technology.
7. Work organization (extent of female contribution to production activities).
8. Family structural variables (lineage and locality, division of domestic labor).

Of these eight factors, says Chafetz, environmental threat is a major variable in explaining sex stratification, especially in preindustrial societies. In general, however, technology may have the greatest impact on the way in which societies distribute social goods to men and women.

Chafetz concludes with an assessment of sex stratification based on degree of significance of eight independent variables for seven major societal types. She predicts low degrees of sex stratification in hunter-gatherer and simple horticultural societies, high stratification in advanced horticultural, pastoral, agrarian, and early industrial societies, and low stratification again in postindustrial settings. Several variables have nearly linear relationships to sex stratification: degree of gender stratification, male participation in family labor, extent of female involvement in or control of work, and proportion of female life cycle devoted to childbearing and nurturance.

Finally, Blumberg (1978) suggests that female status alone predicts other dimensions of female social position. She argues that four indicators of female economic power, along with selected political and ideological variables, influence women's lifestyle choices: (1) female economic power (relative control of means of production, relative control of surplus, relative labor productivity, relative labor indispensability), (2) male force, (3) ideology of male supremacy, and (4) economic power related to kinship. She hypothesizes that these factors contribute to women's degree of lifestyle choice or discretion to initiate marriage, initiate divorce, initiate premarital sex, and maintain household authority. By studying more than 150 societies, Blumberg found that economic power and male force explained almost all the variance in lifestyle choice.

These universalistic hypotheses about gender segregation and female status can be questioned on methodological grounds (Narroll 1968). As with other cross-national data analyses, these are suspect because many data are missing or unreliable. A second objection to these theories is that societies vary greatly internally, and conceptual and empirical efforts to type them ultimately distort reality. There is, however, a theme sufficiently consistent in these attempts to understand women's position to warrant attention and possible application to West Indian societies.

COMPARATIVE GENDER STRATIFICATION
AND CARIBBEAN SLAVE WOMEN

Comparative theories of economic change and gender stratification can tell us much about slave womens' life chances, but some synthesis of findings about the material foundations for women's position is needed. As societies were uprooted by the slave trade, with a scarcity of food and other resources, slave communities lent themselves to male dominance, much like other agrarian societies (Blumberg 1978) and those influenced by external crises and disasters (Sanday 1981). Within slave societies horticulture, with its historically greater economic and political benefits for women, sometimes flourished because slaves were required to produce their own food. This granted females economic power and status by, in Blumberg's terms, allowing them relative control over a means of production and its surplus product. It was reinforced in the Caribbean by frequent male absence from family life and African women's highly visible roles in many areas of agriculture and marketing (Goody 1976; Boserup 1970; Chafetz 1984).

More of women's labor was required in the fields as the ending of the slave trade cut off the supply of bonded workers. Better processing technology created a greater demand for sugar cane, increasing the need for women's labor, their indispensability, and their economic status, as Blumberg's (1978) and Chafetz's (1984) analyses would predict. Moreover, women's time spent in childbearing and rearing necessarily lessened. The ideology of male dominance, an important factor according to Blumberg for predicting lifestyle choice, mitigated this influence in the assignment of higher-status jobs to men. In general, horticulture and simple agriculture offered women more economic and social power than work in plantation agriculture, in keeping with Chafetz's theory.

Women's indispensability and resulting status is demonstrated in female slaves' opportunities for sexual relationships with white males. The scarcity of white women encouraged white male–black female liaisons that brought material benefits, status, and often freedom to female slaves. This situation differentiates slavery from most other agrarian and industrial socioeconomic systems but is not without historical and cross-cultural precedent. Migratory males frequently leave behind females, who become vulnerable to but benefit from liaisons with middle- and upper-status males, often of different skin color (Kuznesof 1979, 1980). Female migrants, increasingly common in the world today, also find advantage in relationships with men who are of different economic and social status from themselves.

Three different systems of production, then, contribute to our understanding of the position of Caribbean slave women: horticulture, agriculture, and industrialism. Horticulture, or gardening, along with marketing generally brought women relative economic power, as materialist students of gender inequality have found in other settings (Chafetz 1984; Boserup 1970; Goody 1976; Blumberg 1978). Settled agriculture reinforced male hierarchy through both peasantlike farming controlled by slaves and the preference for male slaves in fieldwork and craft and artisanal positions on the plantation, a finding consistent with the materialist study of women in agrarian societies. Finally, industrial patterns of labor organization are found in plantation agriculture, intensified by the mechanization of processing. Females were badly needed for sugar cultivation, yielding them independence from male kin. They were entitled to goods and benefits independent of family organization or status, again as predicted in the literature on gender and economic change. This autonomy is also found among slave women in domestic service who used household positions to gather resources. The continuing access of males to skilled positions gave them an advantage over women slaves, particularly on estates that began sugar production later with highly rationalized patterns of organization and technological development.

Two production systems of Caribbean slave society, then, encouraged social equality of males and females but on quite different terms. To the extent that horticulture occupied West Indian slaves, the economic contributions of males and females were recognized, yielding bases for economic power and social status to both genders. Industrial influences on plantation agriculture enhanced gender equality among fieldworkers, but male labor was valued for high-status occupational tasks, meaning that females' social autonomy often led to marginalization, with high-status males differentially able to attract mates and construct kinship ties.[2]

Can we then conclude that slave women were sometimes comparatively advantaged? Yes, a hideous social system spawned some advantages to women relative to men and relative to women in social formations influenced by other systems of production. But, in fact, neither males nor females had opportunities for mobility or resource gain in many settings. On small plantations males were deprived of chances for skilled work, and on many of these estates male access to land and food production was also restricted, with horticulture and marketing opportunities rare. Moreover, the equality of males and females that developed on large-scale plantations in advanced stages of Caribbean sugar production rested on the shared access of most slaves to only the most rudimentary of goods.

MARXISM AND GENDER STRATIFICATION

Comparative theories of gender stratification and economic development contribute to our understanding of slave women's position, but they do not provide a full explanation or analysis. They do supplement the general Marxian categories used throughout this book, enriching their too often slender application to gender stratification. Several points of synthesis can be usefully pursued. First, in proposing that capitalist and noncapitalist modes of production combined in New World slavery, the means and organization of production and distribution must be more fully described for women's place to be clear. The gender and racial segmentation and fragmentation of labor forces evident in advanced capitalism are also present in other modes and systems of production, including those of New World slavery.

The work of women in the reproduction of the labor force must be recognized not only for its intrinsic value but also for its functional relationship to other dynamics of social transformation. Slave women's roles in horticulture and simple agriculture were obviously crucial to the continuation of slave-based plantation production of cash crops. But they were also linked in an essential way to women's willingness and capacity to have children and their ability to rear them (Chafetz 1984). Hence, to the degree that women supported slavery through the production of use-value, they were also more likely to reproduce the labor force.

Then there is the matter of ideology. There are several particular areas in which the slaves' and the Europeans' beliefs shaped material interests: the apparently continuing disinclination of some Spanish slave owners to purchase females; the friendships that developed between slaveholders and slaves, resulting in sentimental manumissions; the likelihood that children sometimes had more emotional than economic value for slaves; the different ways in which petty agricultural labor and domestic work were organized in the U.S. South and in the Caribbean.

It is confounding to try to specify a dominant ideological theme for slavery in the Caribbean or in the U.S. South because women's position has been studied so little. If, for example, we understand New World slavery as a form of capitalism, then we assume superstructural components associated with capitalism—individualism and competition. These values reflect men's working and investment experiences, not women's more cooperative, collective forms of organization (Nicholson 1986; Hartsock 1983). Male-centered ideas about ideology are not wrong in this case but in need of qualification. Likewise, if we understand slavery as a precapitalist mode of production, as Genovese (1976) does for the U.S. South, other problems arise. The characterization of slavery as seigneurial seems to assume mutual rights and obligations between superordinate and subordinate men, reproduced in relationships between slave men and women. In the West Indies, however, bondwomen's increasing social autonomy, extensive participation in field labor, and casual relationships to slave men undermined patriarchy.

The ideologies and cultures of Caribbean slaves were complex and made more difficult to discern by the paucity of primary materials left by the slaves. There seems little doubt that ideological development and change turn on the articulation of beliefs and values generated by or influencing categorically different social formations and modes of production. In general, patriarchy and its ideological blend of male hierarchy and obligation to subordinate females gave way gradually to the ideology of social equality, even as new forms of gender hierarchy emerged. This process, neither smooth, consistent, nor inexorable, resulted in the peculiar mingling of ideological tendencies we see throughout New World slave culture (Smith 1953; Wolf 1982; Brathwaite 1971; James 1963). Again, however, a Marxian perspective provides a general framework for the analysis of ideology that theory and research on gender stratification and economic change make meaningful.

THEMES IN SLAVE STUDIES

In Chapter One I discussed three major areas of slave studies and analyzed them to determine how their theoretical frameworks and research traditions are influenced by the exclusion from study of women and gender. What general theoretical insights or principles have been reinforced by this investigation of women's contributions to Caribbean commodity and food production, slave family organization, and reproduction of the slave population?

The first area of theoretical debate considered is the comparative treatment of male and female slaves by their masters. By extending empirical scrutiny beyond questions of both physical abuse and punishment to include access to food and housing and labor productivity, we can draw these conclusions: (1) Women often were punished in the same ways as men and were considered more troublesome workers. They benefited from some improved treatment if pregnant or lactating but generally only during the amelioration period. (2) Women had less access to food because they were believed to require less sustenance than working men and indeed generally enjoyed better health and greater longevity. (3) The labor productivity of women nearly equaled that of men and sometimes was apparently the same. In general, then, differences in treatment were not profound. But variation occurred and is best explained *not* by reference to the ideological proclivities of various colonial powers, as argued by Tannenbaum and others (although Spanish attitudes toward women may have limited their presence on Cuban and Puerto Rican estates, especially early in the seventeenth century) but by the overall labor needs and intensity of sugar production and the physical demands on slaves, with little differentiation between males and females. Arid lands and those with little food production also strained physical well-being, as food imports and rations were small and sometimes scarce.

Finally, two exogenous variables influenced male and female slaves' relative access to social goods and therefore their quality of life. Plantation size determined to a great extent the number of positions available for skilled workers, mostly males. Even on an intensely worked nineteenth-century plantation in Cuba or Surinam, for example, males had more opportunities than females for social goods if a large skilled work force was retained. By the same token some societies had large resident European populations, where both men and women benefited from positions as servants but with women often able to get more and different kinds of benefits from this sort of arrangement. Finally, some slave masters were sadistic, a personality variable we can neither measure nor predict. Cruel slave owners were not necessarily committed to getting more out of slaves; they often appear to have had an excessive need to control subordinates, a pattern we now recognize among the dominant in many non-wage-based work settings and in the nuclear family (Rodney 1981; Martin 1983).

Is slavery best understood as a capitalist or a precapitalist mode of production? The rising productivity of slaves and general capacity of Caribbean slavery to endure, even with the use of women's and children's labor, point to the positive effect of highly rationalized production organization and technology on what is best understood as a capitalist firm. However, the study of women in New World slavery, especially in the West Indies, points significantly to the precapitalist or noncapitalist elements of slave systems, reminding us of their scope and contribution to plantation-based commodity production. Women were *not* always in control of petty agriculture but sometimes did lead their families in the production and marketing of food products. Their labor always contributed significantly to this realm. Horticulture was women's domain, often a major supplement to food rationed by slave masters. It kept slaves alive and hence supported the capitalist plantation.

Women's status in subsistence production is meaningful to the categorization of slavery as capitalist or noncapitalist by enhancing our understanding of Caribbean plantations as a dominantly capitalist but ultimately mixed system of production. This unification of systems or modes of production has been advanced in Marxian studies in terms of articulation of modes of production (Foster-Carter 1978; Wolf 1982; Attewell 1984). Our inquiry into women's position reinforces the crucial assumption that capitalism dominates social formations, as we observe that women's domain in the household, in horticulture, and in agriculture shrank as capitalist rationalization seized hold. However, the concept of articulation, with its suggestion that capitalism will inevitably overcome other systems of production, is a static one. We see throughout the Caribbean that, where capitalist commodity production faltered, the peasantry reasserted itself. Small-scale farmers were dependent on paid plantation work, but their involvement in the subsistence sector was considerably greater than during slavery. This was especially true in Haiti, where the slaves' revolt destroyed the capitalist plantation sector. A theoretical structure such as the "articulation of modes of production" is vulnerable both to systemic changes in a variety of directions and to the actions of members of the underlying population.[3]

Finally, in what ways has the study of women slaves altered our perceptions of the phenomenological position of slaves? As posited in Chapter One, the findings suggest that slave women were often doubly oppressed, as slaves and as wives and daughters. Two ideal typical constructs, slavery and patriarchy, describe women's subordination. Whether understood as ownership or in other terms (such as Patterson's natal alienation, dishonor, and subjection to force), slaves and women in patriarchal societies shared these dimensions of oppression. Patriarchy and slavery are not, of course, identical relationships of subordination, but they are similar in several ways: the isolation and separation of the subordinate population from the social life of the dominant group, the use of violence against the subordinate group, the provision of laws that confer ownership rights on the superordinate, and the difficulties of slaves and women in gaining access to goods except through masters or through husbands and fathers (Omvedt 1986; Blumberg 1978; Patterson 1982; Finley 1968, 1980; Davis 1966).

The debate among scholars (Patterson 1982; Finley 1968, 1980; Davis 1966) over what theoretical construct best describes the degraded status of slaves seems sterile in light of women's at least occasional double oppression. The phenomenological status of slaves is certainly multidimensional and perhaps too variable to permit constant categorization or definition.

CONCLUSIONS: SLAVERY, CAPITALISM, AND PATRIARCHY

A unifying theme of this work is that ideological and material "structures," as currently constituted in slave studies, do not explain much about Caribbean slave women's position. We can create new analytical structures to include women, postulating perhaps that agrarian patriarchy combined with slavery in its capitalist form to produce complex structures of subordination. But, as I have argued, a more analytically fluid and flexible approach to categorization is required.

Three historical trends make it difficult to construct theoretically appropriate patterns of analysis for Caribbean slave societies. First, variation among social settings, a function of the stage of capitalist development, colonial influences, the demographic makeup of slave populations, ecology, and access of the population to food, is great. Second, these and other factors contributed to movement away from simple slave societies dominated by agriculture and patriarchy, as in the Bahamas, to the highly rationalized, industrial patterns of Cuban plantation agriculture, where slave women were relatively autonomous from males and other kin.

Most important is the third constraint against constructing constant analytical structures—slaves did rebel.[4] Bondwomen participated in slave revolts (Mathurin 1975), and women slaves undoubtedly rebelled against their fathers, husbands, lovers, older brothers, and other men of influence. Slave rebellions and revolts are increasingly studied, and we know more than ever about slaves' physical retreats into marronage, about poisoning and other individual acts of violence against slave masters, and the like (Genovese 1979; Fouchard 1981; Mathurin 1975; Kopytoff 1976; Marshall 1976; Baralt 1981). Much has been made as well of slave culture as a form of revolt against slavery, with the generally unsatisfying results described in Chapter Five on the slave family. We know less about women's insurgency against patriarchy. Perhaps the formation of liaisons with European males was viewed by fellow slaves as a rebellion against the slave community—or, alternatively, as a wise and lucky move for a slave woman with few other opportunities to improve her life chances and those of her children. On the other hand, some forms of slave revolt, such as poisoning (especially common in the French West Indies), were often slave women's province (Debbasch 1964). Here the proximity to the slaveholder and his family that was needed to commit an act of violence—rather than individual social or economic gain—was perceived as an advantage of domestic service. The point remains that structures are subject to change through human action, and slaves had a continuing effect on slavery, as slave women had on the forces of patriarchy.[5]

We cannot solve here what is a major and historical problem in the social sciences, the relationship between social structure and social action. We find that structural-functional theories, with their overemphasis on a social structure informed by a single value or ethos, have been discredited, only to be replaced by other "structuralisms" (for example, structural anthropology and structural Marxism), again stressing ideological influences on the social system (Giddens 1976, 1981, 1982; Attewell 1984). Materialist theories can also be totalistic and inappropriate for complex and textured interpretations of social phenomena. In response, uncritical theories of social action have developed, with daily life itself held to be rebellion because it indicates a will to survive in hostile circumstances.

The study of powerless groups can only advance efforts toward synthesis. Slave women, along with children and older slaves, were generally more vulnerable to hegemonic institutions than were bondmen. Their study can reveal much about how the institutions of slavery came into being, took form, and ultimately influenced slaves' responses. I have scratched the surface of information available about women slaves. For any particular setting endless stories can be told from demographic findings, legends about women slaves, and surviving plantation records. Let us hope that historians and historical sociologists and anthropologists will proceed in unearthing and interpreting these data, for only when we know more about women and other often ignored but significant groups can we resolve the current contradictions in social theory that frustrate our understanding of social organization and change.

NOTES

CHAPTER ONE. A THEORETICAL OVERVIEW

1. Other works on gender and women in Caribbean slavery include Bush (1986), Mathurin (1975), Martinez-Alier (1974), and Patterson (1976).

2. There has been violence against women wherever they are held as the property of men (Martin 1983). As later discussion reveals, male slave "ownership" of female slaves was usurped in slavery and perhaps reasserted where, as in the U.S. South, slave families achieved some independence from masters. Although not a constant theme in seventeenth- through nineteenth-century commentary, bondmen's abuse of slave women is occasionally noted or suggested. See, for example, Moreau de Saint Méry (1958, vol. 1, p. 57) and Mrs. Carmichael (1834, vol. 1, p. 266).

3. In the U.S. South, male slaves controlled provision grounds and distributed earnings in a patriarchal way associated historically with agrarian societies. "Garden patches were assigned to the husbands and the money earned from sale of crops from these patches was held in his name" (Fogel and Engerman 1974, p. 142).

4. "In the Jamaican slave kinship network, the maternal bond was the key element, for a grown son tended to live with his mother until her death or stayed as close as possible in the house next door" (Dunn 1977, p. 48).

5. "Mothers were of fundamental importance in child rearing—in Africa as well as in the slave quarters—and the control of the kitchen and the involvement of women in the informal market networks developed by West Indian slaves reinforced the mothers' role in the slave households. But fathers remained much more important than is suggested" (Craton 1982, p. 49).

6. The significant exception is the Spanish West Indies, where eighteenth- and nineteenth-century prices of females were about one-third those of males.

7. Hindess and Hirst (1975) criticize Genovese's emphasis on the internal contradictions of U.S. slavery and argue that political pressures from western farmers brought about its end.

8. Mintz's (1974, 1978) stress on the growing of provisions as integral to the success of some Caribbean slave systems has influenced my thinking on slave-based plantation economies in the New World and women's place in them. The implications for women slaves are significant, as production of provisions, especially on private plots, offers a context and an explanation for women's economic strength. This point is made, of course, in much academic literature on households in the world economy, distinguishing as it does women's fundamental roles in production from the apparently mundane tasks of sustaining a household. Mintz (1978) also points out inherent contradictions between the slaves' nutritional self-sufficiency in much of the region and the slaveholders' need for slaves' labor time to be spent in commodity production.

9. Other important explanations grounded in the dynamics of capitalist growth rather than the intrinsic failures of slavery include emphasis on the acceptable alternatives to slavery available in technology and contract labor (Moreno Fraginals 1978; Rodney 1981).

10. "From the standpoint of the grower, the greatest defect of slavery lies in the fact that it quickly exhausts soil. The labor supply of low social status, docile and cheap,

can be maintained only by systematic degradation and by deliberate attempts to suppress its intelligence. Rotation of crops and scientific farming are therefore alien to slave societies'' (Williams 1966, p. 7).

11. Such a synthesis has been discouraged by the political and ideological importance of stressing the unique and fixed status of slaves. The unfortunate result is a deep insensitivity to women's experiences, expressed in the claim that status and implicitly race were always more significant at the legal and symbolic levels than was gender.

12. This view is not far from one claiming that ''primitive communist'' societies use women as a unit of trade; only here it is suggested that men's traditional right to subordinate exchange has been usurped by slave owners. The result is equality of male and female slaves. Leacock's comments are relevant: ''Only when the genders in primitive communist societies are understood as economically independent exchanges of goods and services, can the full force of capitalist relations in subverting the labor of women, and therefore transforming the entire structure of relationships in such societies, be appreciated'' (Leacock 1983, p. 280).

Chapter Two. Women in New World Slavery

1. The Brazilian case is not considered here. Its structural differences from the U.S. South and the Caribbean and internal complexity merit extensive commentary. Suffice it to say here that Brazil is frequently grouped with the Caribbean and Latin America in contrasts between the U.S. South and other slave societies in the Americas. Comparison to Spanish colonies, with large settler populations, has a long tradition (Genovese 1965; Tannenbaum 1946; Sio 1965). Recent research asserts the integrity of Brazilian slavery and its relationship to the cultivation of sugar and other forms of production by slaves (see Klein 1986 for a general review).

2. Slave women's position in U.S. and Caribbean urban settings was probably more similar than that of fieldworkers. Cities generally offered slave women more autonomy and independence than residence on plantations (Jones 1986; Mathurin 1974).

3. Fox-Genovese and Genovese (1983, p. 59) state that slavery, with its economies of scale, offered ''financial advantages'' but could not ''lay the foundation for sustained growth and qualitative development.''

4. Genovese (1979, p. xv) qualifies his terminology: ''Never an independent mode of production or form of government, slavery in the Americas constituted a social formation and a particular set of social relations of production within a declining seigneurial ('feudal') and a rising capitalist mode of production, under the governance of the attendant political relations of property and authority.'' See Dupuy (1985) for further discussion of the suitability of the ''slave mode of production'' to the Caribbean, particularly the French West Indies.

5. In 1860 slaves accounted for 47 percent of Louisiana's population, 45 percent of Alabama's, 44 percent of Georgia's, 31 percent of Virginia's, 25 percent of Tennessee's, and 20 percent of Kentucky's (Genovese 1979, p. 15).

6. There remains extensive debate on the profitability of slavery, the role of planting classes, and other political forces, including the abolition movement, in the demise of slavery in the U.S. South. Wallerstein (1976) makes the important and finally irrefutable point in discussing these debates: that, whatever the first cause, there was an inexorable movement away from slavery in the mid-eighteenth century that underscores the unsuitability of this form of labor organization to the world's emergent twentieth-century political economies and their ideological superstructures.

7. Dunn (1972, pp. 16–17) argues that the militancy of the Spanish and indigenous Caribbean peoples discouraged the British from settling larger islands and from cultivating crops that could make the fortunes they had hoped to find in the wild Caribbean. They became instead "modest tobacco and cotton farmers" in the early seventeenth century on the smaller and apparently less desirable Barbados and on St. Christopher, Nevis, Antigua and Montserrat, and the Lesser Antilles.

8. Half of householders owned slaves in tidewater counties of coastal Virginia and Maryland of the 1750s, indicating a concentration of slaves and that most slaves were on small plantations (Kulikoff 1986, pp. 6, 332).

9. Blacks in the Chesapeake area probably maintained their populations in the 1720s or 1730s (Kulikoff 1986, p. 5), in contrast to the West Indies where larger estate size, the rigorous sugar planting regimen, and related demographic and physiological factors impeded the reproduction of slave populations, often until after emancipation.

10. Fogel and Engerman's (1974, p. 29) breakdown is: United States, 36 percent; Brazil, 31 percent; British Caribbean, 15 percent; Spanish America, 11 percent; French Caribbean, 4 percent; Dutch, Danish, and Swedish islands, 2 percent. This period did *not* constitute a peak in slaveholding in the British, the French, or most other islands in the Caribbean, although it did in the United States, Cuba, and Dutch-held Surinam.

11. There are three island groups in the Caribbean. The Greater Antilles are the largest islands and run in a line southeast from the tip of Florida. They include Jamaica, Cuba, Hispaniola (now Haiti and the Dominican Republic), and Puerto Rico. The Lesser Antilles are made up of many small islands and are located in an arc east and south of the Greater Antilles. The most notable and frequently discussed in slave studies are the Leewards (St. Christopher [also called St. Kitts], Nevis, Montserrat, Antigua); the Windwards (Dominica, Grenada, St. Vincent, St. Lucia); Trinidad, Barbados, Guadeloupe, and Martinique; and the Virgin Islands (particularly St. Croix, St. John, and St. Thomas). The Bahamas are the third island group, located significantly northeast of the other islands. Bermuda, north of the West Indies and directly east of South Carolina in the Sargasso Sea, is of interest as an example of the use of slaves by European settlers in maritime work. Guyana and Dutch Surinam, also of importance in the study of Caribbean slavery, are countries on the northeast coast of South America. The development of slave-based sugar production there and colonization by European powers with other regional interests have led to their inclusion in many studies of the Caribbean.

12. Dunn (1972, p. 188) notes that Barbados's "sugar fetched a higher price per acre or laborer, paid lower English import duties, and suffered less from a glutted home market" than did its principal U.S. mainland competitor, Chesapeake tobacco.

13. Dirks (1987, p. 12) argues that plantation agriculture is made unique by the repetitive tasks demanded of the work force and the close watch needed over workers. Small-scale cash crop farming belies this and many other generalizations about the plantation.

14. African slave women were often subfecund, like their West Indian counterparts. Voluntary fertility control apparently played a large role in this condition, but the general health and welfare of the slaves—presumably influenced by their workload—may well have had an impact (Meillassoux 1983).

15. Fogel and Engerman (1974, p. 141) maintain that in the cotton culture of the U.S. South slave women did relatively little field labor and rarely worked in the plow gangs (see also Jones 1982). Others offer evidence of the varied nature of women's work in cotton cultivation and its frequent significance (White 1985).

16. Dunn (1977, p. 54), for example, finds that women "did much of the heavy labor at Mount Airy" in early nineteenth-century Virginia, "but more of them worked in craft or domestic jobs, and nearly half were excused from employment." On the comparable Mesopotamia sugar estate in Jamaica, "female slaves did much more of the basic labor" than at Mount Airy.

CHAPTER THREE. GENDER RATIOS AND CARIBBEAN SLAVERY

1. Although these data are not necessarily indicative of a majority of women, a majority of men is equally unlikely.

2. The reasons for the preponderance of local births among U.S. slaves have not been clearly distinguished or agreed on, although commentary is extensive. The close of the slave trade was important, but there are other pertinent factors: masters' encouragement of slave marriage and reproduction (Fogel and Engerman 1974); smaller units of production, also fostering the formation of nuclear families (Fogel and Engerman 1974; Jones 1982); less time between births, perhaps occasioned by shorter periods of breast feeding (Klein and Engerman 1978); and comparatively less oppressive work for male and female slaves alike (Dunn 1977).

3. Jesuit and Bethlemite friars were an exception to the Cuban rule, importing women and forcing them to marry slave men. The Jesuits followed the same practice in Martinique and were well known for the high birth rates on their estates (Peytraud 1973, p. 208). Spain expelled the Jesuit order from Cuba in 1767, in part because of their experiments in the humane treatment of slaves (Marrero 1983, p. 7).

4. Deerr (1949–1950, p. 277) reports resulting gender ratios of 1.46 males to 1 female in Guadeloupe in 1730 and 1.39 males to 1 female in Saint Domingue in 1754. The latter figure differs substantially from Debien's (1974, p. 366) estimate of the female slave population in Saint Domingue in the eighteenth century, at only 5 percent, and Moreau de Saint Méry's (1958, vol. 1, p. 57) eighteenth-century claim that as many female slaves were found in Saint Domingue as males.

5. Other societies were similarly dominated by youthful slaves. Since the 1600s most new slaves to the French West Indies were between 24 and 30 years old (Debien 1974, p. 366). The same "bulge in the middle age range" was found in the British West Indies (Craton 1974, p. 199).

6. In the early 1800s Pinckard (1970, vol. 3, p. 354) observed the public sale of slaves from a Dutch vessel in Demerara, with women valued at from 700 to 800 guilders, and men from 700 to 900 guilders. Demerara was developing as a sugar-producing society and slave women were still substantially outnumbered by males in the 1816–1818 registration period, with 1.3 males for every female (Roberts 1977, p. 154).

7. Records from the ship of Captain Lawrence Spain, arriving at Christianbourg castle on December 15, 1726, indicate that 50 males left Africa, valued at 48 rigsdalers each, along with 25 females, each also priced at 48 rigsdalers. They were sold at an equal price in St. Thomas (Westergaard 1917, p. 130).

8. Yet Knight (1970), Genovese (1965), and Moreno Fraginals (1978) have all stressed the national bourgeois character of Cuban planters in contrast to the mercantile orientation of other West Indian slaveholders. This interpretation implies more regard for cost savings, particularly in the interest of reproduction of the labor force, than Cuban slaveholders exhibited in their decided preference for male slaves.

9. DuTertre (1958, vol. 2, p. 462) describes three kinds of Africans who were sold to international slave traders: (1) war prisoners, (2) criminals condemned to death, and (3) thieves condemned to banishment. Labat (1930, vol. 2, p. 36) adds to these groups

the slaves of princes, along with stolen people. See also Gaston-Martin (1948, pp. 59–60) and Jesse (1961, p. 139).

10. "The proportion of female slaves in Cuba was always very low, usually estimated at one-third the number of males. A certain resistance existed in Cuba against having female slaves on the plantations, since they were thought a source of distraction; nor were slave marriages generally thought desirable" (Corwin 1967, p. 15).

11. Church records reveal that the ratio of slave marriages to population in Cuba was nearly the same as that for whites in the early 1800s (Klein 1967, pp. 96–97).

12. The slaves could not be prohibited from forming unions, often recognized by slaveholders, if not by law. Such unions were always vulnerable to separations through the sale of a partner. The fragile nature of slaves' conjugal unions supports Patterson's argument that slaves were bondless in the symbolic order and undermines the significance of Klein's (1967, p. 38) contention that the Spanish West Indian planters' recognition of the slaves' "legal personality" offered rights to "personal security, property, marriage . . . parenthood."

13. Klein (1983) offers evidence that refutes other explanations of why males were preferred to female slaves, for example, that females were more costly and difficult to ship or experienced higher mortality in passage. See also Robertson and Klein (1983), Meillassoux (1975, 1983) and Terbourg-Penn (1986) for discussions of women's significance in African slavery.

14. After the revolution gender ratios in British areas of Saint Domingue changed dramatically as a result of flight from plantations and the termination of slave imports. Using data from 1796 and 1797, drawn from 200 plantations housing more than 15,500 slaves, Geggus (1982, p. 292) found that men slightly outnumbered women on coffee estates, with 103 males for every 100 females. On sugar estates the ratio was 93 males for every 100 females.

CHAPTER FOUR. HOUSEHOLD ECONOMIES

1. Ligon (1657) claimed that slaves' houses in Barbados were never more than 5 feet square. Descriptions of slaves' dwellings are remarkably similar for the region. On St. Croix, for example, houses were of "withes, daub and wattle style. Upright poles were laced with branches and a daub thrown on made from clay or cow dung base" (Lewisohn 1970, p. 118; see also Flinter 1834, p. 247; Carmichael 1834, vol. 1, pp. 124–130; Fouchard 1981, p. 51; Diaz Soler 1974, p. 163; Tomich 1976, p. 224).

2. House building remains the prelude to family formation in some areas of the Caribbean today (Dirks and Kerns 1976).

3. Moreton (1793, pp. 150–151) repeats a slave song in which a man laments his life without the domestic help of a wife.

4. DuTertre (1958, vol. 2, p. 475) reported that young French West Indian slave children wore no clothing. Children were naked in St. Vincent in the 1830s (Carmichael 1834, vol. 2, p. 10). A traveler to the Danish Virgin Islands in 1758 found most field slaves unclothed (Hall 1975, p. 180). In urban Antigua in the late 1700s, Janet Schaw observed women with "nothing on their bodies" (1939, p. 87). Atwood (1791, p. 260) noted that slaves had clothes on the English estates of Dominica, unlike the French. Stedman (1971, p. 370) found black women slaves naked above the waist but mulatto slave women clothed. See also Leslie (1740, p. 36), Pinckard (1970, vol. 1, pp. 229, 258–259), and Schoelcher (1948, p. 34).

5. Infant mortality increased, as women could not nurse their children sufficiently (Ortiz 1975, p. 260).

6. Mintz (1974, p. 187) mentions the cultivation of fruit trees, herbs, and "delicate crops." Brathwaite (1971, p. 133) describes Jamaican kitchen gardens with plantains, ackee, okra, yams, eddoe, mangos, and oranges. The *jardin-case* of the French West Indian slave included Guinea sorrel, spinach, cucumbers, peppers, gourds, and Chinese yams (Debien 1974, pp. 183–189).

7. The Code Noir and Penal Code forbade free Saturdays in place of rations, but both were ignored by planters (Tomich 1976, p. 206). Slaveholders in the Danish Virgin Islands also traded days for rations, despite legal prohibitions enacted in 1755 (N. Hall 1977, p. 176).

8. Slaves rarely produced estate crops for sale. Mintz (1983, p. 234) describes this phenomenon in British Guiana: "Though its very sparse settlement prevented the growth of a flourishing internal market system comparable to that of Jamaica or Saint-Domingue, the slaves did grow some substantial part of their own food, and were able to sell off their surpluses. (Of rather special significance was the practice of cultivating rice on unused lands near the plantation, and selling the crop.)"

9. On St. John slaves' grounds frequently bordered estates, forming slave settlements. These small communities were a source of support for slaves in the production of subsistence goods, in child care, in food provision, and in the fomenting of resistance (Olwig 1985).

10. Scott (1985) questions the emphasis of Moreno Fraginals (1977) and others on the establishment of *barracones* in nineteenth-century Cuba and the eradication of *conucos,* or provision grounds. She maintains that single-sex barracks were found in Havana and Matanzas only. Provision grounds remained common, she argues, citing a nineteenth-century observer's noting of storage areas for slaves' harvests on estates with barracks housing.

11. Sturge and Harvey (1838, p. 47) were told that estate cultivation of food required five months yearly, making it more dear than importation.

12. Beckford (1790, pp. 138–139) describes the division of labor that emerged as slaves restored an estate damaged by a hurricane. The field gang worked together to rebuild houses. Women planted the estate provision grounds, and with their children gathered produce while the men built fences.

13. Slaves left provision grounds to friends and kin whenever masters would comply.

14. Court records reveal that on St. John women tended pigs, fished from shore, and may occasionally have controlled boats that bondmen used to fish (Olwig 1985, pp. 49–50).

15. In asserting the significance of the growing of provisions to later Caribbean peasant economies, Mintz (1983, p. 227) argues that even in the midst of the revolution Saint Domingue's slaves established private areas for food cultivation and robust markets. The revolutionary leadership struggled to return former slaves to restored estates and sugar cultivation.

CHAPTER FIVE. PLANTATION WORK

1. Some domestic positions allowed the worker little supervision. Mrs. Carmichael (1834, vol. 2, p. 20) and her friends among Trinidad's planting families found domestics in town harder to rule than "country negroes."

2. Dunn (1977, pp. 56–57) cites logs from the Newton estate on Barbados to indicate that job tasks were more mixed than titles indicate. It is possible, then, that women did more different kinds of work than the historical record seems to suggest.

3. An association of slave women with healing and knowledge of physiology may explain the assignment of a woman to the role of executioner in Bermuda in 1652 (Packwood 1975, p. 11).

4. A Cuban slave could be freed at baptism for $25.00. Women sought a "respectable male" for godfather, one who might free the child (Tannenbaum 1946, p. 57; see also Campbell 1976, p. 248).

5. The actual proportion of freed men and women in total populations of the British West Indies was comparatively small: about 2.9 percent in Jamaica in 1800 and 2.6 percent in Barbados in 1801 (Cohen and Greene 1972, p. 4). The proportion of free persons of African descent per 100 slaves was 0.8 in St. Kitts, 1.9 in Nevis, 2.6 in Montserrat, 2.7 in St. Vincent, 3.2 in Jamaica, 3.5 in Barbados, 3.6 in Antigua, 4.0 in Grenada, 5.0 in Tobago, 12.8 in Dominica, and 16.6 in Trinidad (Hart 1980, p. 135).

6. Elderly and "superannuated" slaves were often freed throughout the Caribbean, frequently to save the cost of maintaining unproductive slaves (Hoetink 1972, p. 67; Bowser 1972, p. 22).

7. Manumissions, often dependent on access to income, particularly for males, were more highly associated with urbanism for males than for females in the British West Indies (Higman 1984, p. 382).

8. "In nearly all slaveholding societies female slaves were manumitted at a higher rate than males, whatever their overall manumission rate, primarily because of their frequent sexual relations with the master or with other free males" (Patterson 1982, p. 263).

9. The same was true in Dutch Surinam. "The numerical superiority of colored over Negro free people, and the fact that there were nearly twice as many women as men in this group, clearly indicates that the composition of the category 'free people' was predominantly determined by masters' preference for manumitting their colored mistresses and their offspring. The colored men among the manumitted had mostly been house or artisan slaves, and the latter had some opportunity to earn income of their own with which to try to buy their freedom" (Hoetink 1972, pp. 62–63).

10. Klein (1986, p. 224) summarizes the impact of these changes in the French and British West Indies: "By the 1780's, the three major islands of Saint Domingue, Martinique, and Guadeloupe had only 30,000 free colored population among them, compared with over 575,000 slaves and 52,000 whites. The British West Indies were no better, with only 13,000 free colored for all the islands, compared with 53,000 whites and 467,000 slaves." This trend reversed, of course, in the early nineteenth century, with the French Revolution and British West Indies amelioration measures.

11. Craton's (1974, p. 209) synthesis of the records of six Jamaican plantations lists five gangs of diminishing strength, all at least 50 percent female: the great or first gang, the second gang, the third gang (the gross or weeding gang), the vagabond gang, and the pen Negroes.

12. Girls aged 15 to 18 years were more highly valued at l'Anse-à-l'Ane than boys of the same age in the 1750s. Among adults, male field workers were priced at a higher rate than females, by about 300 livres, with the prices of both dropping after age 40 (Debien 1960, pp. 37, 42). We can infer that young women's childbearing capacity and increased role in export commodity production were acknowledged by planters in these pricing and labor use patterns.

13. Throughout the region women's work in coffee cultivation more nearly resembled that of men than did their work in sugar cultivation (Knight 1970, p. 67; Diaz Solar 1974, p. 156), much as in the United States.

14. Individual plantations conformed to varying degrees to the Cuban sugar harvest routine. Bremer (1853, vol. 2, p. 312) wrote that at Ariadne estate shifts changed every

seven hours and that the mill was turned off two nights weekly. At the large St. Amelia Inhegno slaves were freed from labor one night a week and a few Sunday mornings.

15. Martinique and Guadeloupe adopted technology in the 1800s that increased their processing capacity. Steam-powered mills were largely replaced by hydraulic ones, increasing the demand for raw cane and either the number of field hands or labor productivity. Plows were not used in Martinique and Guadeloupe, demanding more field labor power than in many competing sugar producers (Schnakenbourg 1980, p. 175; Tomich 1976, p. 106).

CHAPTER SIX. WOMEN AND THE SLAVE FAMILY

1. James (1963, p. 16) notes an apparent cruelty among slaves, particularly toward kin. Slaves in Saint Domingue poisoned one another ''to keep the number of slaves small and prevent their masters embarking on larger schemes which would increase work.''

2. Monk Lewis has charmed modern readers with his iconoclastic observations about Jamaican slavery. He often saw in Europeans' moral outrage at slaves' behavior a denial of their own ethical transgressions. He notes, for example, that the slaves were guilty of the same ''fashionable peccadillos'' as their masters. ''Negroes . . . are not without some of the luxuries of civilised life; old men of sixty keeping mistresses and young ones seducing their friends' wives'' (M. Lewis 1834, pp. 220–230).

3. Patterson further contends that males mated exogamously; estates traced descent through women (Patterson 1976, p. 59).

4. ''For the Negro child, in particular, the plantation offered no really satisfactory father-image other than the master. . . . the very etiquette of plantation life removed even the honorific attributes of fatherhood from the Negro male, who was addressed as 'boy'—until, when the vigorous years of his prime were past, he was allowed to assume the title of 'uncle' '' (Elkins 1976, p. 130).

5. In urban Trinidad, on holdings of more than 20 slaves, families of *any* type were relatively rare (Higman 1978, p. 168).

6. Women in these units were less fertile than those in conjugal ones (Debien 1960, p. 48).

7. Patterson (1976, p. 50) acknowledges that stable unions existed among Caribbean slaves, resulting in ''statistical regularity in mating and familial patterns.'' He argues finally, however, that normlessness prevailed.

8. ''Therefore, in assessing the nature of slave family and its place in the continuum we emphasize not the ways that slavery destroyed or distorted family, but the ways in which the slaves' own forms of family triumphed over adversity. In this light, we evaluate slavery not by the manner in which it controlled and shaped slaves' destinies, but by the degree to which it allowed slaves to make family lives of their own'' (Craton 1979, p. 35).

9. This pattern was especially strong on large holdings, distant from Nassau. Close to the city land units were often too small for conjugal families to form, and female-headed households predominated (Craton 1979, p. 11).

10. Indeed, Higman (1978, pp. 165–167) found fewer nuclear families in Trinidad than in Jamaica, which he attributes to Trinidad's larger number of Africans (with high mortality) and more urbanized population. Gautier (1985, p. 89) reports a disproportionate number of marriages and co-resident unions among skilled workers on Bisdary estate in Guadeloupe in 1759. The 32 artisans and workers made up 36 percent of slaves living alone, 48 percent of those in concubinage, and 68.7 percent of

married slaves. The share of slave marriages is, however, particularly high on this estate, which was once owned by Jesuit priests who encouraged it.

11. Polyandrous unions might seem likely given demographic preconditions, but the material foundations of such unions were absent because of the relatively low social status of women slaves.

12. African polygynous systems generally were found in areas where women farmed and thus enjoyed a fair degree of independence from men (Goody 1976, p. 32).

13. Boserup (1970) traces three patterns of gender division of labor among African peasants: female farming, male farming, and mixed systems. In the first, men assist only by felling trees, a pattern occasionally referred to in the literature on West Indian slavery. Women generally have the larger role in farming in the mixed systems as well. Boserup (1970, p. 22) concludes: "The available quantitative information about work input by sex seems to indicate that even today *village* [emphasis mine] production in Africa south of the Sahara continues to be predominantly female farming." The introduction of the plow to raise agricultural productivity increased males' labor commitment and lessened females'.

14. In Higman's (1978) analysis of families among African slaves registered in early nineteenth-century Trinidad, the greatest number of polygynous units was found on the largest plantation. This finding suggests that, with many women available and with the greater opportunities for resource maximization sometimes offered by larger estates, African men sought multiple spouses. Higman also found more polygyny and nuclear families among the Igbo than in other polygynous African groups. Higman attributes this pattern to the large number of Igbos in Trinidad and their low gender ratio.

15. With data from the Human Relations Area Files, Goody (1976) discerned a strong correlation among societies with complex agriculture, diverging inheritance, and monogamy.

16. Describing *le contre-pouvoir féminin*, Gautier (1985, p. 51) comments that "[African] women lived in an essentially feminine milieu," which protected them from male mistreatment.

17. Citing Bettelheim's (1943) analysis of concentration camp behavior, Elkins argues that no inmates attained true autonomy; all formed personalities in reaction to their situations. Bettelheim's ideal of informed action is itself a reactive stance, suggests Elkins (1976, p. 135), one possible only for those who assumed an alternate role, in Bettelheim's case, that of the detached, scientific observer.

18. Elkins also notes that a range of behavior was possible for slaves, citing Goffman's and others' typologies for individual responses to oppressive institutions. He argues, however, that a modal personality type is a legitimate sociological construct and can be expected to emerge from a structural setting. For U.S. slaves that type, Elkins contends, is the docile and dependent "Sambo."

CHAPTER SEVEN. FERTILITY

1. Even among U.S. slaves, childlessness (wrongly labeled "sterility" by Klein and Engerman 1978) was high. Still the U.S. slave birth rate was unusually high, but births in the British West Indies were similar to European rates at the time (Fogel and Engerman 1979, p. 568).

2. Abénon (1973, p. 315) notes further that child mortality was actually higher in eighteenth-century France than in the Caribbean. Fogel and Engerman (1974, pp. 123-124) make a related point about U.S. slave infant mortality in contrast to white

infant mortality. About 183 per 1,000 slave infants aged 1 year and younger died in 1850, compared to the only slightly lower rate of 177 per 1,000 infant deaths among white southerners.

3. Caribbean slaves were also virtually immune to some diseases.

4. Geggus (1978, p. 26) notes that this strain of yaws was associated with venereal disease.

5. Rice eating was a recognized cause of beriberi in Southeast Asia and in Cuba. Pellagra is often associated with a diet heavy in corn consumption.

6. Dirks (1987, pp. 86–87) cites eighteenth- and nineteenth-century sources to argue that hookworm was common among British West Indian slaves. He also claims that women ate ''fine clays'' more frequently than men and that dropsy in women was often accompanied by amenorrhea, or cessation of menstruation.

7. Fearing tetanus, Jamaican slaves believed that newborns were not of this world for nine days. Some West Africans shared a belief that life begins after nine days (Brathwaite 1971, p. 213; Patterson 1969).

8. Kiple and Kiple (1981) remind us that many adult Africans suffer lactose intolerance, leaving them without dairy sources of vitamin D and calcium. Nursing mothers passed vitamin D deficiencies to their infants. Many suffered from sickle cell anemia as well, causing iron deficiencies (Kiple and Kiple 1977, pp. 285–287).

9. These diseases caused 11 percent of deaths among white children to 9 years of age (Kiple and Kiple 1977, p. 290).

10. There is some debate among students of the Caribbean about the relative contributions of low fertility and high mortality in accounting for natural decreases. Eblen (1975) compared U.S. and Cuban fertility rates and concluded that, given similar age and gender distributions, Cuban fertility would have equaled that of U.S. slaves. Kiple (1984) agrees, contending that in the British West Indies infant mortality was the key source of natural decrease. Roberts (1957) and Higman (1984, p. 314) argue instead that neither mortality nor fertility alone consistently accounts for population change in British colonies.

11. Fogel and Engerman (1974, p. 137) argue further that U.S. slave women bore first children late, at 22.6 years, after establishing marriages. White (1985, pp. 97–98) disagrees, claiming first births to have been at age 18 or 19, with a 2½-year gap between children, little different from the 30-month gap between Jamaican slave children (Craton 1977, p. 98). DuTertre (1958, vol. 2, p. 473) reported that seventeenth-century French West Indian slave mothers bore children at 20-month to 2-year intervals.

12. On three Jamaican properties, from 1817 to 1822, colored fertility was greater than that of blacks, almost five times greater among females aged 15 to 19 (Higman 1976a, p. 154). Craton (1978, p. 340) notes that at Jamaica's Worthy Park, fertility declines were associated with a decline in miscegenation, more likely to mean colored women, not black women, with white men.

13. Fogel and Engerman (1979, p. 570) report a greater fertility gap between African and Creole slave women in the United States than in the Caribbean.

14. ''Fertility and longevity depend less on the slaves' origins than on the plantations' prosperity'' (Siguret 1968, p. 225). Dunn (1987, p. 815) notes that African women lived longer than Creoles on Mesopotamia but that the latter experienced higher fertility. ''The Africans tolerated the labor regimen on Mesopotamia well but did not breed, whereas the local slaves did breed but showed less tolerance for the labor system.''

15. Olwig (1985, pp. 34, 54–55) cites evidence from Danish colonial records that slave women complained that ''the planters made it difficult for them to bear and rear

children and lead a secure family life.'' Some also found it difficult to have their babies, nurse them, and to care for provision grounds. See also Dirks's (1987, p. 201) critical comments about the ''modern speculation'' that slave abortions were politically motivated.

16. Blassingame's comments (1972, p. 81) on similar planter attitudes in the United States remind us that the need to maintain order sometimes superseded ideological and material motives in the treatment and management of slaves. ''It is obvious that most slaveholders did not care about sexual customs of their slaves as long as there was no fighting and bickering.'' Slave owners encouraged monogamy as a way to discipline slaves yet punished them by forbidding visits to other plantations to see spouses (Blassingame 1972, pp. 82, 88).

17. In Trinidad suckling infants were fed arrowroot or flour, oatmeal, and pap every two days and castor oil every three or four days (Carmichael 1834, vol. 2, p. 189). French West Indian slave babies were fed nothing but breast milk for the first five to six months in the seventeenth century (DuTertre 1958, vol. 2, p. 473). This may have changed as the pressure on women to work and separate from newborns increased (Gautier 1985).

18. Babies were weaned to less protein but more carbohydrates (Kiple and Kiple 1977, p. 288).

19. Lunn et al. (1984) found that increasing food supplements to pregnant and then nursing mothers in Gambia resulted in reductions in plasma PLR (pituitary hormone concentration) and earlier resumption of ovulation. A comparison of supplementation during pregnancy and nursing with none shows that the birth rate increased 37 percent.

20. Sheridan (personal communication) responded that slaves in the British West Indies easily concealed health practices from European doctors who, during the seventeenth and eighteenth centuries, came to estates no more than twice a month. Cared for by African nurses and midwives, slave women could end unwanted pregnancies and recover from reproductive diseases and injuries and from the loss of newborns without the knowledge or interference of whites. Planters' frequent anti-natalism also shielded these dimensions of slaves' private lives until the early nineteenth century, when European abolitionist pressure brought scrutiny to slaves' health and medical treatment.

21. The incidence of infanticide by slaves was overstated by white southerners, and many deaths of slave infants are now understood to have had other causes, including perhaps Sudden Infant Death Syndrome (SIDS) (White 1985, pp. 87-89).

CHAPTER EIGHT. FECUNDITY

1. From 10 percent to 25 percent of pregnancies end in ''recognised spontaneous abortion before 28 weeks,'' whereas 2 percent of pregnancies end in ''perinatal deaths after 28 weeks' gestation'' (Miller et al. 1980, p. 555).

2. It is also possible, as Lady Nugent thought, that colored women actually aborted pregnancies rather than suffer miscarriages, perhaps to keep their youthful appearances and attract white males. Europeans often freed their offspring or at least allowed them to remain in domestic work. But there were no guarantees of favored treatment for a woman or her child, and outside of those in long-established unions, colored women may generally have feared loss of status and banishment to fieldwork with pregnancy. Nevertheless colored women frequently had higher fertility than black women because of better health or by intent.

3. Estimates of both gonorrhea and syphilis among U.S. slaves are derived from army induction records showing that 35 percent of black recruits from ages 31 to 35 had syphilis. McFalls and McFalls (1984, p. 470) suggest that these figures overstate black males' syphilis rate. Assuming a ratio of 1.4 infected males to 1 female, about 21 percent of black females had syphilis in the 1940s.

4. Keller et al. (1984, p. 181) offer slightly different estimates of the impact of gonorrhea on fertility. In 15–50 percent of cases, they indicate, gonorrhea spreads to the uterus and fallopian tubes, impairing fertility.

5. Blacks were more susceptible to tuberculosis than whites, and black children were more prone to whooping cough than white children. Tuberculosis spreads in densely populated areas. Hence urbanized populations generally have greater immunity to the disease than nonurbanized groups such as African slaves.

6. Handler and Corruccini's (1983) analysis of dental fragments from slaves at the Newton estate on Barbados suggests that children experienced malnutrition not prenatally but after weaning, at age 3 or 4. The prenatal nutritional environment does not bear directly on conception but does suggest that infant loss resulting from inadequate nutrition was rare.

7. A peasant family of 5, where all but the youngest child works, is said to require 2,000 calories per capita daily (Kleinman 1980, p. 124).

8. Kiple (1984, p. 58) claims that Ibo women were among the Africans "most subject to 'obstructions of the menstrua' or amenorrhea, a phenomenon often linked to malnutrition."

9. Frequency of intercourse is related to conception in this way. If we assume other conditions, in particular, that both partners have optimal health and fertility, then intercourse three times weekly results in conception in less than six months 51 percent of the time; twice weekly intercourse leads to pregnancy in less than six months 46 percent of the time; once weekly, 32 percent; less than once, 17 percent (Keller et al. 1984, p. 5). Lack of conjugal residence or stable union, illness, and work commitments all reduced opportunities for intercourse and hence rapid conception.

10. Male subfecundity accounts for one-third to one-half of infertility among couples. Male age has a dramatic impact on fertility, with conception occurring among 75 percent of couples in 6 months when the male is under 25 years of age; in 23 percent of couples in 6 months when the male is over age 40. These data do not take into account reduced frequency of intercourse among older men or the age of the woman (Keller et al. 1984, p. 4).

11. Sturge and Harvey's (1838, p. 5) testimony about a Bridgetown prison official's cruelty to a pregnant woman, discussed in Chapter Nine, casts doubt on the universality of changed attitudes toward pregnancy and childbirth.

12. As Higman (1984, p. 355) suggests, British West Indian amelioration policies had a more discernible positive effect on fertility than on mortality. Where infant mortality fell, the effect is probably reflected in the higher fertility. Infant deaths were often unrecorded by planters (Roberts 1977, p. 147).

13. Gautier (1985, p. 129) refers to noncompliance in Guadeloupe, where the local Conseil found government-imposed amelioration rules disregarded by many planters.

14. Gender ratios favored women, although only slightly, in Montserrat as early as 1729 (Sheridan 1973, pp. 172–175). Gender ratios were equal in much of Barbados by the last quarter of the eighteenth century. But, as Craton (1978) points out, a preponderance of females can indicate their aging as well as high levels of male mortality from overwork, neither of which contributes to fertility.

15. There are interesting exceptions to all of these trends. In the 1870s, at the height of Antigua's prosperity, Schaw (1939, p. 88) saw slaves busy with their own grounds on

Sundays, hiring themselves out, and on Thursdays marketing their crops. She visited an estate whose proprietor, Colonel Martin, claimed not to have bought a slave for 12 years and that 52 slave women were pregnant. The quantity and quality of land available for provisions is suggested by Schaw's comment (p. 130) that "there is a great want of shade, as every acre is under sugar."

16. In the French West Indies the number of women increased near the end of the Colonial Period, but among adults males continued to outnumber females (Debien 1974, p. 42).

17. Debien's (1974, pp. 347-351) survey of plantation inventories from Saint Domingue reveals both high levels of infant and child death and low fertility. At la Sucrerie la Barre, 14 boys and 6 girls were listed in 1776, but only 7 boys and 4 girls survived to 1790. At Galbaud du Fort aux Sources, with an average of 120 slaves from 1741 to 1772, only 2 births were recorded per year; after 1772, with from 150 to 190 slaves, 1 or 2 births were recorded yearly. At la Caféière Mauleurier aux Matheux, 42 deaths occurred from 1786 to 1791 and only 20 to 22 births.

18. Infant mortality was also higher in maternal than conjugal families at l'Anse-à-l'Ane.

19. Planters eventually came to depend on provision grounds to avoid collective food cultivation and the problems of food importation. Mrs. Carmichael (1834, vol. 2, p. 230) reports that by 1832 at her Laurel Hill estate few slaves had fewer than six acres of provision land producing two crops per year. Generally, however, it appears that Trinidad's slaves were not well nourished during the first three decades of the nineteenth century, regardless of whether they consumed rations or food grown on individual gardens and farms.

20. Lamur (1977, pp. 171-172) compares the population of Catharina Sophia with that of plantations with more than 30 slaves and with Surinam's free population. The birth rate was slightly lower for other plantations, but mortality was higher on Catharina Sophia, although age distributions varied. In general, Catharina Sophia's work force had more young adult women and more older males than large plantations in Surinam.

21. Land in tobacco doubled, from slightly more than 2,000 cuerdas in 1830 to 4,000 cuerdas in 1896 (Scarano 1984, p. 5).

22. Barbuda's population fell by 15 percent from 1774 to 1790. An estate manager blamed low fertility on a shortage of males and venereal disease. Age and gender ratios naturally improved, and venereal disease "[ran] its course," producing a dramatic change in fertility and mortality (Lowenthal and Clarke 1977, p. 517). The demographic profile was obviously integral to this change and the impact of venereal disease ambiguous.

23. African fertility was low at the time (Boserup 1970).

24. By the 1850s the crude birth rate at Worthy Park in Jamaica had doubled from that of the late days of slavery (Craton 1977, p. 287). Marriage became common in rural Jamaica, as peasants purchased land and withdrew from plantation work (Phillippo 1843).

25. McFalls and McFalls (1984, p. 467) note that childlessness moved in the opposite direction, increasing until the 1930s and then dropping until 1960.

26. Dirks and Kerns (1976) shed light on this hypothesis in their longitudinal research on marriage and mating patterns in a rural community in Tortola in the British Virgin Islands. Through six successive stages of economic change, the tendency to marry (usually accompanying relatively high fertility, but not necessarily) is positively related to availability of cash to males, who build houses preceding a legal union. "The plurality of conjugal forms in Rum Bay can be understood as a response

to an environment in which fully adult and sexually active individuals cannot count on access to income-earning opportunities" (Dirks and Kerns 1976, p. 50).

CHAPTER NINE. SEX, PUNISHMENT, AND PROTEST

1. The reference to Foucault's work (1977, 1978) on sexuality and punishment should not obscure or deny the material roots of these phenomena. Like other structuralist writings, Foucault's give power to ideological factors that this largely materialist analysis subordinates. Bondwomen sought relationships with slave masters primarily for concrete material reasons and only then because such ties were culturally or symbolically valued. At the same time, brutal treatment of slaves—male and female—was generally associated with the slaveholder's perception of poor work performance. The bizarre and sadistic treatment of slaves by their owners is the result, finally if distantly, of the owners' sovereign status in a highly productive but often strained economy.

2. Moreau de Saint Méry (1958, p. 53) found Congolese women in Saint Domingue especially free sexually, although he wondered if the generally decadent atmosphere had not encouraged this tendency.

3. The ratio of white men to white women varied historically and regionally, even within colonial areas. Twelve white men resided in Saint Domingue in the 1600s, for example, for every white woman. By the eighteenth century in Saint Domingue, among white Creoles the gender ratio was two men for every woman; among Europeans, from four to five men for every woman. In eighteenth-century Martinique, there were 120 white men for every 100 white women. The gender ratio of white men and women approached equality in Guadeloupe in the mid-eighteenth century (Gautier 1985, p. 33).

4. "The girls here [in Surinam] who voluntarily enter into these connections are sometimes mulattoes, sometimes Indians, and often negroes. They all exalt in the circumstances of living with a European, whom in general, they serve with the utmost tenderness and fidelity, and tacitly reprove those numerous fair ones who break through ties more sacred and solemn" (Stedman 1971, p. 17).

5. The Spanish slave codes "guaranteed slave women and children against violations and abuse by masters" (Klein 1986, p. 191). The 1755 Reglement in the Danish West Indies fined a master 2,000 pounds of sugar for the rape or sexual exploitation of a slave (N. Hall 1977, p. 176). The Code Noir levied 2,000 livres of sugar against the master or overseer who bore a child with a female slave (Tomich 1976, p. 217).

6. Frère Saint-Gilles observed in 1687 that slave women were pushed to "debauchery" by a lack of food and clothing (Peytraud 1973, p. 199).

7. European male attitudes toward their children varied. Mrs. Carmichael (1834, vol. 1, p. 91) claimed that a man who would not free his child was "justly detested." Lady Nugent (1907, p. 274) noted that her staff's mixed children were obviously not freed by the "thoughtless young men." Black women involved with European men were thought to use abortifacients in Antigua in the 1770s (Schaw 1939, pp. 112-113) and in the French West Indies (Gautier 1985, p. 175).

8. Mrs. Carmichael (1834, vol. 1, pp. 28-31) claims that white children in St. Vincent were "tyrannical to slaves" and everyone else, so badly were they reared.

9. Clinton (1982, p. 188) refers to slave narratives to suggest that southern white women punished slaves far less often than did slave masters or their agents. Violence by mistresses against slaves was most common on small estates. Gautier (1985, p. 35) suggests that in the French West Indies slave masters were motivated to abuse slaves

primarily to increase work productivity, whereas white women's domestic power, magnified by confinement in the home and their husbands' frequent absences, led to the physical harassment of slaves.

10. Patterson (1972, p. 286) comments, "Jamaican society was no place for the fair sex, and the evidence indicates that those white women who survived were hardly the fairest specimen of their race. In the absence of wives, mothers, daughters, and sisters, the Jamaican great house never became the sanctified fortress of southern 'gynocracy.'"

11. Devèze (1977, p. 297) points out that the image of a gay and empty life of Caribbean slave-owning females is at odds with what is occasionally revealed in "detailed studies." Country estate houses were often simple wooden structures requiring care by the slaveholder and his family.

12. Clinton's comment (1982, p. 209) on this phenomenon in the U.S. South is acute: "Despite white women's exaggerated modesty, the body of an unclothed black gave the plantation mistress little offense. The relationship between the plantation mistress and slave was never personal; this dehumanized naked object could present no threat to a woman's propriety."

13. A common form of torture of women in twentieth-century fascist regimes is the physical and sexual abuse of their children and violence against unborn children. Males, by contrast, are threatened with sexual abuse of their wives and lovers (Bunster-Burotto 1986).

14. Mathurin (1975, p. 30) claims that by the late 1700s women outnumbered men in some Jamaican Maroon communities. In "Nanny Town" there were more women and children than men, according to a British soldier who was a prisoner there (Tuelon 1973, p. 22). Large populations of women have been noted in other Maroon communities. The Maroon band at Bahorruco in Saint Domingue, freed in 1785, had 71 males and 58 females, making up 30 couples and children, a widow, a man with children, 4 women with children, and 11 men and women alone (Gautier 1985, p. 232).

15. Edwards (1966, vol. 1, pp. 540–541) writes that in Jamaica the polygamous male Maroons treated daughters cruelly and offered them to male visitors.

16. Debien (1973, p. 126) suggests that women mostly ran away in pairs to nearby areas. In the United States male runaways outnumbered females, but more women than men were truants (White 1985, pp. 70–75).

17. There may be a pattern of women slaves, particularly domestics, who betrayed conspirators. Craton (1982) cites three such cases in the British West Indies. Although slave men also informed masters of likely rebellions, the intimate relations of slave women to some white men surely strained their loyalty to the slave community. See also Schoelcher (1842, p. 106).

18. Concubines and new wives in African slavery were reared for such a role, not meant to float between the status of chattel and mistress (Robertson and Klein 1983; Patterson 1982).

19. See Douglas (1966) for a lengthy discussion of how violation of female purity can bring danger to others. This ideology contrasts with the honor/shame dichotomy associated with Latin America and other societies, in which males gain from the honored position of some females and the shamed position of others (Martinez-Alier 1974). The attitudes of European men in the Caribbean appear to be close to the honor/shame complex, as Martinez-Alier argues for late nineteenth-century Cuba, with white women honored and slave women shamed. A problem with the application of this concept to slavery, however, is that it turns on women's choice to observe the code of honor or to reject it, which bondwomen lacked.

20. Mathurin (1974, p. 343) argues that by the end of slavery in Jamaica the black woman had come to symbolize slavery, its tensions, and its crises. Responsible for the bulk of agricultural work, receiving "neo-natality . . . indulgencies," she was reviled by white Creole society.

CHAPTER TEN. CONCLUSIONS

1. "Many theories of sexual inequality pose the wrong question. Instead of asking what variables account for variation in *degree* of sex inequality, they address the issues of 'How did the subordination of women to men come about?' or 'What accounts for female subordination to males?' The first question presupposes an era in history in which females were not subordinated to males; the second assumes that females have always been subordinated; and both utilize a simple dichotomy—subordination vs. non-subordination" (Chafetz 1984, p. 2). See Nicholson (1986, pp. 8-9) for a critique of cross-cultural studies of women's position that focuses on the resulting positivism and the dualism objected to by Chafetz.

2. Materialist writings are generally mute on this point, suggesting that further analysis of ideology may be helpful. The marginalization of population groups is a special problem of advanced industrial societies and has been addressed by Marxist feminists (Bonacich 1981).

3. See Attewell (1984) for a brief but penetrating critique of the "mode of production" approach and its failure to address specific historical cases. It has been more successfully applied to precapitalist modes of production in Africa, where the mix of lineage and trade-based slavery has been studied by Meillassoux (1975), Bloch (1980), Terray (1975), and others.

4. Scott (1985) links these points in arguing that Cuban slaves' rebellions shaped emancipation. This in itself suggests that the growing of provisions, petty trade, and kinship relations—all phenomena that enabled slaves to organize insurgency—were more common in nineteenth-century Cuba than current commentary, influenced heavily by the work of Moreno Fraginals (1977, 1978), allows.

5. This debate is significant in Marxist-feminist studies. Barrett (1980) argues that ideological structures finally explain the depth of gender stratification in advanced capitalism. Brenner and Ramas (1984) counter that biological factors predispose even industrial societies to women's economic subordination and social isolation. Omvedt (1986) and Delphy (1984) contend that patriarchy remains a legitimate material structure for explaining women's subordination in the contemporary West. Proponents of all these viewpoints call for more comparative historical research, which may alter the terms of debate rather than confirm a perspective.

REFERENCES

Abénon, Lucien-René. 1973. "Blancs et libres de couleur dans deux paroisses de la Guadeloupe (Capesterre et Trois-Rivières), 1699–1779." *Revue française d'Histoire d'Outre-Mer* 60(220):297–329.

Aimes, Hubert H.S. 1967 [1907]. *A History of Slavery in Cuba, 1511 to 1868*. New York: Octagon Books.

Anstey, Roger. 1975. "The Volume and Profitability of the British Slave Trade," in *Race and Slavery in the Western Hemisphere*, S. Engerman and E. Genovese, eds. Princeton, N.J.: Princeton University Press, 3–31.

Attewell, Paul A. 1984. *Radical Political Economy since the Sixties: A Sociology of Knowledge Analysis*. New Brunswick, N.J.: Rutgers University Press.

Atwood, Thomas. 1791. *The History of the Island of Dominica*. London: J. Johnson.

Baralt, Guilermo A. 1981. *Esclavos rebeldes: Conspiraciones y sublevaciones de esclavos en Puerto Rico (1795–1873)*. Río Piédras: Ediciones Huracán.

Barclay, Alexander. 1828. *A Practical View of the Present State of Slavery in the West Indies*. London: Smith, Elder and Co.

Barrett, Michèle. 1980. *Women's Oppression Today: Problems in Marxist Feminist Analysis*. London: New Left Books.

Bean, Richard N. 1977. "Food Imports into the British West Indies: 1680–1845." *Annals of the New York Academy of Sciences* 292:581–590.

Beckford, George. 1972. *Persistent Poverty*. New York: Oxford University Press.

Beckford, William. 1790. *A Descriptive Account of the Island of Jamaica*. London: T. and J. Egerton.

Bennett, J. Harry, Jr. 1958. *Bondsmen and Bishops: Slavery and Apprenticeship on the Codrington Plantations of Barbados, 1710–1838*. Berkeley: University of California Press.

Bentson, Margaret. 1969. "The Political Economy of Women's Liberation." *Monthly Review* 21(September):13–27.

Bettelheim, Bruno. 1960. *The Informed Heart*. Glencoe, Ill.: Free Press.

———. 1943. "Individual and Mass Behavior in Extreme Situations." *Journal of Abnormal Psychology* 38(October):417–452.

Blassingame, John W. 1972. *The Slave Community*. New York: Oxford University Press.

Bloch, Maurice. 1980. "Modes of Production and Slavery in Madagascar: Two Case Studies," in *Asian and African Systems of Slavery*, James Watson, ed. Oxford: Basil Blackwell, 100–134.

Blumberg, Rae Lesser. 1978. *Stratification: Socioeconomic and Sexual Inequality*. Dubuque, Iowa: Wm. C. Brown.

Bolles, Lynn. 1983. "Kitchens Hit by Priorities: Employed Working Class Jamaican Women Confront the IMF," in *Women, Men and the International Division of Labor*, J. Nash and M. P. Fernández-Kelly, eds. Albany: SUNY Press, 138–160.

Bonacich, Edna. 1981. "Split Labor Markets and Black-White Relations, 1865–1920." *Phylon* 42(December):293–308.

Bongaarts, John. 1980. "Does Malnutrition Affect Fecundity? A Summary of Evidence." *Science* 208(May):564–569.

Bongaarts, John, and Robert G. Potter. 1983. *Fertility, Biology and Behavior*. New York: Academic Press.

Boserup, Ester. 1970. *The Role of Women in Economic Development.* New York: St. Martin's.

Bowser, Frederick P. 1972. "Colonial Spanish America," in *Neither Slave nor Free,* David W. Cohen and Jack P. Greene, eds. Baltimore, Md.: Johns Hopkins University Press, 19-58.

Brathwaite, Edward. 1971. *The Development of Creole Society in Jamaica, 1770-1820.* Oxford: Clarendon Press.

Bremer, Fredricka. 1853. *The Homes of the New World,* 2 vols. Mary Howett, trans. New York: Harper and Brothers.

Brenner, Johanna, and Maria Ramas. 1984. "Rethinking Women's Oppression." *New Left Review* 144(March-April):35-71.

Brereton, Bridget. 1981. *A History of Modern Trinidad, 1783-1962.* London: Heinemann.

Bunster-Burotto, Ximena. 1986. "Surviving beyond Fear: Women and Torture in Latin America," in *Women and Change in Latin America,* June Nash and Helen Safa, eds. South Hadley, Mass.: Bergin and Garvey, 297-325.

Bush, Barbara. 1986. "The Family Tree Is Not Cut: Women and Resistance in Slave Family Life in the British Caribbean," in *Resistance: Studies in African, Caribbean and Afro-American History,* Gary Y. Okihiro, ed. Amherst: University of Massachusetts Press, 117-132.

———. 1981. "White 'Ladies,' Coloured 'Favourites' and Black 'Wenches': Some Considerations on Sex, Race and Class Factors in Social Relations in White Creole Society in the British Caribbean." *Slavery and Abolition* 2(December):245-262.

Campbell, Mavis. 1976. "The Price of Freedom: On Forms of Manumission." *Revista/Review Interamericana* 6(Summer):239-252.

Cancian, Francesca M., Louis M. Goodman, and Peter Smith. 1978. "Capitalism, Industrialization and Kinship in Latin America: Major Issues." *Journal of Family History* 3(Winter):319-336.

Carmichael, Mrs. A. C. 1834. *Five Years in Trinidad and St. Vincent,* 2 vols. London: Whittaker and Co.

Carrington, Selwyn H. H. 1987. "The American Revolution and the British West Indies Economy." *Journal of Interdisciplinary History* 17(Spring):823-850.

Chafetz, Janet. 1984. *Sex and Advantage.* Totowa, N.J.: Roman and Allenheld.

Charlton, Sue Ellen. 1984. *Women in Third World Development.* Boulder, Co.: Westview Press.

Chilcote, Ronald H. 1984. *Theories of Development and Underdevelopment.* Boulder, Co.: Westview Press.

Clinton, Catherine. 1982. *The Plantation Mistress: Woman's World in the Old South.* New York: Pantheon.

Cohen, David W., and Jack P. Greene. 1972. Introduction to their *Neither Slave nor Free.* Baltimore, Md.: Johns Hopkins University Press, 1-18.

Colthurst, John Bowen. 1977. *The Colthurst Journal.* Woodville K. Marshall, ed. Millwood, N.Y.: KTO Press. (Written in 1835-1838.)

Corwin, Arthur F. 1967. *Spain and the Abolition of Slavery in Cuba, 1817-1886.* Austin: University of Texas Press.

Cox, Edward L. 1984. *Free Coloreds in the Slave Societies of St. Kitts and Grenada, 1763-1833.* Knoxville: University of Tennessee Press.

Craton, Michael. 1982. *Testing the Chains: Resistance to Slavery in the British West Indies.* Ithaca, N.Y.: Cornell University Press.

———. 1979. "Changing Patterns of Slave Family in the British West Indies." *Journal of Interdisciplinary History* 10(Summer):1-35.

———. 1978. "Hobbesian or Panglossian? The Two Extremes of Slave Conditions in the British Caribbean, 1783–1834." *William and Mary Quarterly* 25(April):324–356.

———. 1977. *Searching for the Invisible Man: Slaves and Plantation Life in Jamaica.* Cambridge, Mass.: Harvard University Press.

———. 1974. *Sinews of Empire.* New York: Anchor Books.

———. 1971. "Jamaican Slave Mortality: Fresh Light from Worthy Park, Longville and the Thorp Estates." *The Journal of Caribbean History* 3(November):1–27.

Curet, José. 1985. "About Slavery and the Order of Things: Puerto Rico, 1845–1873," in *Between Slavery and Free Labor: The Spanish-Speaking Caribbean in the Nineteenth Century,* M. Moreno Fraginals, F. Moya Pons, and S. W. Engerman, eds. Baltimore, Md.: Johns Hopkins University Press, 117–140.

Curtin, Phillip D. 1985. "Nutrition in African History," in *Hunger and History,* R. I. Rotberg and T. K. Rabb, eds. Cambridge: Cambridge University Press, 173–184.

———. 1970. *Two Jamaicas.* New York: Atheneum.

———. 1969. *The Atlantic Slave Trade.* Madison: University of Wisconsin Press.

David, Bernard. 1973. "La population d'un quarter de la Martinique au debut du XIXᵉ siècle d'après les registres paroissiaux: Rivière-Pilote 1802–1829." *Revue française d'Histoire d'Outre-Mer* 60(220):330–363.

Davis, David Brion. 1974. "Slavery and the Post-World War II Historians," in *Slavery, Colonialism, and Racism,* Sidney W. Mintz, ed. New York: W. W. Norton, 1–16.

———. 1966. *The Problem of Slavery in Western Culture.* Ithaca, N.Y.: Cornell University Press.

Debbasch, Yvan. 1963. "Le Crime d'empoisonnement aux îles pendant la période esclavagiste." *Revue française d'Histoire d'Outre-Mer* 50(179):137–163.

Debien, Gabriel. 1974. Les esclaves aux Antilles Françaises (XVII-XVIIIᵉ siècles). *Basse-Terre: Société d'Histoire de la Guadeloupe.*

———. 1973. "Marronage in the French Caribbean," in *Maroon Societies,* Richard Price, ed. New York: Anchor Books, 107–134.

———. 1962. *Plantations et esclaves à Saint-Domingue.* Université de Dakar.

———. 1960. "Destinées des esclaves à la Martinique." *Bulletin de L'Institut Français d'Afrique Noire* (Dakar) 26, série B, 1–91.

Deerr, Noel. 1949–1950. *The History of Sugar,* 2 vols. London.

Delphy, Christine. 1984. *Close to Home: A Materialist Analysis of Women's Oppression.* Diana Leonard, ed. and trans. Amherst: University of Massachusetts Press.

Devèze, Michel. 1977. *Antilles, Guyanes, La Merdes Caribes de 1492 à 1789.* Paris: Société d'Édition d'Enseignement Superieur.

Diaz Soler, Luis M. 1974. *Historia de la esclavitud negra en Puerto Rico.* Río Piédras: University of Puerto Rico Press.

Dickson, William. 1789. *Letters on Slavery.* London.

Dirks, Robert. 1987. *Black Saturnalia.* Gainesville: University Presses of Florida.

———. 1978. "Resource Fluctuations and Competitive Transformation in West Indian Slave Societies," in *Extinction and Survival in Human Populations,* C. D. Laughlin, Jr., and Ivan A. Brady, eds. New York: Columbia University Press, 122–180.

Dirks, Robert, and Virginia Kerns. 1976. "Mating Patterns and Adaptive Change in Rum Bay, 1823–1970." *Social and Economic Studies* 25(March):34–54.

Dobb, Maurice H. 1947. *Studies in the Development of Capitalism.* New York: International Publishers.

Dookhan, Isaac. 1975. *A History of the British Virgin Islands 1672 to 1970.* Epping, Essex, England: Caribbean Universities Press.

Douglas, Mary. 1966. *Purity and Danger.* New York: Praeger.

Drescher, Seymour. 1987. *Capitalism and Antislavery: British Mobilization in Comparative Perspective*. Oxford: Oxford University Press.

————. 1977. *Econocide: British Slavery in the Era of Abolition*. Pittsburgh, Pa.: University of Pittsburgh Press.

Dunn, Richard S. 1987. " 'Dreadful Idlers' in the Cane Fields: The Slave Labor Pattern on a Jamaican Sugar Estate, 1762-1831." *Journal of Interdisciplinary History* 17(Spring):795-822.

————. 1977. "A Tale of Two Plantations: Slave Life at Mesopotamia in Jamaica and at Mount Airy in Virginia, 1799 to 1828." *William and Mary Quarterly* 34(January):32-65.

————. 1972. *Sugar and Slaves: The Rise of the Planter Class in the English West Indies, 1634-1713*. New York: Norton.

Dupuy, Alex. 1985. "French Merchant Capital and Slavery in Saint-Domingue." *Latin American Perspectives* 12(Summer):77-102.

————. 1983. "Slavery and Underdevelopment in the Caribbean: A Critique of the 'Plantation Economy' Perspective." *Dialectical Anthropology* 7(3):237-251.

DuTertre, F. I. Baptiste. 1958 [1667-1671]. *Histoire générale des Antilles*, 3 vols. Fort-de-France, Martinique: Société d'Histoire de la Martinique.

Eaves, Charles Dudley. 1945. *The Virginia Tobacco Industry (1780-1860)*. Lubbock: Texas Tech Press.

Eblen, Jack E. 1975. "On the Natural Increase of Slave Populations: The Example of the Cuban Black Population, 1775-1900," in *Race and Slavery in the Western Hemisphere: Quantitative Studies*, S. L. Engerman and E. D. Genovese, eds. Princeton, N.J.: Princeton University Press, 211-247.

Edwards, Bryan. 1966 [1819]. *The History, Civil and Commercial, of the British West Indies*. New York: AMS Press.

Eisner, Gisela. 1961. *Jamaica, 1830-1930: A Study of Economic Growth*. Manchester: University of Manchester Press.

Elisabeth, Leo. 1972. "French Antilles," in *Neither Slave nor Free*, David W. Cohen and Jack P. Greene, eds. Baltimore, Md.: Johns Hopkins University Press, 134-171.

Elkins, Stanley M. 1976. *Slavery: A Problem in American Institutional and Intellectual Life*, rev. ed. Chicago, Ill.: University of Chicago Press.

Eltis, David. 1987. *Economic Growth and the Ending of the Transatlantic Slave Trade*. New York: Oxford University Press.

Ely, Roland T. 1963. *Cuando reinaba su majestad el azúcar*. Buenos Aires: Editoral Sudamericana.

Engerman, Stanley L. 1973. "Some Considerations Relating to Property Rights in Man." *Journal of Economic History* 33(March):43-65.

Farley, Rawe, n.d. *The Rise of Village Settlements in British Guiana: Apprenticeship and Emancipation*. Department of Extra-Mural Studies, University of the West Indies.

Fergus, Howard A. 1975. *History of Alliouagana: A Short History of Montserrat*. Montserrat: University Centre.

Finley, M. I. 1980. *Ancient Slavery and Modern Ideology*. New York: Viking.

————. 1968. "Slavery," in *Encyclopedia of the Social Sciences*. New York: Macmillan, 307-313.

Flinter, George D. 1834. *An Account of the Present State of the Island of Puerto Rico*. London: Longman.

Fogel, R. W., and S. L. Engerman. 1979. "Recent Findings in the Study of Slave Demography and Family Structure." *Sociology and Social Research* 63(April):566-589.

————. 1974. *Time on the Cross*. Boston, Mass.: Little, Brown & Co.

Foster-Carter, Aiden. 1978. "The Modes of Production Controversy." *New Left Review* 107(January–February):47–78.

Foucault, Michel. 1978. *The History of Sexuality*. Robert Hurley, trans. New York: Pantheon.

———. 1977. *Discipline and Punishment: The Birth of the Prison*. Alan Sheridan, trans. New York: Pantheon.

Fouchard, Jean. 1981. *The Haitian Maroons*. A. F. Watts, trans. New York: Blyden Press.

Fox-Genovese, Elizabeth. 1986. "Strategies and Forms of Resistance: Focus on Slave Women in the United States," in *In Resistance: Studies in African, Caribbean and Afro-American History*, Gary Y. Okihiro, ed. Amherst: University of Massachusetts Press, 143–165.

Fox-Genovese, Elizabeth, and Eugene D. Genovese. 1983. *Fruits of Merchant Capital: Slavery and Bourgeois Property in the Rise and Expansion of Capitalism*. New York: Oxford University Press.

Franco, José L. 1979. "Maroons and Slave Rebellions in the Spanish Territories," in *Maroon Societies*, Richard Price, ed. New York: Anchor Books, 35–48.

Frucht, Richard. 1977. "From Slavery to Unfreedom in the Plantation Society of St. Kitts, West Indies," *Annals of the New York Academy of Sciences* 292:379–388.

Furley, Oliver W. 1965. "Moravian Missionaries and Slaves in the West Indies." *Caribbean Studies* (July):3–16.

Galenson, David W. 1982. "The Atlantic Slave Trade and the Barbados Market, 1673–1723." *Journal of Economic History* 42(September):491–506.

Gaston-Martin. 1948. *Histoire de l'esclavage dans les colonies françaises*. Paris: Presses Universitaires de France.

Gautier, Arlette. 1985. *Les soeurs de solitude*. Paris: Éditions Caribéennes.

Geggus, David P. 1983. "Slave Resistance Studies and the Saint Domingue Slave Revolt: Some Preliminary Considerations." Occasional paper. Latin America and Caribbean Center, Florida International University.

———. 1982. *Slavery, War and Revolution: The British Occupation of Saint Domingue 1793–1798*. Oxford: Clarendon Press.

———. 1978. "The Slaves of British-Occupied Saint Domingue: An Analysis of the Workforces of 197 Absentee Plantations, 1796–1797." *Caribbean Studies* 18(1–2): 5–41.

Genovese, Eugene D. 1979. *From Rebellion to Revolution*. Baton Rouge: Louisiana State University Press.

———. 1976. *Roll, Jordan, Roll*. New York: Vintage.

———. 1971. *The World the Slaveholders Made*. New York: Vintage.

———. 1965. *The Political Economy of Slavery*. New York: Pantheon.

Giddens, Anthony. 1982. *Profiles and Critiques in Social Theory*. Berkeley: University of California Press.

———. 1981. *A Contemporary Critique of Historical Materialism*. Berkeley: University of California Press.

———. 1976. *New Rules of Sociological Method: A Positive Critique of Interpretative Sociologies*. London: Hutchinson.

Gisler, Antoine. 1965. *L'esclavage aux Antilles Françaises (XVIIe–XIXe siècle)*. Fribourg, Suisse: Éditions Universitaires.

Goody, Jack. 1976. *Production and Reproduction*. Cambridge: Cambridge University Press.

Goveia, Elsa V. 1965. *Slave Society in the British Leeward Islands at the End of the Eighteenth Century*. New Haven, Conn.: Yale University Press.

————. 1960. "The West Indian Slave Laws of the Eighteenth Century." *Revista de Ciencias Sociales* 4(March):75–105.

Green, William A. 1988. "Supply versus Demand in the Barbadian Sugar Revolution." *Journal of Interdisciplinary History* 18(Winter):403–418.

Gundersen, Joan R. 1986. "The Double Bonds of Race and Sex: Black and White Women in a Colonial Virginia Parish." *Journal of Southern History* 52(August): 351–372.

Gurney, Joseph John. 1840. *Familiar Letters to Henry Clay of Kentucky, Describing a Winter in the West Indies.* New York: Mahlon Day and Co.

Gutman, Herbert. 1977. *The Black Family in Slavery and Freedom, 1750–1925.* New York: Vintage.

Guttentag, Marcia, and Paul F. Secord. 1983. *Too Many Women?* Beverly Hills, Calif.: Sage.

Hall, Douglas. 1972. "Jamaica," in *Neither Slave nor Free,* David W. Cohen and Jack P. Greene, eds. Baltimore, Md.: John Hopkins University Press, 193–213.

Hall, Gwendolyn Midlo. 1972. "Saint Domingue," in *Neither Slave nor Free,* David W. Cohen and Jack P. Greene, eds. Baltimore, Md.: Johns Hopkins University Press, 172–192.

————. 1971. *Social Control in Plantation Societies.* Baltimore, Md.: Johns Hopkins University Press.

Hall, Neville. 1980. "Slaves' Use of 'Free' Time in the Danish Virgin Islands in the Later Eighteenth and Early Nineteenth Centuries." *Journal of Caribbean History* 13:21–43.

————. 1977. "Slave Laws of the Danish Virgin Islands in the Later Eighteenth Century." *Annals of the New York Academy of Sciences* 292:174–186.

————. 1976. "Anna Heegaard–Enigma." *Caribbean Quarterly* 22(June–September): 62–73.

Handler, Jerome S. 1974. *The Unappropriated People: Freedman in the Slave Society of Barbados.* Baltimore, Md.: Johns Hopkins University Press.

————. 1972. "An Archaeological Investigation of the Domestic Life of Plantation Slaves in Barbados." *Journal of the Barbados Museum and Historical Society* 34(May): 64–72.

Handler, Jerome S., and Robert S. Corruccini. 1983. "Plantation Slave Life in Barbados: A Physical Anthropological Analysis." *Journal of Interdisciplinary History* 14(Summer):65–70.

Harris, Marvin. 1964. *Patterns of Race in America.* New York: Walker and Co.

Hart, Richard. 1980. *Slaves Who Abolished Slavery: Blacks in Bondage,* vol. 1. Mona, Jamaica: Institute of Social and Economic Research.

Hartsock, Nancy C. M. 1983. *Money, Sex and Power: Toward a Feminist Historical Materialism.* New York: Longman.

Higman, Barry W. 1984. *Slave Populations of the British Caribbean, 1807–1834.* Baltimore, Md.: Johns Hopkins University Press.

————. 1978. "African and Creole Slave Family Patterns in Trinidad." *Journal of Family History* 3(Summer):163–180.

————. 1976a. *Slave Population and Economy in Jamaica, 1807–1834.* Cambridge: Cambridge University Press.

————. 1976b. "The Slave Population of the British Caribbean: Some Nineteenth Century Variations," in *Eighteenth Century Florida and the Caribbean,* Samuel Proctor, ed. Gainesville: University Presses of Florida, 60–70.

Hilliard d'Auberteuil. 1776. *Considérations sur l'état présent de la colonie française de Saint-Domingue, ouvrage politique et législatif.* Paris.

Hindess, Barry, and Paul Q. Hirst. 1975. *Pre-Capitalist Modes of Production.* London: Routledge & Kegan Paul.

Hine, Darlene C. 1979. "Female Slave Resistance: The Economics of Sex." *Western Journal of Black Studies* 3(2):123–127.

Hobsbawm, Eric J. 1959. *Primitive Rebels.* New York: Norton.

Hoetink, H. 1972. "Surinam and Curaçao," in *Neither Slave nor Free,* David W. Cohen and Jack P. Greene, eds. Baltimore, Md.: Johns Hopkins University Press, 59–83.

Humboldt, Alexander. 1960 [1826]. *Ensayo político sobre la isla de Cuba.* La Habana: Publicaciones del Archivo National de Cuba.

James, C. L. R. 1963. *The Black Jacobins,* rev. ed. New York: Vintage.

Jesse, C. 1961. "DuTertre and Labat on Seventeenth Century Slave Life in the French Antilles." *Caribbean Quarterly* 7(December):137–157.

Jones, Jacqueline. 1986. *Race, Sex and Self-Evident Truths: The Status of Slave Women during the Era of the American Revolution.* Paper 162, Wellesley College Center for Research on Women.

———. 1982. " 'My Mother Was Much of a Woman': Black Women, Work and the Family under Slavery." *Feminist Studies* 8(Summer):235–269.

Jordan, Winthrop D. 1968. *White over Black: American Attitudes toward the Negro, 1550–1812.* New York: Penguin.

Keller, David W., Ronald C. Strickler, and James C. Warren. 1984. *Clinical Infertility.* Norwalk, Conn.: Appleton-Century-Croft.

Kiple, Kenneth F. 1984. *The Caribbean Slave: A Biological History.* Cambridge: Cambridge University Press.

———. 1976. *Blacks in Colonial Cuba, 1774–1899.* Gainesville: University Presses of Florida.

Kiple, Kenneth F., and Virginia H. Kiple. 1981. *Another Dimension to the Black Diaspora: Diet, Disease and Racism.* Cambridge: Cambridge University Press.

———. 1980. "Deficiency Diseases in the Caribbean." *Journal of Interdisciplinary History* 11(Autumn):197–215.

———. 1977. "Slave Child Mortality: Some Nutritional Answers to a Perennial Puzzle." *Journal of Social History* 10(March):284–307.

Klein, Herbert S. 1986. *African Slavery in Latin America and the Caribbean.* New York: Oxford University Press.

———. 1983. "African Women in the Atlantic Slave Trade," in *Women and Slavery in Africa,* Claire C. Robertson and Martin A. Klein, eds. Madison: University of Wisconsin Press, 29–38.

———. 1978. *The Middle Passage: Comparative Studies in the Atlantic Slave Trade.* Princeton, N.J.: Princeton University Press.

———. 1967. *Slavery in the Americas: A Comparative Study of Virginia and Cuba.* Chicago, Ill.: University of Chicago Press.

Klein, Herbert S., and Stanley L. Engerman. 1978. "Fertility Differentials between Slaves in the United States and the British West Indies: A Note on Lactation Practices." *William and Mary Quarterly* 35(April):357–374.

Kleinman, David S. 1980. *Human Adaptation and Population Growth.* Montclair, N.J.: Allenheld and Osmun.

Knibb, William, 1832. *Defence of the Baptist Missionaries.* London: J. Haddon and Co.

Knight, Franklin W. 1972. "Cuba," in *Neither Slave nor Free,* David W. Cohen and Jack P. Greene, eds. Baltimore, Md.: Johns Hopkins University Press, 278–308.

———. 1970. *Slave Society in Cuba during the Nineteenth Century.* Madison: University of Wisconsin Press.

Koplan, Jeffrey. 1983. "Slave Mortality in Nineteenth Century Grenada." *Social Science History* 7(Summer):311–320.

Kopytoff, Barbara. 1976. "The Development of Jamaican Maroon Ethnicity." *Caribbean Quarterly* 22(June–September):33–50.

Kulikoff, Allan. 1986. *Tobacco and Slaves: The Development of Southern Cultures in the Chesapeake, 1680–1800.* Chapel Hill: University of North Carolina Press.

Kuznesof, Elizabeth Anne. 1980. "Household Composition and Headship as Related to Mode of Production: São Paulo 1765 to 1836." *Comparative Studies in Society and History* 22(January):78–108

––––––. 1979. "The Role of the Female-Headed Household in Brazilian Modernization: 1765 to 1836." *Journal of Social History* 13(Summer):589–614.

Labat, Père Jean-Baptiste. 1930 [1722]. *Nouveau voyage aux isles de l'amérique (Antilles), 1693–1705,* 2 vols. Paris: Éditions Duchartre.

Lamur, Humphrey. 1977. "Demography of Surinam Plantation Slaves in the Last Decade before Emancipation: The Case of Catharina Sophia." *Annals of the New York Academy of Sciences* 292:161–173.

Lasch, Christopher. 1977. *Haven in a Heartless World.* New York: Basic Books.

Laslett, Peter. 1972. *Household and Family in Past Time.* Cambridge: Cambridge University Press.

Leacock, Eleanor. 1983. "Interpreting the Origins of Gender Inequality: Conceptual and Historical Problems." *Dialectical Anthropology* 7(February):263–284.

Leslie, Charles. 1740. *A New and Exact Account of Jamaica.* Edinburg.

Levine, David. 1983. "Proto-Industrialization and Demographic Upheaval," in *Essays on the Family and Historical Change,* L. P. Moch and G. D. Stark, eds. College Station: Texas A&M Press, 9–34.

––––––. 1977. *Family Formation in an Age of Nascent Capitalism.* New York: Academic Press.

Levy, Claude. 1980. *Emancipation, Sugar and Federalism: Barbados and the West Indies, 1833–1876.* Gainesville: University Presses of Florida.

Lewis, Gordon K. 1968. *The Growth of the Modern West Indies.* New York: Monthly Review Press.

Lewis, Matthew Gregory. 1834. *Journal of a West India Proprietor.* London: John Murray.

Lewisohn, Florence. 1970. *St. Croix under Seven Flags.* Hollywood, Fl.: Dukane Press.

Ligon, Richard. 1657. *A True and Exact History of the Island of Barbados.* London: H. Moseley.

Long, Edward. 1774. *The History of Jamaica,* 2 vols. London: T. J. Lowndes.

Lowenthal, David, and Colin G. Clarke. 1977. "Slave-Breeding in Barbuda: The Past of a Negro Myth." *Annals of the New York Academy of Sciences* 292:510–535.

Lunn, Peter G., Stevan Austin, Andrew M. Prentice, and Roger G. Whitehead. 1984. "The Effect of Improved Nutrition on Plasma Prolactin Concentrations and Postpartum Infertility in Lactating Gambian Women." *American Journal of Clinical Nutrition* 39:227–235.

Manigat, Leslie F. 1977. "The Relationship between Marronage and Slave Revolts and Revolution in St. Domingue-Haiti." *Annals of the New York Academy of Sciences* 292:420–438.

Marrero, Levi. 1983. *Cuba: Economía y sociedad.* Madrid: Editorial Playor.

Marshall, Bernard A. 1976. "Marronage in Slave Plantation Societies: A Case Study of Dominica, 1785–1815." *Caribbean Quarterly* 22(June–September):26–32.

Martin, Del. 1983. *Battered Wives.* New York: Pocket Books.

Martinez-Alier, Verena. 1974. *Marriage, Class and Colour in Nineteenth Century Cuba.* London: Cambridge University Press.

Mathieson, William Law. 1926. *British Slavery and Its Abolition*. London: Longmans, Green.

Mathurin, Lucille (Mair). 1974. *A Historical Study of Women in Jamaica from 1655 to 1844*. Ph.D. dissertation, University of the West Indies, Mona, Jamaica.

———. 1975. *The Rebel Woman in the British West Indies during Slavery*. Kingston: Institute of Jamaica.

McFalls, Joseph A., Jr., and Marguerite Harvey McFalls. 1984. *Disease and Fertility*. New York: Academic Press.

Meillassoux, Claude. 1983. "Female Slavery," in *Women and Slavery in Africa*, Claire G. Robertson and Martin A. Klein, eds. Madison: University of Wisconsin Press, 49–66.

Meillassoux, Claude, ed. 1975. *L'esclavage en Afrique précoloniale*. Paris: Maspero.

Miller, J. F., E. Williamson, J. Glue, Y. B. Gordon, J. G. Grudzinskas, and A. Sykes. 1980. "Fetal Loss after Implantation." *Lancet* 2:554–556.

Millette, James. 1970. *The Genesis of Crown Colony Government: Trinidad, 1783–1810*. Curepe, Trinidad: Moko Enterprises.

Mintz, Sidney. 1983. "Slavery and the Rise of Peasantries." *Historical Reflections* 6(1):213–242.

———. 1979–1980. "Time, Sugar and Sweetness." *Marxist Perspectives* 2(Winter): 56–73.

———. 1978. "Was the Plantation Slave a Proletarian?" *Review* 2(Summer):81–98.

———. 1974. *Caribbean Transformations*. Chicago: Aldine.

Mitchell, Juliet. 1972. *Woman's Estate*. New York: Penguin.

Moreau de Saint Méry, Médéric Louis Élie. 1958 [1797]. *Description topographic, physique, civile politique et historique de la partie française de l'isle Saint Domingue*. Paris: Société de l'Histoire des Colonies Françaises.

Moreno Fraginals, Manuel. 1978. *El ingenio: Complejo económico social cubano del azúcar*. La Habana: Editorial de Ciencas Sociales.

———. 1977. "Africa in Cuba: A Quantitative Analysis of the African Population in the Island of Cuba." *Annals of the New York Academy of Sciences* 292:187–201.

Moreton, J. B. 1793. *West India Customs and Manners*. London: J. Parsons.

Morner, Magnus. 1973. "Legal Equality—Social Inequality: A Post-Abolition Theme." *Revista Interamericana* 3(Spring):24–41.

Morrissey, Marietta. 1986. "Women's Work, Family Formation and Reproduction among Caribbean Slaves." *Review: Journal of the Braudel Center* 9(Winter):339–367.

———. 1981. "Towards a Theory of West Indian Economic Development." *Latin American Perspectives* 8(Winter):4–27.

Mullen, Edward J., ed. 1981. *The Life and Poems of a Cuban Slave*. Hamden, Conn.: Archon Books.

Narroll, Raoul. 1968. "Some Thoughts on Comparative Method in Cultural Anthropology," in *Methodology in Social Research*, Hubert M. Blalock, Jr., and A. Blalock, eds. New York: McGraw-Hill, 236–277.

Nash, June, and Maria Patricia Fernández-Kelly, eds. 1983. *Men, Women and the International Division of Labor*. Albany: SUNY Press.

Nicholls, David. 1985. *Haiti in Caribbean Context*. New York: St. Martin's.

Nicholson, Linda J. 1986. *Gender and History: The Limits of Social Theory in the Age of the Family*. New York: Columbia University Press.

Nisbet, Richard. 1970 [1789]. *The Capacity of Negroes for Religious and Moral Improvement*. Westport, Conn.: Negro Universities Press.

Nistal Moret, Benjamín. 1980. "Ocho documentos legales para el estudio de la esclavitud en Puerto Rico, 1797–1873." *Caribbean Studies* 20(June):81–109.

Nugent, Lady Maria (Skinner). 1907 [1839]. *Lady Nugent's Journal*. Frank Cundall, ed. Kingston: Institute of Jamaica.

Olwig, Karen Fog. 1985. *Cultural Adaptation and Resistance on St. John*. Gainesville: University of Florida Press.

Omvedt, Gail. 1986. "'Patriarchy': The Analysis of Women's Oppression." *Insurgent Sociologist* 13(Spring):30–50.

Ortiz, Fernando. 1947. *Cuban Counterpart: Tobacco and Sugar*. New York: Knopf.

———. 1975 [1916]. *Hampa afro-cubano: Los negros esclavos*. La Habana: Editorial de Ciencias Sociales.

Packwood, Cyril. 1975. *Chained on the Rock: Slavery in Bermuda*. New York: Eliseo Torres and Sons.

Padgug, Robert. 1977. "Commentary." *Annals of the New York Academy of Sciences* 292:613–618.

Patterson, Orlando. 1982. *Slavery and Social Death*. Cambridge, Mass.: Harvard University Press.

———. 1976. "From Endo-deme to Matri-deme: An Interpretation of the Development of Kinship and Social Organization among the Slaves of Jamaica, 1655-1830," in *Eighteenth Century Florida and the Caribbean*, Samuel Proctor, ed. Gainesville: University Presses of Florida, 50–59.

———. 1973. "Slavery and Slave Revolts: A Sociohistorical Analysis of the First Maroon War, 1665-1740," in *Maroon Societies*, Richard Price, ed. New York: Anchor, 246–292.

———. 1969. *The Sociology of Slavery*. Rutherford, N.J.: Fairleigh-Dickinson University Press.

Peytraud, Lucien. 1973 [1897]. *L'esclavage aux Antilles Françaises avant 1789*. Pointe-à-Pitre: Emile Désormeaux.

Phillippo, James M. 1843. *Jamaica: Its Past and Present*. London: John Snow.

Phillips, Ulrich B. 1949. "A Jamaican Plantation." *Caribbean Quarterly* 1(April–June):4–13.

Pinckard, George. 1970 [1806]. *Notes on the West Indies*. Westport, Conn.: Negro Universities Press.

Price, Richard, ed. 1979. *Maroon Societies: Rebel Slave Communities in the Americas*. Baltimore, Md.: Johns Hopkins University Press.

Price, Richard. 1976. *The Guiana Maroons*. Baltimore, Md.: Johns Hopkins University Press.

Ragatz, Lowell. 1963. *The Fall of the Planter Class, 1763-1833*. New York: Octagon Books.

Raynal, Guillaume. 1981 [1772]. *Histoire philosophique et politique des deux Indes*. Paris: François Maspero.

Reddock, Rhoda E. 1985. "Women and Slavery in the Caribbean: A Feminist Perspective." *Latin American Perspectives* 12(Winter):63–80.

Riland, John. 1828. *Two Letters, Relative to the Slave-Cultured Estates of the Society for the Propogation of the Gospel*. London: John Hatchard and Sons.

Roberts, G. W. 1977. "Movements in Slave Population of the Caribbean during the Period of Slave Registration." *Annals of the New York Academy of Sciences* 292:145–160.

———. 1957. *The Population of Jamaica*. Cambridge: Cambridge University Press.

Robertson, Claire C., and Martin A. Klein. 1983. "Women's Importance in African Slave Systems," in their *Women and Slavery in Africa*. Madison: University of Wisconsin Press, 3–28.

Rodney, Walter. 1981. *A History of the Guyanese Working People, 1881-1905*. Baltimore, Md.: Johns Hopkins University Press.

Rogers, Barbara. 1979. *The Domestication of Women*. New York: St. Martin's.

Rubin, Gayle. 1975. "The Traffic in Women: Notes on the Political Economy of Sex," in *Toward an Anthropology of Women*, Rayna Reiter, ed. New York: Monthly Review Press, 157–210.

Saco, Jose Antonio. 1893. *Historia de la esclavitud de la raza africana en el Nuevo Mundo y en especial en los países américo-hispanos*. La Habana.

Safilios-Rothschild, Constantina. 1977. "The Relationship between Women's Work and Fertility: Some Methodological and Theoretical Issues," in *The Fertility of Working Women*, Stanley Kupinsky, ed. New York: Praeger, 355–368.

Salaff, Janet. 1981. *Working Daughters of Hong Kong*. New York: Cambridge University Press.

Sanday, Peggy Reeves. 1981. *Female Power and Male Dominance: On the Origins of Sexual Inequality*. New York: Cambridge University Press.

Scarano, Francisco A. 1984. *Sugar and Slavery in Puerto Rico: The Plantation Economy of Ponce, 1800–1850*. Madison: University of Wisconsin Press.

———. 1977. "Slavery and Free Labor in the Puerto Rican Sugar Economy: 1815–1873." *Annals of the New York Academy of Sciences* 292:553–563.

Schaw, Janet. 1939. *Journal of a Lady of Quality*. New Haven, Conn.: Yale University Press.

Schnakenbourg, Christian. 1980. *Histoire de l'industrie sucrière en Guadeloupe aux XIXe et XXe siècles: La crise du système esclavagiste (1838–1847)*. Paris: Éditions L'Harmatten.

Schoelcher, Victor. 1948 [1830]. *Esclavage et Colonisation*. Paris: Presses Universitaires de France.

———. 1842. *Des colonies françaises, abolition immédiate de l'esclavage*. Paris.

Schwartz, Mildred A. 1987. "Historical Sociology in the History of American Sociology." *Social Science History* 2(Spring):1–16.

Scott, Eugenie C., and Francis E. Johnston. 1985. "Science, Nutrition, Fat, and Policy: Tests of the Critical-Fat Hypothesis." *Current Anthropology* 26(August–October):463–473.

Scott, Rebecca J. 1985. *Slave Emancipation in Cuba: The Transition to Free Labor, 1860–1899*. Princeton, N.J.: Princeton University Press.

Sheridan, Richard B. 1985. *Doctors and Slaves*. Cambridge: Cambridge University Press.

———. 1976. "'Sweet Malefactor': The Social Costs of Slavery and Sugar in Jamaica and Cuba, 1807–1854." *Economic History Review* 24(May):236–257.

———. 1973. *Sugar and Slavery*. Baltimore, Md.: Johns Hopkins University Press.

———. 1965. "The Wealth of Jamaica in the Eighteenth Century." *Economic History Review* 18, 2d ser. (August):292–311.

———. 1964. "Planter and Historian: The Career of William Beckford of Jamaica and England, 1744–1799." *The Jamaican Historical Review* 4:36–58.

Siguret, Rosalind. 1968. "Esclaves d'ingoteries et de caféières au quartier de Jacmel (1757–1791)." *Revue français d'Outre Mer* 55(20):199–230.

Silié, Rubén. 1976. *Economía, esclavitud y población: Ensayos de interpretación histórica del Santo Domingo español en el siglo*. Santo Domingo, República Dominicana: La Universidad Autonoma de Santo Domingo.

Sio, Arnold. 1976. "Race, Colour and Miscegenation: The Free Coloured of Jamaica and Barbados." *Caribbean Studies* 16(1):5–21.

———. 1965. "Interpretations of Slavery: The Slave Status in the Americas." *Comparative Studies in Society and History* 7(3):289–308.

Skocpol, Theda. 1984. "Emergent Agendas and Recurrent Strategies in Historical Sociology," in *Vision and Method in Historical Sociology*, T. Skocpol, ed. New York: Cambridge University Press, 356–391.

————. 1987. "Social History and Comparative Sociology." *Social Science History* 2(Spring):17–38.

Smith, Joan, Immanuel Wallerstein, and Hans-Dieter Evers, eds. 1984. *Households and the World-Economy.* Beverly Hills, Calif.: Sage.

Smith, M. G. 1953. "Some Aspects of Social Structure in the Caribbean about 1820." *Social and Economic Studies* 1(August):55–80.

Solow, Barbara, and Stanley L. Engerman, eds. 1987. *British Capitalism and Caribbean Slavery: The Legacy of Eric Williams.* Cambridge: Cambridge University Press.

Stampp, Kenneth M. 1956. *The Peculiar Institution.* New York: Vintage.

Stedman, John Gabriel. 1971. *Narrative of a Five Years' Expedition against the Revolted Negroes of Surinam.* Amherst: University of Massachusetts Press.

Stewart, J. 1823. *View of the Past and Present State of the Island of Jamaica.* Edinburgh: Oliver and Boyd.

Sturge, Joseph, and Thomas Harvey. 1838. *The West Indies in 1837.* London: Frank Cass.

Tannenbaum, Frank. 1946. *Slave and Citizen.* New York: Vintage.

Terbourg-Penn, Rosalyn. 1986. "Women and Slavery in the African Diaspara: A Cross-Cultural Approach to Historical Analysis." *Sage* 3(Fall):11–15.

Terray, Emmanuel. 1975. "Classes and Class Consciousness in the Abron Kingdom of Gyaman," in *Marxist Analysis and Social Anthropology,* Maurice Bloch, ed. London: Malaby Press, 85–136.

Thompson, Edgar T. 1975. *Plantation Societies, Race Relations and the South: The Regimentation of Populations.* Durham, N.C.: Duke University Press.

Tilly, Charles. 1984. "Demographic Origins of the European Proletariat," in *Proletarianization and Family History,* David Levine, ed. New York: Academic Press, 1–85.

————. 1978. "The Historical Study of Vital Processes," in *Historical Studies of Changing Fertility,* C. Tilly, ed. Princeton, N.J.: Princeton University Press, 3–56.

Tomich, Dale. 1976. *Prelude to Emancipation: Sugar and Slavery in Martinique, 1830–1848.* Ph.D. dissertation, University of Wisconsin.

Tuelon, Alan. 1973. "Nanny—Maroon Chieftainess." *Caribbean Quarterly* 19(December):20–25.

Tulloch, A. M., and H. Marshall. 1838. *Statistical Report on the Sickness, Mortality and Invaliding among Troops in the West Indies.* London.

Turnbull, David. 1840. *Travels in the West.* London: Longman.

Turner, Mary. 1982. *Slaves and Missionaries: The Disintegration of Jamaican Slave Society, 1787–1834.* Urbana: University of Illinois Press.

Wallerstein, Immanuel. 1980. *The Modern World-System, Vol. 2, Mercantilism and Consolidation of the European World-Economy in the Sixteenth Century.* New York: Academic Press.

————. 1976. "American Slavery and the Capitalist World-Economy." *American Journal of Sociology* 81(5):1199–1213.

————. 1974. *The Modern World-System. Vol. 1, Capitalist Agriculture and the Origins of the European World-Economy in the Sixteenth Century.* New York: Academic Press.

Walton, John. 1984. *Reluctant Rebels.* Cambridge: Cambridge University Press.

Ward, Kathryn B. 1984. *Women in the World-System.* New York: Praeger.

Watkins, Susan Cotts, and Etienne van de Walle. 1985. "Nutrition, Mortality and Population Size: Malthus' Court of Last Resort," in *Hunger and History,* R. I. Rotberg and T. K. Rabb, eds. Cambridge: Cambridge University Press, 7–27.

Watson, Karl Stewart. 1975. *The Civilised Island, Barbados.* Ph.D. dissertation, University of Florida.

Wessman, James W. 1980. "The Demographic Structure of Slavery in Puerto Rico: Some Aspects of Agrarian Capitalism in the Late Nineteenth Century." *Journal of Latin American Studies* 12(2):271–289.

Westergaard, Waldemar. 1917. *The Danish West Indies under Company Rule.* New York: Macmillan.

White, Deborah G. 1985. *Ar'n't I a Woman? Female Slaves in the Plantation South.* New York: Norton.

Williams, Eric. 1966. *Capitalism and Slavery.* New York: G. P. Putnam's.

Wolf, Eric R. 1982. *Europe and the People without History.* Berkeley: University of California Press.

Wood, Peter H. 1974. *Black Majority: Negroes in Colonial South Carolina.* New York: Norton.

Wright, Gavin. 1987. "Capitalism and Slavery on the Islands: A Lesson from the Mainland." *Journal of Interdisciplinary History* 17(Spring):851–870.

Wynter, Sylvia. 1967. "Lady Nugent's Journal." *Jamaica Journal* 1(December):23–34.

INDEX

Abortion, 109, 112, 114, 117, 119, 120, 138, 153, 177n2, 177n20; concealing of, 155; incidence of, 115–116; motivation for, 177n15; punishment for, 152. *See also* Infanticide

Absenteeism, 20–21

Abuse, 7, 106, 144, 146, 151–152, 157, 163, 167n2, 174n1, 175n16, 180n5, 180–181n9, 181n19; child, 149, 181n13; description of, 3–4; during pregnancy, 152, 156, 178n10, 181n13; reactions to, 156

Amelioration, 125–130, 133, 134, 137, 140, 152, 163, 173n10, 178n12, 178n13; impact of, 130, 142

Antigua, 169n7, 169n11, 171n4, 178n15; birth rates on, 132; free colored on, 173n5; manumissions on, 71, 72; nuclear families on, 91; slave markets on, 53

Arango y Parreño, 36

Arawaks, 32

Bahamas, 169n11; birth rates in, 124, 132; domestic labor in, 65; family patterns in, 86; fertility in, 140; nuclear families in, 87, 89, 90, 132; sugar production in, 131

Barbados, 60, 133, 169n7, 169n11; abuse on, 152; amelioration on, 140; birth rates on, 101, 126, 127, 132; contraception on, 114; diseases on, 107; domestic labor on, 64; field labor on, 73; free colored on, 173n5; gang system on, 74; gender ratios on, 42, 178n14; housing on, 50, 171n1; manumissions on, 71; miscegenation on, 149; mortality rates on, 104, 122; nuclear families on, 85, 86, 91, 93, 94; polygamy on, 89; productivity on, 78; promiscuity on, 84; provisions for, 51, 55, 56; slave prices on, 37; sugar production on, 26, 169n12; working conditions on, 76, 77

Barracones, description of, 49–50

Beckford, Richard, 36

Bermuda, 54, 66, 69, 169n11; domestic labor on, 64; family patterns on, 86; hiring out on, 70; nuclear families on, 89

Birth rates, 11, 111, 112, 117–118, 131, 143, 170n2, 170n3, 175n1, 176n11, 179n20, 179n24; decrease of, 16, 101; economic incentives and, 141; fertility and, 100,

101–104, 113, 140; sugar production and, 132–139

Boiling house, description of, 76

Bondwomen. *See* Slave women

Brazil, 32; sugar production in, 26

Breast feeding, 114, 170n2, 176n8, 177n17. *See also* Fertility, controlling

British Guiana, 32, 43, 172n8; gender ratios in, 34; provisions for, 56; sugar production in, 33

British Honduras, 32

British Leewards, 60, 133; birth rates in, 127, 132; domestic labor in, 66; islands of, 169n11; nuclear families in, 93; promiscuity in, 83; provision grounds in, 51; provisions for, 55–56; slave markets in, 53; sugar production in, 26, 131; working conditions in, 77

British Virgin Islands, 54; working conditions in, 76

British West Indies, 41, 55, 59, 68; abuse in, 152; amelioration in, 178n12; birth rates in, 101, 103, 124, 126, 127, 175n1; contraception in, 114; domestic labor in, 66; fertility in, 109, 136; free colored in, 173n10; gender ratios in, 170n5; housing in, 48, 50; malnutrition in, 123; manumissions in, 67, 71, 173n7; mortality rates in, 104, 105, 107, 122, 176n10; nuclear families in, 86, 87, 88, 89, 91, 99; polygamy in, 99; promiscuity in, 84; prostitution in, 69; provision grounds in, 51; slave prices in, 37; sugar production in, 131; working conditions in, 76

Canary Islands, sugar production in, 26

Capitalism, slavery and, 3, 7–12, 162, 164, 165–166

Caribs, 32

Cédula of 1798, 41

Childbearing, 6, 13–14, 16, 19, 81, 111, 119, 146, 159, 162, 173n12; benefits of, 100, 127; conditions for, 125–126; encouragement of, 14–15; health and, 121. *See also* Pregnancy

Child rearing, 50, 81, 167n5, 177n17; kinship and, 117

Children: abuse of, 149, 181n13; household